Children's First School Books

THE LANGUAGE LIBRARY

EDITED BY DAVID CRYSTAL

Children's First School Books

INTRODUCTIONS TO THE CULTURE OF LITERACY

Carolyn D. Baker and Peter Freebody

Basil Blackwell

Copyright © Carolyn D. Baker and Peter Freebody 1989

First published 1989

Basil Blackwell Ltd
108 Cowley Road, Oxford, OX4 1JF, UK

Basil Blackwell, Inc.
3 Cambridge Center
Cambridge, Massachusetts 02142, USA

British Library Cataloguing in Publication Data

A CIP catalogue record for this book is
available from the British Library.

Library of Congress Cataloging in Publication Data

Baker, Carolyn D.
    Children's first school books: introductions to the culture of
literacy/Carolyn D. Baker and Peter Freebody.
        p.   cm. — (The Language library)
    Bibliography: p.
    Includes index.
    ISBN 0-631-15926-6 — ISBN 0-631-15927-4
(pbk.)
        1. Textbooks.   2. Reading (Primary)   3. Educational anthropology.
I. Freebody, Peter.   II. Title.   III. Series.
LB3045.B35   1989
371.3′2—dc19

Typeset in 11 on 13 pt Garamond
by Setrite Typesetting Ltd.
Printed in Great Britain by
Billing & Sons Ltd, Worcester

Contents

List of Tables

Preface

The project we report here began with our curiosity about the 'special language' contained in materials produced for early reading instruction, but it did not end there. In this book we have treated that language as worthy of detailed study in itself — as a special corpus of text written in and for our time — and as a valuable and unique key to an understanding of literacy as a cultural accomplishment.

Our examinations of the language in the beginning reading books used in schools follow some familiar paths as well as introducing several new orders of interest in the nature and uses of these materials. Working from our detailed textual analyses, we have addressed a number of practical and theoretical issues that overlap more than they are distinct: how language and school-knowledge are put on paper for initial access by young children; what types of problems students and teachers may encounter in using early school materials; how the books code social relationships between children and adults — relationships that are, importantly, the very context of their use; and what the relation is between these apparently simple introductory school books and contemporary theorizing about literacy, schooling and society. These orders of interest are captured in our concept of 'school-literate culture', which conveys our attention to the specific institutional circumstances in which literacy is taught and learned. Thus, while this work forms part of a tradition dealing with problems of teaching and learning from books and about books, it is also an attempt to employ textual analyses in the connection of practice and theory.

A number of the analyses we report are somewhat technical,

but we have continually tried to write for an audience of interested teachers as well as researchers and students working in the areas of language, literacy and education. We have done this partly in the hope that a range of practitioners, including teachers, may find some of the analytic techniques themselves, and not just the conclusions we draw from them, useful in their work.

The reader will find a range of methodological strategies (both quantitative and qualitative) in use in this book. This is partly due to the fact that early reading materials and the uses to which they are put invite description at several distinct levels, and partly because the two authors come to the issue of literacy learning in school from different research backgrounds. This project represents an interleaving of sociological/interpretive and cognitive/linguistic perspectives, and it would now be impossible to disentangle our separate contributions. Since, in the end, each sentence (including this one) was written by both of us in one way or another, the order of authorship reflects a quirk of the alphabet rather than differing degrees of input into the project.

We would prefer that this book not be read simply as an extended research report. Rather, we have treated the corpus of beginning reading materials as a unique literary genre in order to explore the ways in which children first encounter the written word in formal schooling. We have tried to document the ways in which the books' language may be different from other uses of language, in particular the oral language children bring to school. Our aim has been to detail a 'culture' of literacy as it is introduced and practised in our schools.

The reader will note, as the book progresses, that we have often adopted a critical stance towards both the materials provided for early literacy instruction and the uses to which they are put. It is perhaps worth outlining briefly our starting position on these issues. We begin with the view that literacy is best regarded not as a unitary abstraction but rather as sets of practical activities engaged in by many different people in many different interpersonal and cultural contexts. The uses and forms of the written word are thus potentially as varied as such contexts permit.

As with activities related to other abstractions (e.g., learning, schooling, loving, thinking), however, the members of any given culture may operate largely as if their set of literacy practices directly reflects a single-faceted 'essence' that is literacy — an essence that is generally unexamined. Thus it is difficult for us both as practitioners (students, writers, teachers and researchers) and as observers (parents, employers and educational managers) to appreciate the extent to which our day-to-day activities and interpretations are congruent with only one of many possible options.

Literacy instruction in our society is accompanied and apparently guided by a rich and idealized rhetoric. Most practitioners would accept that literacy learning is crucial to personal and cultural growth and enlightenment, as well as to individual occupational fulfilment. The objective of this book is not to present complaints about current practice, but rather, in part, to excavate some conceptions guiding modern literacy instruction so that such instruction may be more carefully and finely considered in the light of both stated and implicit educational goals. Further, we would hope to show practitioners and observers how some aspects of the materials and methods used in early literacy instruction might both constrain current practice and enable other possible practices in the early school years.

Thus we attempt to provide details of how early school reading materials shape language and experience on paper, and, in turn, how this shaping process might work against some idealistic aspirations for literacy learning. If the book can do this convincingly, then students, teachers, writers and researchers may come to view some of the ways in which their own practices and interpretations reflect the tension between our society's rhetoric about literacy and our schools' socializing agenda. This seems to us a prerequisite for the development of more enabling practices on all our parts.

We have been greatly assisted in the preparation of this work by a number of people, and we are happy to be able to thank them here. The initial germ of this project came from postgraduate research work by Jan Gay, who developed a basic word recognition list from a corpus of early materials currently in use. Jan kindly allowed us to build on her sample and was involved in some of our early analyses. We then contacted those publishing houses that had recently produced early reading books in Australia and asked whether they could supply us with additional materials for use in our project. We are grateful for their assistance. The sources we have used are itemized in the Materials Reference List.

Some sections of this book are adaptations of papers we have published earlier, in the *Harvard Educational Review* (Freebody and Baker, 1985), *Language in Society* (Baker and Freebody, 1986), the *British Journal of Sociology of Education* (Baker and Freebody, 1987), *Language and Communication* (Freebody, Baker and Gay, 1987), the *Australian Journal of Reading* (Baker and Freebody, 1988), and in chapters contributed to books published by Australian Professional Publications (edited by Pauwels; see Freebody and Baker, 1987) and Falmer Press (edited by de Castell, Luke and Luke; see Baker and Freebody, 1989). We are grateful to these publishers for allowing us to rework our earlier papers.

We also thank the administration, staff and students of those schools involved in this project for their friendly cooperation in the collection of classroom data.

A number of other individuals contributed directly to the preparation of this work. Christine Perrott allowed us to 'borrow' some of her transcripts, and Carmen Jones carefully typed some sections of the work under unfair pressure. We thank both of them for their help.

We were lucky to have the assistance of Colin Fraser, a computer programmer extraordinaire, who gave generously of his time and talents in developing the search and analysis routines upon which some sections of the book depend heavily. His patience in suffering our many garbled requests and his perspicacity in actually making sense of most of them made possible the extensive description of the corpus that we provide. Colin deserves thanks bordering on extravagance for his contribution.

The University of New England provided financial support through its Internal Research Grant scheme; also, the Behavioural Studies computer facilities were well suited to the conduct of a project such as this.

Finally, we thank David Crystal, our series editor, for his editorial advice, and our patient publisher at Basil Blackwell, Philip Carpenter, for his faith in the value of this project, and for his polite and encouraging 'get-on-with-it' letters.

C. D. B.
P. F.

Introduction

In our society learning to read is widely regarded as the most central objective of early schooling. Not only does instruction in reading accompany and often precede instruction in writing, but also the ability to read is viewed as essential for managing most of the academic tasks students will face throughout their school lives. This central place given to reading is reflected in the widespread attention paid by parents, schools and the community to the nature and outcomes of reading acquisition, and in the fact that a student's acquisition of reading skills is, in general, closely monitored and taken to be an important indicator of educational achievement and potential.

In addition, decades of educational research have been devoted to the study of the reading process. Researchers have put considerable effort into identifying sources of difficulty in learning to read, planning and developing instructional materials, and refining instructional and assessment practices. The work we report here complements this tradition of attention to reading, but is distinct in that it presents a close analysis of the reading materials children receive in their early schooling and attends also to children's encounters with these materials.

The books written for children in their first years of school look simple. As parents and teachers of young children know, these books for the most part contain short, common words in curt, grammatically simple sentences, and a lot of staccato conversational exchanges. Moreover, many of the stories in first school books are either commonly known fairy tales and rhymes, or depict familiar character-types engaged in routine everyday activities.

One explanation of this apparently simple language and familiar, mundane content might be that these books are used largely as vehicles for instruction in the technical aspects of reading acquisition — for example, in decoding skills. This account might in turn serve to deflect attention away from a critical analysis of the substance of the books. That is, it may be suggested that the language and structure of the stories presented are not to be treated as topics of learning, in the sense of content learning or learning about the literary forms of stories, but are rather best seen as vehicles for learning about some of the basic technicalities of written language. This claim, that the language and structure of the stories are not intended to be topics of learning, supports an assumption that the stories themselves are a form of 'idle discourse'.

There are, however, at least two reasons for making the nature and content of first school books objects of critical attention. The first is a practical one: it relates to how the books are used in classrooms. The stories do in fact become incorporated into lesson content. Teachers may extract material from a text the students have read or listened to as a basis for decoding instruction; but, as we will show in chapter 7, the text is often used as a stimulus for general questioning or discussion about the sequence of events, the characters' motives, students' preferences for characters and other issues associated with the substance of the story. Many of the assumptions built into stories are largely accepted rather than challenged in discussions in reading lessons. The intellectual problems presented to students often relate to the activities depicted in a story as if they were a 'slice of life' rather than results of graphic and literary crafting. This last feature endows early literacy instruction with a particular orientation to the written text, and forms a significant component of the organization of teacher—student relations. In summary, it is not as idle discourse that beginning reading texts are effectively used.

A second reason for directing critical attention to the content of first school books relates to their potential multiplicity of functions. Clearly, the books are written to help in the reading instruction of young children, however broadly the notion of reading is conceived. The books, in addition, are important stepping stones in a child's progress from facility with the conventions of oral, conversational communication towards facility with written, literary communication. More broadly still, as we will argue further, the books play a central role in the child's introduction to the culture of schooling. If the proposition that 'schooling is a matter of mediating the relationship between children and the printed text' (Olson, 1977b: 66) has any force, then the first school books children encounter can be regarded as documents of the particular form of the child−text relationship that schooling is trying to effect. The books are not neutral or content-free, however simple they appear. They portray characters in social relationships in distinct ways, and they locate the child-reader in a particular relationship with book knowledge and, more broadly, with school learning.

Functionally then, the texts of first school books invite analysis both as informative records of pedagogical theory and as sources of socialization, over and above their use in teaching decoding skills. It seems important, therefore, to approach the task of examining first school books in some detail, in the light of their multiple purposes, in order to understand more fully the particular forms and contents of our society's version of becoming 'school-literate'. In this book we turn our attention to this task. We present and discuss a series of detailed analyses of the texts of school books written for children in the earliest years of their schooling.

Previous examinations of the vocabulary and illustrations in beginning school reading books have been concerned with, among other things, issues of gender portrayals (e.g., Women on Words and Images, 1972), and with the nature and significance of story grammars and implicit social ideologies in basal readers (e.g., Luke, 1988a). The work we report here is distinctive in a number of ways. First, our analyses are based on an extensive, representative corpus, containing the texts of a large number of beginning reading books in recent or current use, including basal readers as well as other types of early school reading materials. Second, our interpretations are guided by a theoretical orientation to the broader functions of school-literacy which emphasizes the ways experience is represented through oral and written language. This orientation guides our selection and analysis of various aspects of the written language in the books, and gives our interpretations a distinctive flavour.

While we acknowledge without reservation the importance and salience of illustrations in early reading materials (as documented by Ninio and Bruner, 1978), we give detailed attention here to the nature of the written texts. This selective focus is derived largely from our theoretical and analytical interests. Further work incorporating more attention to relations between words and illustrations is clearly warranted.

Our analyses are focused on written texts in current use, and thus provide descriptions of the nature and possible uses of early reading materials in our specific time and culture. We are sensitive throughout the book to the reflection in early reading materials of current conceptions of child—adult relations, of school knowledge and practice, of the literate uses of language and of other ideational components of contemporary culture. A sense of the cultural specificity of these reading materials is heightened when considered in relation to Luke's (1988a) sociological and historical analysis of post-war literacy materials and practices.

The study presented here of the written texts of early school reading materials, therefore, provides some detailed analyses of an extensive corpus of written text, but is by no means exhaustive of the many lines of theoretical, analytical or practical interest along which these materials could be approached. We will, in this and subsequent chapters, elaborate further on the reasons why beginning reading books warrant extensive analysis, and on how such an examination could contribute to our understanding of the ways in which children are introduced to the culture of literacy as that culture is effected in our schools.

It is a commonplace that teachers and parents of young children have an interest and an investment in the nature of the first school books children encounter. One major practical concern faced by teachers and parents derives from the purposes to which the books are generally put in the classroom and the home — that is, teaching and learning the skills of reading, and developing enjoyment of books. Therefore the criteria usually applied to these books include readability, suitability, interest value and attractiveness. These criteria are relevant and important. However, consideration of these books need not be limited to criteria that relate only to practical instructional uses and to children's enjoyment. As indicated by our discussion above, our interest goes beyond the issue of whether certain materials may lead to more rapid reading acquisition than others, incorporating a broader view of the place of the books in the enculturation process.

The critical nature of children's first sightings of the terrain of school culture should not be underestimated. Early school reading materials are important and visible features of that terrain. We take it that school learning is largely about the induction of children into selected areas of knowledge that are conveyed in specialized ways. The nature and use of early reading materials are important in this process, in that, their apparent simplicity aside, they instantiate school-literate culture.

Some previous work on reading acquisition has attempted to locate problems in learning to read *in* the child through descriptions of idealized, individualized versions of the cognitive task of reading (cf. Rumelhart, 1977; Schallert, 1982). There is also some recent work that has pointed to problems *in* the interactions that occur between teachers and students in reading-related classroom activities. The examination of the social organization of reading lessons, for example, has cast some light on the processes of reading acquisition and instruction as interactional issues (e.g., Cazden, 1981; Heap, 1985; McDermott, 1976). Thus, to date, it has typically been to cognitive-management theories of reading or to interactional accounts of what teachers do with students that teachers and researchers have turned to find and to develop descriptions of children's reading problems or descriptions of reading activities.

One usually unintended implication of these internal-psychological and interactional traditions is that parents and teachers may behave as if they trust that there are few problems in the texts themselves, other than 'readability', 'suitability', or 'interest'. Some earlier studies that have examined aspects of the vocabulary and illustrations in early reading materials in some depth (e.g., Beck et al., 1979; Willows et al., 1981) have tended to study corpuses based on two or three major series of basal readers, and have presented highly selective and methodologically restricted analyses of the language and pictures in the books. In the work reported here, we focus largely on the texts themselves, and on inferring a description of the tasks involved in learning to read from materials of the kind typically encountered by children in their first school books. This direction of attention is motivated partly by the observation that, while appearing simple, these books present some complex and subtle textual problems. In general, the analyses that follow cast doubt on the proposition that the more simply a text is written the easier it is to read and understand. We also take it that the way a text is written is a construction of its readership, not just an adjustment (of vocabulary or style) to that readership. In this sense it is not easy to separate the nature and suitability of the texts from assumptions about the readership for whom they are written. This point will be developed more fully in our discussion of how the concept of 'the child' is constructed in beginning reading books.

In the following chapter we provide an introduction to the various theoretical issues we have brought together for purposes of analysing these texts. Some of these issues are concerned with continuities and discontinuities between oral and written language forms. We raise questions about the extent to which learning to read can be tied to oral language conventions, and how these texts attempt to relate the task of learning to read to the oral conventions with which children are assumed to be familiar. Other issues we explore derive from work concerned with the nature of knowledge as encapsulated in print: the 'autonomy' and the 'authority' of the text are ideas we address in the chapters to follow.

Another set of theoretical sources on which we draw is concerned with the methods of socializing children into school culture and adult culture. We ask at various points in the book how the materials that are found in children's first school books present a portrayal of childhood which the child-readers of these texts may or may not recognize. In summary, chapter 1 sets out the theoretical sources which guide the subsequent analyses, and which are the mainsprings of the analytic methods that we employ throughout the book.

Our analyses of the beginning reading books are guided by a number of questions. Each of these questions forms the basis of a chapter to follow. We will briefly outline here the sequence of chapters and the issues addressed in each.

In chapter 2 some details of the general vocabulary content of children's first school books are presented. For example, we present some initial analyses of word frequencies, and draw out some implications of these. We compare the vocabulary used in children's first school books with that used in school texts written for the later years of schooling, and with the oral language of children of the age of the readership of the beginning school reading books. These analyses are designed to outline the nature of the contrasts between oral and written language as documented in the various language samples. We conclude that written language displays intellectual and communicational functions that are, in certain critical and observable ways, distinct from those displayed in spoken language. We give attention to forms of language in early school reading books that appear to be transitional across oral and written forms.

In chapter 3 we address the question, 'How is the social world presented in the beginning reading books?'. We draw attention to the nature of the characters, activities and events portrayed in the books. We also undertake some detailed analyses of gender descriptions and gender differences assigned to characters, and of the expression of emotion by various kinds of characters in the books. Thus, this chapter develops our response to the issue of whether these portrayals of social life concur with other available descriptions of children's culture. We take it that many of the books are written in order to achieve some parallel between children's everyday lives and the materials that they encounter in their first school reading books. Hence we ask whether the 'worlds' portrayed in the texts are comparable to those inhabited by the readership.

The central role of the author in children's first school books is addressed in chapter 4. One major role of the author in these books is to narrate stories. Since it is the case that these books contain a great deal of reported talk among characters in the books, one additional aspect of the narrator's work is to introduce characters, give them things to say, and generally choreograph their interactions. Beginning reading materials also contain first person texts which involve different kinds of authorial practice. We will attempt to show how an analysis of the author's role in the books is relevant to the introduction of children to the 'authority' and 'autonomy' of school texts (as described by Olson, 1977a, b, 1980). We describe those ways in which that 'authority' and 'autonomy' is gently but pervasively introduced in the first reading material that children encounter in school.

Chapter 5 undertakes an analysis of how characters in the books talk with one another — how oral language is put on paper. Here, leaving narration aside for the most part, we examine the kinds of utterances that various characters produce — the way, for example, children and adults are shown to speak to each other. We examine the models of the speech community found within the texts and contrast them with what is known about how children converse with each other and with adults in everyday life. This is an important aspect of the possible discontinuity between the everyday world of the child and the worlds portrayed in these books, in the light of the prevalence of reported speech. This chapter also describes some possible problems in reading texts which contain reported talk on paper.

In chapter 6 we draw together and elaborate some of our earlier observations about the nature of 'the child' as portrayed in the texts. We show how the child (as both character-type and implied reader) is placed at the centre of the social worlds shown in the texts. We take the view that 'the child' is a social and not a natural construct, and that it is especially pertinent to document how a version of the nature of contemporary childhood is itself embedded in the organization of these texts. We raise the question of whether any children or particular groups of children may encounter difficulties in concurring with the versions of childhood that they as readers find reflected back to them from the books.

In chapter 7 we supplement our descriptions of the beginning school reading books with a report of data concerned with how teachers orient children to the written word through classroom talk. That is, we look at the nature of teacher questioning in the process of teaching children how to read. We are interested here mainly in how teachers design conversation about text and what teachers alert children to in their encounters with beginning school reading books. We attempt to assess how those activities may shape children's views of stories and of textual knowledge, and thus inform broader issues of reading acquisition and reading comprehension.

Chapter 8 presents some conclusions and implications of our analyses. In particular, we attempt answers to the broader questions we have posed throughout the foregoing chapters. These questions include: how is school literacy best described; what are the ways of expressing, knowing and interpreting their own behaviour and the social and physical world around them that children might develop from their contact with beginning reading books; might children find difficulty with the content of these materials on the various grounds we have described; and in what ways might teachers and writers of beginning reading books present the task of learning to be literate?

To conclude this introduction, it is appropriate to give a brief description of the beginning reading corpus that forms the basis of our analyses, so that the reader can form a view of both the generalizability and limitations of our findings and interpretations. Included in the survey were early school reading books in common use in a representative educational division of New South Wales, Australia. This division contains 65 classes of children in their first and second years of schooling. Also included in the corpus were books published recently by some of the major relevant publishing houses in Australia (see Materials Reference List). A total of 163 basal and supplementary readers comprised the beginning reading books corpus. Many of these books are identical to or adaptations of books published in the United Kingdom, the United States, Canada and New Zealand.

The size of this corpus enables us to address the variety of questions outlined above. The range of questions invites the use of a diversity of analytic methods, and is informed by a number of theoretical considerations developed more fully in the first chapter. An important point to be kept in mind is that no individual child or group of children would encounter more than a small subset of these or similar books in the course of being taught to read or being read to. We cannot claim that our findings and interpretations would apply proportionately to any particular subset of these books; nor would we claim that all children's beginning reading programmes would display each of the characteristics we will describe; nor is every young reader exposed to each of the linguistic and social features of the books. On the other hand, it is precisely because of the size and breadth of our collected samples of texts that we feel some confidence in the account we give as a general description of our culture's attempts to introduce children to school-literacy.

1

Background Considerations

We present in this chapter the main elements of the framework within which we would like this work to be viewed. These elements derive partly from previous scholars' attempts to account for three related issues — the relationship between oral and written language; the effects of the printed word on learning and knowledge; and society's attempts, mainly through schooling, to fashion children into students and ultimately into literate adults. Stated in their most general terms, the assertions that we will elaborate in this chapter, and that we will attempt to document in our analyses, are: first, that children's beginning school books can be seen as stepping stones from conventions of oral language to conventions of written language use; second, that these books begin to build a transition from 'oral-language' ways of documenting and communicating experience and knowledge towards 'literate-language' ways; and third, that the books show to child-readers officially sanctioned versions of themselves — that is, that the books display school-endorsed discourses through which children are to interpret and explain their everyday lives. This third point reflects our view that what is taught in school is constructed through forms of preferred discourse that are themselves inscribed in certain institutional and everyday practices (cf. Whitty, 1985: 37).

But first a Gedanken experiment: imagine a colonial power that is administering a non-literate indigenous people. The colonists take their educational obligations seriously. As part of their educational programme, they produce books from which the indigines are to be taught literacy in a school-type context. In an attempt to make these early literacy experiences more familiar and relevant to the indigenous people, the books depict indigines in everyday contexts at home, at work, talking to their families and neighbours, and generally going about the business of everyday life in the colony. The books also depict the indigenes in the new activities of going to school and interacting with the colonists in other social contexts. Further imagine that the colonists, including the writers of these books, are themselves benign, sympathetic and even affectionate toward the indigines.

The question that arises here is what would the books be like. More specifically, how might the language of the books relate to the oral language practised every day by the indigines? This question pertains not only to the substance of the stories, that is, to what the indigenous characters do and how they talk. If we make the further imaginative leap and hypothesize that the colonists develop a script for the previously unscripted indigenous language, we can ask additionally what sound-grapheme relationship would be put in place. Would graphic symbols attempt to represent words, syllables, or phonemes? Would prosodic contours such as intonation be realized in the graphic system? That is, what resources would the colonists bring to the task of dividing the indigenous sound stream into its constituent, graphically demonstrable parts?

These speculations might be followed by a consideration of the substance of the stories — the cultural content of the books. What categories of characters, what social relationships, what properties of objects and attributes of people would be marked in the vocabulary of the books? What aspects of experience and knowledge would be shown to be important enough to be written about and learned? In other words, would the everyday language and culture of the indigines be presented faithfully, or would it be reshaped in certain subtle or not-so-subtle ways?

Whatever the characteristics of the books used in this (not terribly difficult to imagine) vignette, it is clear that the books would provide a richly informative document of the colonists' perhaps implicit theories of reading, of school learning, of the indigenous readership's culture and of the relationship between the colonial and indigenous cultures. The books would make available an equally if not more revealing document of these theories than would, say, the official statements of educational policy for the colony, or the descriptions provided by colonial administrators. They would be documents for a social anthropology of the colonizing process. While the books might be written apparently about indigenous culture, they would say more about the colonists themselves. Specifically the books would offer the reader a view of the colonists' understandings of how facility with written language is best developed, of the role of written language in the colony's broader educational programmes for the indigines, of the indigines' perceived educational needs, and of the nature of indigenous culture itself.

It would, in fact, be difficult to imagine that the books could avoid a particular reshaping of language, learning and the 'indigine'. We may ask whether or not the indigenous readers would recognize the versions of language in use, the aspects of their experience that are shown to be worth documenting in writing and worth learning about, and the indigenous characters in the books as being their own versions. In addition, we might not expect the reshapings to be random or unsystematic. Rather we might expect them to assume certain forms that systematically portray, to the indigenous people, versions of the components of language and its major uses, of school learning, and of the indigenous culture that are compatible with the colonists' views and culture, and with their needs to develop and maintain a particular kind of relationship with the indigines that they regard as orderly and commonsensical. This little vignette shows that education, through its materials and its practices, is a form of socialization and acculturation.

In fact Speier (1976) has argued that adult–child relations can be viewed as more than analogous to the colonizing process, in that adults define and enforce both the needs and the nature of children. These perceptions, whether from 'commonsense' or from 'scientific' theories of child development and socialization, serve to naturalize and justify adult–child relations as they are practised in the home and at school. These perceptions point to key areas of experience in which children are deemed to be incompetent or, in Speier's terms, 'precompetent'. The supposition underlying these theories and the practices that they inform is that children are adults-in-the-making. The details of that making process can be viewed in conversations, at home and at school, between adults and children, and in the documents produced by adults for and about children (see also Jenks, 1982). From this perspective, all texts produced in and for adult–child contact can be interpreted as documents of acculturation. Television programmes designed for young children illustrate this view clearly. In the play-school/pre-school kind of programme, for example, we find an adult-produced script and an enactment of that script sometimes involving children as participants. Such programmes have both entertainment and strong pedagogical dimensions: in some cases, the interactions between adult and children in the studio are organized in ways that parallel classroom relations. In all of these programmes, we can recognize an adult construction of the nature and needs of children through pitch and intonational patterns, through selections of activities designed to have children practise skills such as naming or jumping, through questions and comments that invite particular kinds of 'thinking', and through the use of constructions like 'magic words', 'mister music' and other figurative devices unlikely to be used seriously in programmes for adults. These activities evidence an implicit theory about what children enjoy, what they like to do or hear, what they cannot yet do, and how their minds and imaginations work. These constructions of childhood are devices in the socialization practices that are designed to make young children gradually more like adults.

We see that the texts of beginning school reading books illustrate similar theories and constructions of childhood. Like the television text, the printed text is a contemporary document of the kinds of adult theorizations that govern how adult—child relations are practised in our culture. Our formulation of this approach to studying the beginning reading books is similar to that suggested by Luke for the historical study of reading textbooks:

> We can read more in historical curricular texts than simply recordings of ideological content, for they stand as reconstructions of everyday communicative transactions between writers and readers, teachers and students. Additionally, the text is a recoverable record of those authorial, pedagogic and interpretive codes that its use presupposed and projected. (1987b: 109)

The Gedanken experiment above signals the many dimensions and levels of the process of becoming school-literate. In the sections that follow we will present ideas concerning oral and written language, literacy and learning, and the reshaping of child culture that have guided our study of beginning school reading books. Our account of previous research and theorizing should not be regarded as an exhaustive one. Our purpose is to draw attention to some interesting interconnections that we will pursue throughout the book. In particular, we will argue that attempting to understand the technical problems presented by the written word leads us to concerns about the issue of how written communication comes to embody experience and to present a view of knowledge. From these we are led to a recognition of the role of print in our society's organized attempts to acculturate the young, along lines that are compatible with adult definitions of order and rationality. It is the interconnectedness of these levels of the process of literacy acquisition, we will argue, that highlights the importance of children's first school books. Our detailed examinations of the content of first school books should be viewed in this context.

CHILDREN'S ORAL LANGUAGE HERITAGE

It is important as a starting point to consider the language abilities that children bring to their initial encounters with formal instruction in literacy, usually at about age 5. These abilities are best seen as practical, conversational competencies, implicating lexical, grammatical and interactional knowledge, rather than the Chomskyan assumption of a generalized, idealized grammatical competence (see Baker and Hacker, 1984, chapter 10). Documenting some of the main features of children's practical uses of language will serve as a guide to some of the distinctive communicative conventions that come into play when the written word is first met. We should point out here that we recognize that children beginning school may be users of a literate language whether or not they can read or write (Olson and Astington, 1986). They may well have participated in literate discourses, in which case their access to written language may be assisted.

There is a considerable body of research that has focused attention on syntactic and lexical development in pre-school children. In a series of classic studies, Brown (1973) demonstrated that the major basic sentence types emerge in English-speaking children by about age 5. This conclusion, supported by considerable detailed analyses of the spoken language of a variety of English children, is compatible with research conducted by Wells and his colleagues in the Bristol Project (Wells 1979, 1981, 1985a). For example, Wells demonstrated (1985a) that all of the major mood options (declarative, imperative, interrogative etc.) are used by the majority of 5-year-olds, and that, within each mood option, a considerable variety of the sentence core structures are employed by the majority of children studied. Similarly, most of the syntactic patterns available in English and all of the major types of language function (representational, control, procedural, expressive, social, heuristic/tutorial) are used by the majority of children by age 5. Also, a substantial context-sensitive variability in the form of utterances attests to a sophisticated grammatical repertoire available to the average 5-year-old. Thus, while there is still much vocabulary, stylistic variation and culturally appropriate form yet to be acquired by the 5-year-old child, the heavy duty structures and functions of oral language are appropriately demonstrated by most children before they begin school.

As Cazden (1981) and others have pointed out, the grammatical repertoire of children is only one aspect of their overall linguistic competence in the pre-school years. Attention needs also to be drawn to the conversational understandings and strategies young children develop in order to communicate successfully.

To illustrate some of these strategies, we will be referring to parts of a transcript presented by Payne and Ridge (1985: 14−15). This transcript should be read as an illustration of what young children can do with oral language. It describes the talk of two sisters playing shop − the older, Sally (aged almost 8 years) in the role of shopkeeper, and the younger, Ann (aged 4½ years) in the role of customer. The pretend game of shop begins as Ann, carrying a doll, arrives at the (shop)room. (Transcript notation conventions are shown in appendix 2.)

Example 1.1

     0   Ann   ((*five knocks at the door*))
     1   Sally   Come i:n
     2   Ann   <u>He:llo</u>
     3   Sally   D-yer-know-what
     4   Ann   What
            ((*pause circa 3 seconds*))

5	Sally	You can ha:ve — <u>some</u>thing free
6	Ann	What we don't have to pay
7	Sally	Yes — you can have <u>one</u> thing free
8	Ann	Oh — thank you
9	Sally	Pick it na
10	Ann	Whoops-a-daisy — — — I was want, — this — this stand this is one thing cos it goes togevver doesn't it // ((*The stand is a doll's carry cot stand, and the carry cot goes with it*))
11	Sally	( ) yeh — now you don't have to pay for it
12	Ann	Thank you — — darling — — would you be quiet I've just brought you a new stand you kno:w — — — don't want you saying it doesn't — you don't like it — — else you'll get a smack// ( )
13	Sally	Ah she <u>will</u> because it's very comfortable you know
14	Ann	Thank you — — thank-you-very-much ((*sing-song voice*)) — — <u>darling</u> and I must never say that again you're always very cheeky ((*pause circa 2 seconds*)) ((*singing*)) If you like — — have you got a baby
15	Sally	<u>Me</u>
16	Ann	Yes
17	Sally	Have <u>I</u> got-a-baby
18	Ann	Yes
19	Sally	No — — I don't like babies yer-see ((*said quietly*))
20	Ann	Have you got children
21	Sally	No — — yes — — I-have-<u>one</u>//but they've left home
22	Ann	How old is it — — what
23	Sally	They're — — they are nineteen

((*pause circa 3 seconds*))
[transcript continues]

Payne and Ridge presented this transcript as a basis for detailing some of the subtleties and accomplishments in the organization of talk among young children. These accomplishments have been documented by a number of researchers, and we will briefly summarize some of their findings below, drawing at times on the 'Sally and Ann' transcript.

In one study of children between the ages of 2 and 4 years, Pellegrini, Brody and Stoneman (1987) applied Grice's description (1975) of conversational principles to the children's talk. Grice argued that certain maxims need to be followed in order for successful communicative exchanges to take place. He itemized the major subcategories of this 'cooperative principle' thus: quantity (say enough but not more than enough), quality (say what is true and only what you have evidence for), relation (say what is relevant to the topic at hand) and manner (speak clearly and without ambiguity). Pellegrini and others found that children as young as 2 years of age rarely violated the quality and manner maxims in conversations with siblings and parents. That is, generally, very young children speak truthfully and clearly. Moreover they found that children's 'violations' of the quality and relation maxims decreased significantly with age. Further, most of the quantity violations that were found, particularly among 2- and 3-year-olds, were non-responses or non-verbal responses to utterances from the parents to which the child may have felt no need to respond. For example, Pellegrini and others note an occasion on which a father said to his son 'This baby doll is silly'. His son did not respond verbally to this utterance, perhaps feeling that it required no particular verbal response on his part.

A similar example can be drawn from the transcript quoted above: in what sense can Ann's question in utterance 14 above, 'have you got a baby', be seen as a violation of the relation maxim? Rather, these responses can be seen as successful attempts on the part of the children to indicate non-acceptance of the topic provided by the previous speaker or to change the topic. Such 'violations' of idealized maxims appear to be fundamentally principled. Grice's model itself seems to derive from a 'literate' conception of conversation, in which the four aspects of the cooperative principle are made salient criteria for evaluating speakers. This is reminiscent of a point made by Michaels (1981, 1985) and Gee (1985) that, in hearing children's oral accounts, a teacher may expect and prefer topic-centred, 'literate' narratives. It seems that similar evaluative criteria are built into many developmental-linguistic accounts of children's communicative competence. All such theories are produced from within and as part of literate culture. One problem with accounts such as Grice's is that they may obscure a view of what children can do well, because either an adult-centred or a school-centred perspective has been adopted.

It seems reasonable to conclude from Pellegrini and others' study that young children, only one year after the appearance of their first single word utterances, display considerable understanding of the basic cooperative mechanisms involved in conversational communication, and, further, that children between 2 and 5 years of age demonstrate a considerable working mastery of all of the basic assumptions that underpin successful conversational exchanges.

Mishler (1976) has also examined in some detail certain aspects of the conversational competence of 5-year-old children. He found (*a*) that the average length of utterance of 5-year-old children and adults did not differ, (*b*) that 5-year-old children were able to vary and adapt their speech style depending on the context and the co-speaker/s, (*c*) that 5-year-olds displayed the ability to produce repairs and to recycle or rephrase in response to apparently unsuccessful utterances, (*d*) that young children were able to use appropriate stress and intonation to punctuate and emphasize their utterances, and (*e*) that they were able to employ successfully appropriate opening and closing gambits in conversations. Mishler concluded from these analyses that, using these particular criteria of conversational competence, 5-year-olds and adults are not markedly different.

The 'Sally and Ann' transcript in example 1.1 above evidences such observations. For example, Payne and Ridge (1985: 20–1) consider at length the interactional sensitivity and significance of what might appear to be, on first (adult) glance, an 'inappropriate' opening routine — knocking on a door to gain entry into a shop. Ann's knocking, and Sally's 'Come in' can alternatively be viewed as an effective recognition first of Sally's prerogative to open the game proper, and second of their prior joint description of the problem of when morning has arrived. Within the context of this game, these moves are highly principled and successful.

Such a conclusion is supported in further work by Black (1979) who adapted Cicourel's (1972) categories of interactional competence to examine the conversational exchanges of 5-year-old (kindergarten) children. Black replicated Mishler's findings and presented more detailed analyses of children's familiarity with the constraints and conditions that obtain in conversation, for example, who speaks when, what is relevant, and how and when to begin, repair, recycle and terminate conversations. She further examined children's ability to link in an appropriate manner past experiences and prior knowledge with present and possible informational events in a play context. Consistent with all of the data summarized above, Black concluded that 5-year-old children display considerable competence on these criteria, and rarely violate or disrupt a conversational exchange due to failure in understanding or strategy.

This sensitivity to context and to interlocutor applies also to the specialized demands of classroom discourse. Children adapt rapidly to the conventions of classroom conversation, which require sensitivity to the teacher's organization of interaction for instruction and socialization (e.g., MacLure and French, 1980; Mehan, 1979; Willes, 1983).

For example, consider the following sequence, which occurs within a teacher-led 'news' session in a kindergarten classroom:

Example 1.2

((Jacob has announced that 'They're going to fix our bathroom' and the teacher has asked the previous four questions, including questions about when the bathroom will be ready and what colour the tiles will be. We begin with the teacher's fifth question.))

T	When are they going to come to do it?
J	They're already there now.
Ss	((*bid to ask questions*))
J	Yes, Moira?
M	When are you going to do the tiles?
J	When they put the bath in.
S	What shape are they going to be?
J	A circle. Yes, Steven.
St	When are they going to finish it?
J	In a month.
T	Someone's asked that.
S	What type of tiles?
J	Red and blue. Yes, Jane?
Jn	Do you like them?
J	Yes.

(Adapted from Baker and Perrott, 1988: 31)

This transcript shows the children following not only the teacher-established turn-taking rules — and here Jacob takes over the role of distributing chances to speak — but shows that they can make their interests identical to the teacher's interests by asking the same kinds of questions the teacher had asked and by questioning 'to the topic' as it had been previously constructed by the teacher and Jacob. While we remain uncertain whether or not young children are genuinely interested in bathroom renovations, the transcript indicates at least their sensitivity to how the teacher wants classroom discussion to be organized, how questions and answers should be phrased, what kind of knowledge is to be introduced, and when and how much of such knowledge is to be produced (cf. Hammersley, 1977).

Thus, not only are children competent to manage conversations with each other, but their conversational strategies show an awareness of how adult—child social relations can be realized and managed through talk (Sacks, 1974; Schegloff, 1968; Speier, 1982). It seems plausible to conclude, therefore, that the grammatical and interactional competencies of 5-year-old children are in many important respects not significantly inferior to those of adults, even though a considerable amount of lexical and stylistic learning is yet to occur. It is clear also that these competencies reflect a very high degree of context- and interlocutor-sensitivity on the part of young children. Children understand and exploit those adaptable and negotiable aspects of communication afforded by conversations with immediate interlocutors.

Over and above these specific strategies, it is important to realize that conversations are not pre-scripted, even though there are certain opening, maintaining and closing moves that are conventional. In face-to-face conversations, the immediacy of the speakers and the need to construct the exchange cooperatively are associated with a tolerance for imprecision and generality; a focus on 'what is meant' rather than on 'what is said' (Olson, 1982); an anticipation of elaborating or clarifying word and utterance meanings; and an expectation that clarifications of ambiguities will be available in due course (cf. Garfinkel, 1967; Cicourel, 1974).

For example, referring again to the 'Sally and Ann' transcript in example 1.1, a potential ambiguity arises in turns 20–23:

20 Ann Have you got children

21 Sally   No − − yes − − I-have-one// but they've left
            home
22 Ann   How old is it − − what
23 Sally   They're − − they are nineteen
            ((*pause circa 3 seconds*))

The question of how many children Sally has becomes clarified.
Through a few subsequent questions from Ann about where these
children live, it is soon established that 'they' are a single child
plus spouse:

Example 1.3

24 Ann   Oh where are they
25 Sally   They're in − − e:r − Debby
26 Ann   Oh where-do-you-live
27 Sally   In Southam
28 Ann   O:h they <u>must</u> have got married
29 Sally   Yes they have − − − I went to their wedding
            ((*pause circa 4 seconds*))

This elegantly both clarifies and preserves the sense of how a
single child could be described as 'they'. Sally and Ann may be
giving each other special latitude for indecision, anomaly and
subsequent recovery work, given that this is a pretend game. The
management of a pretend game is itself a special kind of interactional accomplishment, drawing on the routine competencies of
children to use language to make sense of each other's utterances
in imaginary or 'real' contexts.

These particular understandings and strategies are afforded by
immediate conversational exchange and in many cases are required
by it. Even when informally called upon to produce monologues
such as explanations or stories, both children and adults use such
interactional strategies and rely upon their interlocutors' use of
them (McKeown, 1986; McKeown and Freebody, 1988).

ENCOUNTERING THE WRITTEN HERITAGE

The studies summarized above describe some aspects of children's
knowledge of and competence within an oral-conversational heri-

tage. When children are introduced to literacy based on written textual materials, the task is therefore not learning language, but learning the special conventions of written language: learning literacy forms. In many respects these new conventions for language use contrast with well-practised oral language skills. Further, some oral language skills may be obscured, denied, or subordinated to the particular literate language forms associated with the school's introduction to the uses of the written word.

Literacy involves the problem of translating and transforming oral language into written language. There are three levels at which this transformation can be described. Each of these levels draws attention to some continuities and contrasts between oral and written language forms. The first level is concerned with how the speech stream is represented graphically. The second level, the interactional, refers to differences between the speaker–hearer and writer–reader relationships. Our descriptions of contrasts at this level are built on the observations made above about children's conversational competencies. The third level, the epistemological, refers to differences in the organization and status of knowledge about the self and the social world conveyed in oral and written forms. In adopting this perspective on the relation between oral and written language, we do not propose that the distinctions we draw are absolute, universal, or logically necessary (see Heath, 1982, 1983; Street, 1984). Oral language can be highly literate (as in, say, a public lecture), while written language can be conversational (as in notes, letters, diaries, and so on). Rather, we use these distinctions heuristically, and as broadly descriptive of the characteristics of oral-conversational language used informally, and written language used formally.

Sounds and letters

The first and most obvious contrast between oral and written language centres on the symbolic systems used in the two modes. The written word is a visible object, encoded in a set of symbols that have an arbitrary and often imperfect relationship to spoken sounds – a relationship that is peculiar to each language. The child learning to read needs to connect the new written symbols with the familiar sounds. There are at least two aspects to this problem. The first involves the management of the principles underlying the relationship between the sounds of the parent tongue and the orthography of the printed word. The second, given a particular principle or set of principles for the sound-grapheme connection, is concerned with the content of that relationship, that is, with the actual connections between sounds and graphemes.

It can be noted that there is no inevitability about either the underlying principles of the sound-grapheme relationship in any particular language, or the nature of the specific relationships themselves. For example, some languages employ largely pictographs (word-grapheme), some rely on syllable-grapheme forms, some employ an alphabetic principle (phoneme-grapheme) and some use combinations of these forms. As Halliday (1980) has pointed out, English is not a strictly alphabetic system, but rather is built on a mixture of syllabic and alphabetic principles. This seems to present to the individual first encountering the tasks of reading and writing English with a somewhat slippery set of analytic problems.

Havelock (1976) has argued that the invention of an alphabetic script by the Greeks (significantly the only such invention in human history) was based on an abstraction. In one sense, Havelock argued, what is heard are syllables. The speech flow can be broken into continuous sounds (vowels) and their attendant starting and stopping sounds (consonants). The consonants, however, do not present themselves readily in the spoken form of the language. It was an act of inventive abstraction on the part of the Greeks, Havelock argued, to see that there were different ways of opening and closing 'sounds'. These particular ways of separating the various aspects of speech such that they come to matter in the graphic form of a language are not the same ways that are used in a range of non-alphabetic scripts, such as Thai or Japanese Kanji. The same spoken language could be represented in different graphic forms. Different principles could be applied for cutting into the sound flow, different symbol systems could be used, and a different theory of the sound-symbol relationship could underlie the script.

Thus English involves some strictly alphabetic strategies and some more holistic recognition strategies, partly accounting for the perennial debate concerning analytic versus holistic methods of early reading instruction. It has been argued (e.g. by Baron, 1979; Byrne, 1986; Bryant and Impey, 1986; Ferreiro and

Teberosky, 1982) that children approach the written script with a 'natural' strategy of treating the graphic unit as equal to a spoken unit, usually a word, or later in the developmental sequence, a syllable. A complex theory of how the sound stream is represented on paper is encountered by all children learning to read. Any representation of an oral language is a recasting of that language into one of many possible visual forms.

This point can be illustrated by observing some of the practices beginning writers use to represent oral language on paper. Walton (1986) provided examples of, in this case, Aboriginal children's early attempts to work with the conventions used in written English. One 6-year-old child, when asked to draw an illustration and write a text for the 'Gingerbread Man' refrain, later produced this sound–symbol correspondence in reading her text aloud:

[written text]:   A R i n t S O O t
[read aloud as]: The gin ger br ead man herun a way

Walton commented:

Adriana wrote her text and then read it trying to give each symbol some meaning and not have any [symbols] left over ... it showed she was persisting in her attempt to work out how the symbols related to the oral text. She used two hypotheses simultaneously: one symbol per word, one symbol per syllable. (Adapted from Walton, 1986: 101 and 103)

(Note that it could be that Adriana believed that 'herun' was a single word, or that she realized that she was rapidly running out of symbols.)

As teachers of young children will have observed, early writing shows the various plausible alternatives that children will attempt in sorting out whether a letter should stand for a word, a syllable, or even a phrase or sentence; whether the sound stream is to be represented horizontally, vertically, or in some other direction; and whether numerals are equivalent to letters, words to parts of drawings, and so on.

Olson (1985) has pointed out that pre-school children differ in the amount of 'metalanguage', or explicit talk about the mechanics of language, to which they have been exposed. We might imagine, also, that the nature of that metalanguage would be different for scripts that have different sound-grapheme relationships. An English-speaking parent or teacher, for instance, may draw attention to particular phonemes in the child's oral production of words, while we would expect a Thai-speaking parent or teacher to provide a different metalanguage, focusing perhaps more on the coordination of intonation and modulation, since it is these characteristics that also have significance when the graphic script of Thai is encountered.

An implication of these observations is that an initial task for reading-instruction texts is to aid an awareness of both the underlying principles and the specific contents of the script's particular sound-grapheme relationship. This awareness, in turn, both extends and modifies the language as it is heard and used in its oral form.

We might also expect first school books to present to novice readers substantive story lines that are sufficiently accessible and engaging that readers would be highly motivated to develop facility with the nature and contents of the sound-grapheme relationship. In short, these books, perhaps more than any other materials, might be expected to embody the promise that the slippery task of cracking the code will be more than worth it when the author's voice is faithfully heard.

Speakers and readers

It is the separation of the writer from the reader that gives rise to the distinctive interactional demands imposed by the written word. That is, the central elements of the distinction between oral-conversational competence and competence with written text are corollaries of the separation in time and space of the reader and the writer, in contrast with the immediacy of conversationalists. It is this separation which affords writing its particular genius and its three major advantages over conversational communication — its portability, its production at leisure and its status as a crafted object.

The written word is portable across time, space and culture; its benefit is that it is potentially permanent and available to people who are out of earshot of the writer. Only with the comparatively recent development of electronic media is this portability of the verbatim text available in the oral mode. The writer's audience can be somewhat indeterminate. That is, a writer of a public document such as a school book may hypothesize an audience and implicitly construct a fictive audience in which the potential reader needs to participate; none the less, compensations need to be made concretely, in the written text, for the lack of immediate negotiation of meaning between reader and writer. Other forms of written text (e.g., a private letter) might share only some of these problems.

Second, the writer generally has the time and sometimes the need to choose words precisely, to make relationships among ideas explicit, and to sequence the ideas in a 'considerate' manner (Kantor, 1978). As a result, written discourse is a crafted artefact — an object capable of being redrafted, reflected upon and sub-sequently altered. In this sense the written word is like the ritual monologues of certain pre-literate or primary oral cultures, except that it is less reliant on remembered stereotypic phrases, and more capable of generating novel combinations of utterances to heighten awareness of and response to the topic. This invites a relatively higher focus on the text itself as an object, and a diminished focus on the writer or the writer's unseen intentions. 'What is said' may become more important than 'what is meant', partly because of the visibility of the written word and the assumption that the actual wording matters.

The following example from an oral reading activity (taken from Heap, forthcoming) illustrates this point. The student (S) is reading from a book and the teacher (T) comments on the reading:

Example 1.4

S   "IT LOOKS COLD OUT THERE" SAID NICK. "I DO NOT
T   /Alright, it <u>means</u> do not/
S   /I <u>DON'T</u> HAVE A COAT, I CAN'T COME WITH YOU
T   /Good ((*said quietly*))

Written texts, especially where they are closely studied, as in schools, provide for this concern with accuracy. Misreading is also a problem in oral texts, of course, but where words are recorded rather than remembered, the issue of an accurate repro-duction can, to some extent, be resolved by direct appeal to the record.

The separation in time and space of writer and reader that characterizes written communication may be compared with the proximity of speakers when they are engaged in ordinary conversation (Perera, 1984). But the differences between these forms of communication are not absolute. That is, people can pass written notes to one another in a pseudo-conversational manner and people can speak through an electronic medium while they are spatially apart. Similarly television newsreaders 'speak' to listeners by reading from a written, highly condensed and structured script. The written form of communication does not logically require, but rather typically entails the separation of writer and reader, as can any permanent recording. The degree and nature of this separation in time and space gives rise to the need for a number of conventions and strategies that are distinct from those associated with successful oral-conversational communication (Rubin, 1980).

The oral/written comparisons we have introduced so far refer to ends of a continuum: informal oral-conversational language compared with, say, a published text. Between these extremes there are many forms of oral and written language which share the characteristics noted in various ways (Rubin, 1980).

Olson (1982) has drawn attention to the shift in focus from what is meant (in oral conversation) to what is said (in written text), and to the discourse characteristics that are consequent upon the separation of writer and reader. He argued that, while everyday oral communication is heavily and expressively value-laden, written text attempts to be value-free, focusing on the criteria of 'truth' rather than of social acceptability. Olson pointed out that written text appears to strive for an autonomy and authority principally because of its anonymity with respect to both writer and reader, in contrast to the personally grounded and context-based assumptions operating in everyday conversational exchange.

Demonstration of this point concerning the anonymous, authoritative attitude of some written text is readily available in the following extract, taken from the first page of an upper primary/lower secondary school reference book on the early Dutch discoveries of Australia.

Everyone recognises Captain James Cook as Australia's greatest discoverer-hero, and indeed he was. But he was not Australia's only hero, nor was he the earliest ... (Murdoch, 1974: 7)

To effect a meaning for the first sentence of this extract, a particular conception of knowledge is required: knowledge can be divided into what 'everyone' knows and, at a different and more authoritative level, into what is 'the case'. The fact that the utterance 'indeed he was . . .' can be made is shown here explicitly not to be dependent upon the agreement of people, in this case 'everyone'. Thus, the text claims a status for the knowledge it presents that is distinct from and more definitive than the knowledge that is constructed and held by 'everyone' — the text is, somehow, the voice of History. It is also possible that the term 'everyone' is meant here to connote 'people who are not specialist historians', and the definitive confirmation of their folk wisdom is to signify that, in this case, specialist historians happen to agree. What is privileged in this latter interpretation is the specialist community in whose voice the text is speaking (cf. Freebody, 1984). The result of such characteristics of written textual language, Olson asserted, is that the text claims for itself an unchallengeability across time, space and the cultural and linguistic resources of a potentially diverse readership.

Tannen (1982) has argued that the principal distinction between oral and written language is that oral language typically attains its cohesion and its relevance partly through those paralinguistic features that arise from the immediate environment, from the prosodic qualities of the speech, and from non-verbal exchanges between the interlocutors. Written language, on the other hand, is characterized by a reliance on lexicalization for its cohesion. That is, the texture and the significance of written discourse is almost exclusively reliant on the actual written words themselves, since texture and significance cannot emerge through paralinguistic accompaniments. While the written mode does afford some paralinguistic devices (e.g., italics for emphasis), these are limited in scope and in immediacy compared to those available to conversants.

The forms taken by this lexicalization process in written language have been studied by, among others, Chafe (1985). He found that conversational language is characterized by short idea units that relate to the immediate conscious intentions of speakers, while written language displays a prevalence of idea units that are expanded by adjectival and clausal conjoining, by nominal packing and by inventive, non-repetitious phrases and clauses. Studies of compositional processes in an elementary school classroom (e.g., Michaels, 1985, 1987) demonstrate how some of these conventions are conveyed through a teacher's corrections of students' written drafts.

Chafe argued further that writing affords a detachment that is not generally displayed in conversational exchange. Speakers in a conversation display through the language a higher involvement with their own view, with the views and the understandings of the listener, and with the informational content itself. Written discourse (in particular expository, informational text), on the other hand, strives, partly through such devices as the passive voice and the abstract nominalizing of the topic, to express its detachment from the writer, the reader and the content. This detachment in turn relates to the distinctive criteria for and demonstrations of evidence that are commonly found in the two forms of discourse. Chafe claimed that written discourse, because of the deliberation with which it may be constructed and because of its attempts to be readily transportable, tends to display explicit attempts to embody its own reliability and validity. As Tannen (1985) has pointed out, this detachment and formality of epistemological status results in the reader's having to 'recontextualize' the writer's purposes through a recognition of a text's structure and its relationship to other similar kinds of text.

Perhaps the most compelling image of the contrast between oral and written discourse has been provided by Halliday (1980), who speculated that the complexity of oral-conversational language is choreographic in nature, displaying a fluidity, a reliance on the interplay between the speakers and a transience in time and space. Written discourse on the other hand displays a complexity which Halliday characterized as crystalline. It is not only transportable, but intricate in a static, crafted manner. Further, he argued that each mode tends to represent the world in its own discourse image. That is, conversational language tends to create and organize a fluid reality as it proceeds, while written language seems to reflect a more static reality, comprised of products.

[written language] defines the universe as product rather than as process ... The cost of this perspective may be some simplifying of the relationship among its parts, and a lesser interest in how it got the way it is, or in where it is going next. (Halliday, 1980: 97)

Ways of knowing

It can be seen that the above sample of accounts of comparisons between oral and written language forms has led directly to the proposition that such differences implicate different ways of knowing as well as different ways of uttering. If the above contentions about the interactional differences between oral and written communication are warranted, then certain distinctions in the way we learn and know in oral versus written modes are entailed. In these terms, the worlds presented in oral and written discourses are distinct in their fundamental parameters: the conversational world is a happening world while the textual world appears to have happened.

The strong case for profound differences in the epistemological bases of primary oral versus literate cultures has been developed most fully by Ong (1958/1983, 1982). Ong has addressed himself to the issue of the ways in which thought, understanding, learning and memory are different in literate cultures from their counterparts in primary oral or non-literate cultures. Ong has argued that the printed word has served to dissociate knowledge from ordinary (oral-dialogic) human exchange and discourse, and has given it a quasi-monologic status:

By removing words from the world of sound where they had first had their origin in active human interchange and relegating them definitively to visual surface, and by otherwise exploiting visual space to the management of knowledge, print encouraged human beings to think of their own interior conscious and unconscious resources as more and more thing-like, impersonal and religiously neutral. Print encouraged the mind to sense that its possessions were held in some sort of inert mental space. (1982: 131–2)

Ong contended that it was the printed word that afforded the particular developments of modern mathematics and science in the Renaissance period, and catalysed their growing dominance as educational materials. These parallel processes constituted a departure from the concept of knowledge as it was embodied in dialogic, oral interaction, towards a concept of knowledge as reliant on the individualistic and visual aspects of experience. Learning in the Renaissance shifted radically from discourse-knowledge to observation-knowledge (Ong, 1958/1983: 151). The strong form of the argument here is that understanding, problem-solving and remembering are experiences which are carried out through dialogic processes in primary oral circumstances — that is, with other people through communicative exchange; but the opportunity afforded by books to display knowledge as static and spatialized (that is mapped or diagrammed on the page) has been grasped by the Western educational system, particularly since the time of the European Renaissance academies. The result is that written textual knowledge is now central in the educational process. The argument proceeds that this form of text- or observation-knowledge is not well suited to capturing the fluidity and oppositional nature of knowledge, even for those topics that seem epistemologically well tailored to such static representation, for example, mathematics and science. Rosen, some years ago, issued a complaint about the language of school textbooks and the way they present knowledge: 'Instead of the new formulations representing hard-won victories of intellectual struggle, or even partial victories, there are not even half-hearted skirmishes' (1972: 112).

It is the anonymity of the source of the written word in textual materials that allows them to be treated as clear windows on the topic. From this point of view, one consequence of early literacy exposure could be to have the definition and status of the text legitimized and unquestioned. The language forms of, the content of, and the classroom discussions surrounding books serve to establish written discourse as neutral observation on the topic; the legitimacy of a text's perspective and vantage point is rarely treated as a problem. The discourse in school books is generally not treated as a crafted product, the crafting of which can be observed in the written language. Thus the written word asks for, and is generally treated as if it warrants, the status of an unquestionably veridical vantage point on the topic — displaying a capacity to convey its meanings in a paralinguistic and perspectival void, and providing sufficient context within itself for its unequivocal interpretation. The texbook, in these respects, can be seen as a form of communicative discourse that is radically different from spoken language. The implication for the transformation of children into students and literate adults is that, in the face of depersonalized, universalized, 'crystalline' truths, the child is invited to become the recipient and reproducer of established knowledge. It might be thought that, if this end is to be achieved,

a number of critical redefinitions need to be accomplished by
students: (i) redefinition of language from a means of conveying
the fluidity of experience to language as a means of recording the
given; (ii) a redefinition of experience itself to be centrally structured in a way compatible with 'written knowing'; and (iii) a
redefinition of books as sanctioned devices for effecting these two
processes.

THE SCHOOL-LITERATE CHILD

Much of this chapter has been concerned with describing some
relations between oral and written language, and with addressing
certain aspects of encountering a written heritage and the conventions of print. In this section we turn to some preliminary observations about the special nature of the content of materials designed
for learning to read in early schooling.

Beginning school reading materials are not merely technical
devices for effecting a transition from competence with oral-
conversational uses of language to scribal competence or facility
with literate discourse. They are also cultural devices for introducing children to some conventions that govern contemporary
shooling. These include, centrally, the issue of how the relation
between *child* reader and written text is provided through the
selection of content for the books. Again in this section we
present some of the conceptual bases which will guide more
specific analyses in later chapters.

It is not surprising that first school books deal with children's
ordinary lives. They are possibly a unique corpus of text in that,
for the most part, they portray to their child-readers images of
children in routine contexts, mostly at school and at home,
engaged in mundane activities. It is hard to imagine adults reading
books about people apparently very like themselves going about
their unremarkable, everyday lives. The first school reading books
appear to attempt to make school reading 'relevant' to the child's
daily experience.

A number of points will be made about this attempt at relevance.
The first is that the familiarity of the mundane is a limited
interpretation of relevance; the second is that the books, being
written by adults, necessarily portray an adult construction of

childhood, in part through conveying an (apparently) child construction of adulthood. This construction is constrained by social distinctions such as cultural background, class and gender; in addition, the depiction by adult writers of apparently ordinary children at home and at school, and the use of these depictions in school lessons amounts to one generation promoting its preferred version of the next. The books written for early reading instruction may be viewed as a special discourse:

The idea of childhood is not a natural but a social construct; as such its status is constituted in particular socially located forms of discourse ... the child is assembled intentionally to serve the purposes of supporting and perpetuating the fundamental grounds of and versions of man, action, order, language, and rationality within particular theories. (Jenks, 1982: 23)

Previous characterizations of the kind of child and the kind of social world produced in modern basal reading series are reviewed in Luke's historical analysis (1987b, 1988a). Luke outlined the close connections between the development of these specialized texts portraying the everyday lives of 'typical' children, the development of a scientific psychology of reading instruction, and the view that literacy had as an aim the efficient adaptation of children to existing orders of knowledge and social organization. Luke has treated the ideological contents of early reading books as preparation for adult citizenship. We emphasize the marking of child status in the prevailing organization of age relations, and preparation for child membership in the classroom community. We view the textual construction of childhood itself (heavily coded in our corpus also through gender categories) to be fundamental to the design and the use of the books. The accomplishment of adult citizenship requires, first, lessons in child and school-child status.

To use Willes's (1983) terms, early schooling turns children into pupils. It is our contention that the importance of learning to read and the non-accidental fact that early reading materials contain portrayals of children behaving at home and at school in routine ways point to the important role of early reading materials in effecting the change from children to pupils. As we will document in later chapters, particular constructions of childhood can be discerned in the materials in these early school texts.

We have raised already the issue of how childhood is described within adult culture. Most commonsense conceptions of childhood and psychological and sociological theories of development posit a particular arrival point in adulthood. There is evident in all such accounts a version of the mature, properly functioning adult, towards which state children progress under the guidance and supervision of adults. This progression then comes to characterize development. Data collected within these theoretical frameworks, therefore, tend to document and itemize children's incompetencies or precompetencies in terms of the final desired state. Recommendations to parents and teachers then come to be based on idealized adult standards for thought and action.

It is in these senses that both commonsense conceptions and scientific accounts of childhood operate in a colonizing fashion. The attention of the colonists is focused on those aspects of indigenous activity and culture which, in comparison with their own, can be defined as different and inferior, but which are open to change through educational, missionary, medical and other forms of intervention. This attention arises not necessarily from a lack of interest in the culture of the indigenes — some aspects of it might be found amusing, noble, or clever — but from the assumption of the superior competence and culture of the colonizing group. Interpretations of child behaviour in terms of the comparison with adults posit the nature of childhood as a stage of precompetence and an early although natural stage of progression towards adult activity, and thus adult status. Early school reading materials may be viewed as part of the colonizing programme. The portrayal of the nature and status of childhood is central to that programme.

SUMMARY

We have argued in this chapter that the acquisition of literacy involves various levels of relation between oral and written language. As initial reading materials, the first school books would be expected to contain features that document methods for effecting a transition from oral to school-literate forms of language use. One level of transition involves the presentation of a particular relationship between oral language and the graphic form that the language community has (from the novice's point of view, idiosyncratically) chosen. Another level implicates the distinct set of interactional competencies required in the successful management of written communication. The written word, as it has come to be used in modern Western schooling, also implicates distinctive ways of learning and knowing in a mode that presents reality in a form distinct from that expressed through dialogic conversational language. We have suggested further that the location of these transitional tensions is not solely in technical or interactional demands, but can be seen to extend into the definition of child-hood and school-childhood in particular. In these senses children's first school books can be seen as serving a variety of both obvious and covert socialization purposes.

The chapters that follow contain detailed examinations and discussions of a corpus of text of reading books produced for children in their first years of schooling. It is important, therefore, that the reader be presented with our view of the broader picture of which research of this type forms a part. For, while we offer detailed examinations of features of the language in beginning school books, our analyses are both informed by and themselves inform our broader concerns with schooling and with contem-porary accounts and constructions of childhood.

As the book proceeds we will be drawing on a variety of theoretical and research sources, not only in the area of literacy but also in other fields pertinent to children, language and schooling. While our presentation of some original analyses of a particular body of data is central to this book, those analyses will be linked continually to various levels of theorizing.

We view the interpretation of our data in an analogous way to that in which rhetoricians have viewed the act of interpretation. A key metaphor in such interpretation has been 'the hermeneutic circle' — the apparent paradox that each element of an utterance (e.g., a word, or a sentence) can be endowed with meaning only in the context of the larger frame in which it appears (e.g., a clause, or a more extended discourse). However, this larger frame itself is in turn constructed and visible only through the individual elements. The solution to this apparent paradox is to draw attention to the persistent interplay among elements (and between the discourse and the context) as the generative mainspring of in-terpretation. The recurrent and often instantaneous shift between figure and ground is the mechanism by which meaning is constructed by both writer and reader. A parallel is found in the ethnomethodological notion of the 'documentary method of interpretation' (Garfinkel, 1967), in which 'particulars' are used to assemble an underlying pattern which is itself the source of the sense and significance of the particulars. Such notions are reflected also in recent interactive theories of reading (e.g., Anderson, 1977; McClelland and Rumelhart, 1981; Rumelhart, 1977).

We take it that the relation between empirical observation, theorizing and practice arises from an analogous interplay. Theoretical accounts of the effects of literacy and schooling on children have often stressed abstract notions such as 'institutional control of knowledge', or broad-gauged programme issues such as 'meaning versus skills emphasis'. It is our position that such abstractions earn their explanatory value only if they are grounded in detailed observations that can in turn be reasonably interpreted in these larger terms. We concur with Whitty, who drew attention to the need for continual mutual interrogation between theoretical and empirical research (1985: 40). This point is also made by Olson in his observations about the necessary explanatory interplay between detailed examinations of school-textual materials and broader accounts of their institutional use and significance:

theories of 'text' that ignore the social, institutional context are inadequate while theories of social structure and authority, which simply talk about the exercise of power without seeing how that authority is created and exercised in particular social contexts such as reading and study, are banal. (Olson, 1983: 130)

This commitment to grounding explanatory notions in the details of daily practice affords increasingly refined directions for relevant observations that, in turn, both make visible and sharpen the outlines of the larger explanatory picture. It is this interplay which permits observers, in this case of literacy and childhood, to develop principled grounds for practice.

2

A Descriptive Outline of the Beginning Reading Corpus

In this chapter we present a description of the vocabulary content of the beginning reading corpus (henceforth called the BR corpus), and we compare some of its central features with those of two other language samples — a collection of the spoken language of children at about the age of entry into formal schooling, and a corpus of the language of school textbooks written for grades three to nine (ages 7 to 14). The purposes of this outline are first to indicate the bases for some of the more interpretive analyses of the BR texts we provide in later chapters, and second to examine at a general level some of those differences that are found in the language used by young children, the language shown to them in their first school books and the language used in texts encountered in the later years of schooling. Pursuing these purposes necessitates the inclusion of some detailed and technical descriptions of the vocabulary content.

Some of the analyses presented in later chapters arose from observation of a number of unexpected characteristics of the BR texts visible in simple word frequency counts. For example, the prevalence of the reportage of direct speech, the differing usage rates of male and female terms, the continual appearance of mothers and fathers, and the striking salience of animal characters were all evident in the word frequency analyses of the corpus, and thus alerted us to some major features of this textual terrain, which we go on to report in more detail in this and later chapters.

We propose that contrasting the BR corpus with the other language samples affords some understanding of the nature of the BR books as transitional between oral—conversational conventions and the conventions of school textbook language. In this chapter these distinctions will be examined at the level of word and word-family frequency counts. Some of the more suggestive structural and thematic distinctions will be highlighted in an attempt to document the contention that oral and written language serve somewhat different intellectual and social functions. The comparisons show specific ways in which first school books can be viewed as transitional from oral conversational to written textual uses of language.

DESCRIPTION OF THE BR CORPUS

For purposes of our analyses of the BR corpus, a word was defined as a string of graphic characters bounded by spaces to the left and right. Letters of the alphabet, apostrophes and hyphens were included, while mathematical symbols, numerals and nonsense syllables used in songs or rhymes were not. The frequency of a capitalized word was combined with that of its non-capitalized counterpart. Using these criteria, it was found that there were 83,838 words of running text in these books (that is, 'word tokens'), and 2,477 different words (that is, 'word types'). Appendix 1 contains the complete word list, arranged alphabetically.

TABLE 2.1 Central tendency values for word and sentence length in the BR corpus

	Words (in letters)		Sentences (in words)			
	Tokens	Types	Decl.	Int.	Excl.	Total
Mean	3.61	5.44	6.46	5.80	3.02	6.11
SD	1.59	1.92	3.76	2.77	3.16	3.79
Median	3	5	6	5	2	5
Mode	3	5	5	4	1	5
Range	1−15	1−15	1−25	1−22	1−21	1−25
Total	83,838	2,477	11,643	818	1,257	13,718

Decl., declaratives; Int., interrogatives; Excl; exclamations.

In table 2.1 the lengths of words and sentences in the BR corpus are indicated. It can be seen first that the mean length of all word tokens in the corpus is very small (3.61 letters); further, the distribution is highly skewed toward the lower end of the scale, such that 79 per cent of all words in the corpus have four letters or less. Most words, therefore, are one-syllable words. This may suggest a policy of ease of decoding on the part of the writers, but it none the less needs to be noted that shortness of a word does not equal its ease or its sound-grapheme regularity. A considerable number of regulating principles would need to be put in place to cope with some of the short, frequently occurring words in the BR corpus, for example, *was, said, come* and *some*; this applies even in the case of words that are not function words or heavy duty substance words, for example, *tea, new, boat, bear* and *dear.*

It is also clear from a comparison of the average length of the unique word types in the corpus with that of the tokens that it is the shorter words that appear more frequently in running text. The central tendency measures of length of types are about two letters greater than for tokens. In addition, the distribution for type lengths is more centrally placed about the mean, such that 74 per cent of the unique word types have a length of six letters or less. So the books, not unexpectedly, are heavily loaded with very short, but not uniformly easy to decode, words. Longer words are present (there are 160 unique words with a length of more than eight letters), but these are not highly or even moderately frequent, in spite of the fact than many of them seem to present no fewer or less daunting decoding problems than do the shorter words (e.g., *blanket, clattering, jumper* and *sprinkler*).

Examination of the lengths of various kinds of sentences is also informative. Declarative statements (any string ending in a full stop) are the most prevalent (85 per cent) in these books. Most of the narrator's sentences are declarative. Declarative sentences are generally a little longer than questions (any string ending in a question mark), and considerably longer than exclamations (any string ending in an exclamation mark). Most of the questions and exclamations are produced by characters in reported direct speech. Declarative informational sentences produced by the narrator and by characters comprise the bulk of sentences encountered.

The median length of all sentences in the books is five words. Thus the term 'staccato', used earlier, seems to be an apt description of much of the language in the BR books. These written sentences represent a segmentation of the conversational or narrative stream into grammatically standard units. Oral conversational language, as exemplified by the Sally and Ann transcript in the previous chapter, does not necessarily occur in such segmented and standardized forms.

In summary, these initial analyses of word and sentence length — showing mostly short words in simple and regular sentences — already implicate the observation that this written script idealizes and transforms ordinary oral language use.

COMPARISONS WITH OTHER CORPUSES

The remainder of this chapter is taken up with presentation of major features of the BR corpus through comparison with two other accessible and detailed language samples — a sample of the spoken language of 4½–5½-year-old white US children (henceforth called the Spoken corpus), and a sample of textbooks written for US school students in all school subject areas between grades three and nine, that is, for ages approximately 7–14 years (henceforth the Grades 3–9 corpus). First, the nature and source of these latter two language samples will be described.

Hall and Nagy (1984) collected samples of the speech of middle- and working-class black and white children attending pre-schools in the United States. A total of 40 children wore wireless microphones sewn into their clothing, and all of their language, and that of nearby children and adults, was collected over a two-day period at home, in pre-school and in transition between these locations. Since a major purpose of these researchers was to document variations relating to ethnicity and social class, they reported data separately for the four ethnicity-by-class groups. Also, they reported separately the language samples obtained from the target children, other children and adults. Our interest, however, is focused mainly on outlining a picture of the language usage patterns of children at around the age they would encounter their first school books; thus we use as our comparison the language of the target children only. Also we note that significant variations have been shown to exist in the language of white and black US children (e.g., by Hall and Guthrie, 1980), so, in the interests of comparability with the BR corpus, we compiled the Spoken corpus used here only from the language of white middle- and working-class target children.

The language sample comprising written school texts for grades three to nine was constructed by Carroll, Davies and Richman (1971). The texts from which this large sample was drawn included textbooks in all major school subjects (reading, literature, mathematics, art, spelling, library references etc.), as well as workbooks used in schools, kits, encyclopedias and magazines. Inclusion of materials in this sample was guided by a large cross-section of school administrators' responses to questions concerning books and other textual materials used in their schools or their districts. The compilers of the corpus believed that the corpus represents 'as nearly as possible, the range of required and recommended reading to which students are exposed in school grades 3 through 9 in the United States (1971: xiii)'.

TABLE 2.2   General characteristics of the three language samples

	Spoken	BR	Grades 3–9
No. words (tokens)	158,217	83,838	5,088,721
No. different words (types)	6,937	2,477	86,741
Mean appearance rate (each word appears once per ...)	23	34	59
% of types of once-occurring words	14.7	30.9	40.4
% of tokens of once-occurring words	0.64	0.91	0.69
No. words accounting for about half of all text	60	49	113

Some general characteristics of the three language samples are provided in table 2.2. It can be seen that, while the average appearance rates per unique word in the Spoken and BR corpuses are comparable, and significantly different from those in the Grades 3–9 corpus, the BR corpus is distinctive in that it presents to the reader a higher percentage of very rare (once-occurring) words (30.9 per cent) compared to the Spoken corpus (14.7 per cent). Also, when the once-only rate in all running text is examined, it is clear that the BR texts present about one-and-a-half times the proportion of rare words (0.91 per cent) than do either of the other language samples. The BR corpus, in comparison with the other two corpuses, has a high proportion of frequently occurring words and a high proportion of very rare words, with a smaller number of words showing moderate appearance rates. The three corpuses, therefore, describe three somewhat different shapes of the distribution of the proportions of words at the various frequency levels.

It is of interest also to compare which words perform the heaviest duty in the three corpuses. Comparing these sets of words allows a view of some of the major thematic and structural preferences operating in the three samples. Table 2.3 presents the 50 most common words in each of the three corpuses, along with their appearance rates per 1,000 words of text, and the cumulative proportion of the text accounted for with the addition of each word. We will draw attention to a number of features of this table, some of which will also be referred to in later chapters.

First, at the highest level of frequency we find the words *I* in the Spoken corpus and *the* in the two samples of written text. In the spoken language of 5-year-olds, the word *I* accounts for about one word in 21, while *the* is about half as frequent. In contrast, the word *the* appears about every 14 words on the average in the written samples, while *I* is substantially rarer, especially in the textbooks for older students (about once per 200 words).

Longer discourses on a single topic would be expected to be more common in written than in spoken language, which by contrast occurs in episodically more fragmented contexts. That is, in everyday spoken language, objects and people would be expected to come and go in more rapid and varied succession than in written language. The exception, of course, is the speaker himself or herself, who remains a constant reference point in everyday, spoken interaction — thus the fact that *I* is the most frequently spoken word. This in turn accounts for the relatively lighter duty

TABLE 2.3 Most common 50 words in the three language samples

	Spoken				BR				Grades 3–9		
Rank	Word	F/1,000	CP	Rank	Word	F/1,000	CP	Rank	Word	F/1,000	CP
1	I	46.73	0.047	1	the	70.06	0.070	1	the	73.32	0.073
2	you	30.01	0.077	2	and	28.17	0.099	2	of	28.69	0.102
3	it	24.74	0.101	3	a	28.15	0.127	3	and	26.31	0.128
4	a	22.62	0.124	4	to	27.76	0.155	4	a	24.56	0.153
5	the	22.39	0.146	5	I	22.48	0.177	5	to	23.85	0.177
6	and	15.77	0.162	6	said	20.50	0.198	6	in	19.48	0.197
7	to	15.21	0.177	7	is	17.84	0.216	7	is	11.96	0.209
8	no	13.23	0.191	8	you	15.12	0.231	8	you	10.01	0.219
9	what	11.68	0.202	9	in	14.30	0.245	9	that	9.32	0.228
10	this	10.72	0.213	10	he	12.37	0.257	10	it	9.29	0.238
11	that	10.11	0.223	11	it	11.71	0.269	11	he	9.09	0.247
12	my	9.91	0.233	12	can	11.13	0.280	12	was	8.04	0.255
13	I'm	9.69	0.243	13	they	9.09	0.289	13	for	7.73	0.263
14	is	9.32	0.252	14	we	8.84	0.298	14	on	7.17	0.270
15	on	9.28	0.261	15	here	8.18	0.306	15	are	6.97	0.277
16	me	9.10	0.270	16	on	7.94	0.314	16	as	6.33	0.283
17	in	8.95	0.279	17	says	7.81	0.322	17	with	5.99	0.289
18	ha	8.93	0.288	18	little	7.78	0.320	18	his	5.75	0.295
19	don't	8.11	0.296	19	go	7.65	0.337	19	they	5.43	0.300
20	one	7.93	0.304	20	for	7.48	0.345	20	I	5.10	0.305
21	ah	7.90	0.312	21	Peter	7.36	0.352	21	at	4.71	0.310
22	he	7.56	0.320	22	at	7.34	0.360	22	be	4.67	0.315
23	have	7.20	0.327	23	come	7.07	0.367	23	this	4.58	0.319

Rank	Word	F/1,000	CP	Rank	Word	F/1,000	CP	Rank	Word	F/1,000	CP
25	yeah	7.08	0.341	25	are	6.26	0.381	25	have	4.37	0.328
26	oh	7.06	0.348	26	see	6.83	0.388	26	or	4.18	0.332
27	want	6.53	0.355	27	look	6.79	0.394	27	had	4.03	0.336
28	know	6.38	0.361	28	big	6.73	0.401	28	by	3.97	0.340
29	go	5.67	0.367	29	she	5.88	0.407	29	one	3.93	0.344
30	it's	5.62	0.373	30	have	5.76	0.413	30	but	3.77	0.348
31	get	5.52	0.378	31	Jane	5.75	0.418	31	not	3.66	0.351
32	right	5.52	0.384	32	my	5.74	0.424	32	what	3.48	0.355
33	see	5.50	0.389	33	will	5.44	0.430	33	all	3.35	0.358
34	like	5.45	0.395	34	up	5.34	0.435	34	were	3.34	0.362
35	here	5.25	0.400	35	not	5.24	0.440	35	we	3.23	0.365
36	not	5.01	0.405	36	of	4.93	0.445	36	when	3.12	0.368
37	look	4.95	0.410	37	like	4.84	0.450	37	your	3.01	0.371
38	up	4.82	0.415	38	get	4.69	0.455	38	said	3.01	0.374
39	now	4.78	0.419	39	ran	4.47	0.459	39	can	3.00	0.377
40	of	4.37	0.424	40	yes	4.29	0.463	40	there	2.99	0.380
41	come	4.31	0.428	41	play	4.27	0.468	41	an	2.89	0.383
42	but	4.17	0.432	42	me	4.22	0.472	42	each	2.81	0.386
43	how	4.14	0.436	43	some	4.22	0.476	43	which	2.75	0.388
44	that's	4.10	0.440	44	this	4.19	0.480	44	she	2.68	0.391
45	I'll	3.99	0.444	45	Jack	4.13	0.484	45	how	2.61	0.394
46	we	3.96	0.448	46	out	4.07	0.488	46	their	2.61	0.396
47	put	3.83	0.452	47	went	4.07	0.493	47	if	2.54	0.399
48	there	3.59	0.456	48	was	3.90	0.496	48	up	2.51	0.401
49	can	3.54	0.459	49	down	3.71	0.500	49	do	2.50	0.404
50	when	3.53	0.463	50	do	3.67	0.503	50	will	2.49	0.406

F/1,000, frequency per thousand words. CP, cumulative proportion of text.

performed by *the* in the oral mode, since *the* generally signals co-reference with, or at least entailment in, a word previously introduced. This reflects the fact that the speaker uses language as an integral operator in and commentator on daily life, while the writer is engaged in the production of an artifice of which one of the characteristics is the pursuit of topic, with people and objects traced through time. This observation supports the point made by Chafe (1985) about the detachment of topic from writer in written language, compared with the involvement typical of oral language. So, in this fundamental respect, the written use of language can be seen as a qualitatively different type of activity in the social world from the conversational use of language.

Similarly, a comparison of the uses of *a* and *the* in the three corpuses points to the more episodic, less consistently topic-driven nature of spoken language. The use of *a* relates often to the introduction of a noun into the discourse, while it is usually preceded by *the* in subsequent references. These two articles have very similar appearance rates in the Spoken corpus, while *the* is about two-and-a-half times more frequent in the written texts.

Just as the marking of the speaker's subjectivity (*I*, *me*, *my* etc.) acts as the major cohering device in spoken language use, the immediacy of the interlocutor acts in conversation as the complementary contextual anchor, as indicated by the significantly greater use of *you* in the Spoken corpus. The BR corpus represents something of an intermediate point between the other corpuses in this respect. In the BR corpus, *you* is used about half as often as in the spoken language of 5-year-olds, but about 50 per cent more often than in the texts for older students. Clearly speakers incorporate more direct reference to their interlocutors than do writers of school text books for the upper grades, and the BR materials provide an intermediate point between the two, partly accounted for by the incidence of reported direct speech in the BR corpus.

The third most frequent word spoken by the young children is *it*, a pronoun which can rely on reference to the extralinguistic environment in a conversational context, but which generally requires prior or immediately subsequent nominal reference in writing. Again, we interpret the two-and-a-half times higher frequency of *it* in spoken language to be attributable to references to the immediate elements of the speaker's environment as the key topics of conversational exchange. Indeed, the combined frequency of pronouns referring to speaker (*I*), interlocutor (*you*) and topic (*it*) amounts to about 10 per cent of all spoken words (a finding replicated in Hart's survey (1974) of the spoken language of 5-year-old children). In contrast, these three terms, which pro-nominally incorporate the immediate salient aspects of the context into the discourse, account together for about 2 per cent of all word tokens in the two written samples.

There is an additional point of contrast between the BR corpus and the other two that suggests that the children's first school books offer a transition between oral-conversational and written uses of language — that is, the frequency of the word *said*. If we combine the frequencies of *said, say* and *says* in the BR corpus, we find that the *say* family fills second place on the word list behind *the* (3 per cent of the text or about once every 33 words on average). This indicates the extraordinary prevalence of the reportage of talk in these early school books. The texts seem to call explicitly and continually on the oral-conversational tradition of the child, in that direct speech is frequently represented. As we document in a later chapter, however, there are important differ-ences between naturally occurring, everyday conversations children may be involved in and the representations of conversations in the BR texts. Also, reporting speech with the use of *said* does not appear to be a major feature of young children's spoken language; the verb does not appear in the first column of table 2.3.

There is a further dimension to the preference for direct speech in the BR books. In literate discourse, we adopt the direct speech form when the actual wording of speeches matters to the com-municational outcome. Otherwise, we typically recount in indirect speech ('she said that . . .') or with a summary interpretation of the message ('he doesn't want to . . .'), and presume sufficiency for practical communicational purposes. Thus the preference for direct speech in the beginning reading books models 'primary orality' (Ong, 1982) or pre-literate oral experience. At this point it is sufficient to note that reported speech is a central feature of the language of beginning reading books. Even when the narrative-based subject areas of the Grades 3–9 corpus (reading, literature, fiction) are examined separately, we find that the appearance of the general speaker-identification terms (e.g., *says, said*) accounts for only eight words per thousand in narrative, about one-quarter as frequently as in the BR corpus. Thus, in the beginning reading books, direct talk and speaker identification are significantly more prevalent than in other written samples.

Certain grammatical distinctions in language use in the three corpuses are also suggested by the differing usage rates of key relational or prepositional terms. The second most frequent word in the Grades 3–9 sample, for example, is *of*, a word with about one-sixth that usage rate in the Spoken and BR corpuses. Since *of* generally indicates either belonging or partitioning, and since belonging terms (generally possessive pronouns or apostrophized nouns) are frequent in both the Spoken and BR samples, we infer that it is mainly the partitioning function of *of* that is under-represented in the language of and for the younger children. That is, structures such as 'the early part of the century . . .' or 'some of the Tudor kings . . .' emerge substantially only in the later textbooks (cf. Perera, 1984).

A final point about the BR list shown in table 2.3 is that we were intrigued by the appearance of *little* in the highest frequency range. It is substantially less frequent in the other samples. Also, in the BR list shown in table 2.3, it is the only two-syllable word apart from *Peter*, and one of the very few substance words. Moreover, it is grapho-phonically irregular. Thus, its prevalence invites some examination.

One partial explanation is that *little* occurs in the names of several popular storybook and fairy-tale characters (for example, Little Red Riding Hood). Such usages account for 89 of the 652 appearances of *little*. Even taking this into account, however, the word *little* is surprisingly prevalent. It seems that size is a dimension which beginning reading books emphasize. Table 2.4 presents the frequency of the four major size descriptors in the BR sample and in the levels covered by the other samples. It is notable first that *little* and *big* appear significantly more frequently in the BR books than in the talk of young children, and second, that the frequency of *little* and *big* significantly decreases with increasing grade level in the Grades 3–9 sample. No such diminution in the use of *small* and *large* is evident.

It may not, therefore, merely be size differences that are empha-sized in the beginning reading books but rather a particular elab-oration of size – not *smallness* but *littleness*. *Littleness* has an additional semantic component: in the *Oxford English Dictionary*, for example, the first two entries for *little* essentially equate it

TABLE 2.4 Frequency of four size-related terms per 1,000 words of text in the three language samples

Corpus	*little*	*big*	*small*	*large*
		Terms		
Spoken	2.00	1.57	—	—
BR	7.78	6.73	0.33	0.02
Grades 3–9				
3	2.11	1.54	0.75	0.50
4	1.45	0.92	0.80	0.54
5	0.99	0.53	0.73	0.62
6	1.17	0.50	0.72	0.61
7	1.00	0.43	0.61	0.51
8	0.78	0.34	0.59	0.46
9	0.68	0.27	0.61	0.57

with *small*, but the third entry reads, 'used to convey an implication of endearment or depreciation, or of tender feelings on the part of the speaker' (1971: 351). To *depreciate*, in turn, is defined as 'to lower in estimation, to represent as of less value, to underrate, to undervalue, to belittle' (218). *Small* conveys no such tenderness or depreciation but more neutrally represents one end of the size dimension. The 'little kitten' is more elaborated than the 'small kitten'. The former, in addition to being small, is also felt to be approachable, warm and harmless. This additional meaning component we might call the 'cuddle factor'. We will have more to say in later chapters about the uses of *little*, in particular its differential attachment to *boys* and *girls*. It is sufficient to note here that littleness and bigness are presented to young children as highly salient characteristics. The prevalence of *little/big* informs young children of the importance not only of size but also of certain qualities that are associated with size and that may, among others things, support a particular organization of child–adult relations (Widdowson, 1976).

A further, simplified contrast of the three language samples is provided in table 2.5, which shows the most frequent 20 word types in the BR corpus (in the centre column), and indicates their frequency rankings in the other corpuses. Some of the comparabilities and contrasts reviewed above among the three corpuses are summarized in this table. It should be kept in mind that the most frequent 20 word types in the BR corpus account for slightly more than one-third of all running text.

TABLE 2.5   Rank orders in the other two language samples of the 20 most frequent words in the BR corpus

Spoken	BR		Grades 3–9
Rank	Rank	Word	Rank
5	1	the	1
6	2	and	3
4	3	a	4
7	4	to	5
1	5	I	20
95	6	said	38
14	7	is	7
2	8	you	8
17	9	in	6
22	10	he	11
3	11	it	10
49	12	can	39
74	13	they	19
46	14	we	35
35	15	here	137
15	16	on	14
>250	17	says	>250
93	18	little	92
29	19	go	106
57	20	for	13

In addition to those contrasts already remarked upon, it is worth noting that the most frequent four words in the BR texts are also very frequent in the textbook corpus. The word rankings for the BR texts seem generally close to those for the Grades 3–9 corpus, in particular in the case of *is, you, in, he, it, on, they* and *for*. Thus, for pronouns and multi-purpose function words, the prevalence rates are notably closer when the BR and Grades 3–9 corpuses are compared. On the other hand, those instances in which the rankings of the BR words are closer to those in the Spoken corpus include *I, here* and *go. Here* is a deictic term, more likely to be used in conversation or to indicate location by a speaker on the scene.

To elaborate further the comparative patterns of frequency in the three language samples, the rates of appearance of a number of common 'word families' were computed. These serve to highlight further some of the differing functions of language use in the three corpuses.

First, table 2.6 shows the appearance rates per thousand words of running text for the various personal pronouns. Each row heading represents a collection of terms. For example, under first person singular has been included *I, I'm, I'll, me, my* and so on. Regarding initially the column totals, it is clear that spoken language is heavily laden with personal pronouns (about one word in 5.5, on the average, of all of the talk of 5-year-old children). The textbooks written for older students contain a personal pronoun rate of about two-and-a-half times less (about one word in 14) than that of the Spoken corpus, while the BR texts occupy a point between these levels of frequency on these measures (about one word in nine on average).

TABLE 2.6 Approximate appearance rates per 1,000 words of personal pronouns in the three language samples

		Spoken	BR	Grades 3–9
Person				
first	sing.	83	36	9
	plur.	8	12	6
second		38	17	14
third	sing.	47	31	32
	plur.	7	13	11
Total		183	109	72

Examining the entries for each person and number shows that it is largely due to the levels of first person singular use that the BR total appears at this intermediate level. Thus, the BR books include substantially less of the '*I–me*' voice than does the Spoken corpus, but substantially more than does the Grades 3–9 corpus. It is worth noting that separate analyses of the Grades 3–9 narrative fiction and expository non-fiction subcorpuses reveal that, while first person singular pronouns appear on an average of nine times per thousand overall, they appear at almost twice that rate in the narrative/fiction subcorpus. Thus, the 'story books' for the older students contain more than four times the rate of first person singular pronoun use than do comparable expository/information texts.

The use of 'I—me' at an intermediate level in the BR books is a significant point in that these books, more than any other documented written corpus, offer a direct embedded personal voice to the child-reader, either through the speech of characters, as in reported dialogue, or through the unique strategy of showing unidentified, unpunctuated apparent speech, a point we pursue in more detail in chapter 4. Many of the stories in the BR corpus contain utterances such as 'I go to school. I like my teacher. I ... etc.'. The reader is thus invited to assume the writer's voice, since no textual devices such as speech identification or inverted commas are provided that might serve to distance that voice by assigning it to a particular character. The act of reading either the omnipresent reported direct speech or the first person voice projected in the BR books can be seen as a hybrid of oral conversation and informational text reading.

Further, when the rates of those pronouns that indicate speaker and interlocutor presence are combined (i.e., first and second person totals), and compared with other-indicating pronouns (third person totals including *he, she, it, they*) for the three corpuses, the intermediate position of the BR corpus again appears. About 70 per cent of all pronouns in the Spoken corpus are first or second person, about 54 per cent in the BR readers and about 40 per cent in the Grades 3—9 corpus. Thus, in the texts for older students, the balance has shifted from marking the presence of speaker and hearer (or writer and reader), to pronominal reference in the third person. Again, the BR texts can be viewed as a transitional point in that shift.

Since the most common verb family in the BR corpus comprises forms of the verb *to be*, some comparison of the tenses of that verb in the three corpuses gives an indication of the temporal framework within the texts. Table 2.7 reports the frequencies per thousand words of running text of the various tense forms of the verb *to be* in the three corpuses.

For both the Spoken and BR corpuses, about 70 per cent of all forms of the verb appear in the present tense (*am, is, are, I'm, she's*, etc.). In the BR books, this appears largely in the reported

TABLE 2.7   Approximate appearance rates per 1,000 words of tenses of the verb 'to be' in the three language samples

Tense	Spoken	BR	Grades 3–9
Present	44	32	21
Past	5	5	12
Future	8	7	3
'Be/being/been'	3	2	7
Total	60	46	43

speech of the characters (e.g., '"This is fun," he said'), in the present tense employed by the narrator in some of the stories (e.g., 'Jane looks on'), and in 'experiential' texts (e.g., 'It's warm in here, in bed'). The texts for the older students also contain a substantial proportion of present tense forms (about half); but they contain more than twice the rate of past tense use than do the other two corpuses. There is also a proportional decrease in the use of future forms in the texts for older children. In both the Spoken and BR corpuses, slightly more future than past forms appear, indicating the more frequent use of language to express intentions and wishes than is the case in the Grades 3–9 corpus. The latter sample is clearly using language proportionally more often to report past events.

However, when the fiction and non-fiction subcorpuses of the Grades 3–9 corpus are examined separately, the pattern of past and present uses of the verb *to be* indicates a cross-over of function. That is, while the total for present tense forms (per thousand words) for the whole Grades 3–9 corpus is 21, the frequency of present tense forms is 15 per thousand in the fiction texts, and 25 in the non-fiction texts. Thus, non-fiction texts contain substantially more present tense uses of the verb *to be*, possibly reflecting more exposition on what 'is' the case. With respect to the past tense forms, this pattern is reversed (12 per thousand overall; but 17 per thousand for fiction and 11 per thousand for non-fiction). If we regard the BR books as fiction, from this analysis we would expect to find more use of the past tense. The fact that we do not find this suggests that one of the distinctive contrasts of the BR texts with fictional materials written for older students is that the former operate predominantly in the present tense.

Looking at the next most frequent verb in the BR corpus, *said* occurs 20 times per thousand words while *says* occurs about eight times per thousand words. We explore the implications of the temporal framework within the stories further in commenting on narrative and expository forms in chapter 4 and on the significance of reported conversation, indexed by the frequency of *said*, in chapter 5. Table 2.2 also indicates the frequency of the verbs *go*, *come*, *see* and *look* in the BR corpus. These appearance rates indicate the extent to which the texts portray routine 'everyday life' activities such as changing physical location, and the importance of attending to the details of the visual environment. We will comment in more detail on the kinds of social worlds and of child-consciousness that the texts assemble, in later chapters.

The appearance rates in the Spoken and Grades 3–9 corpuses of a number of other word families that are very frequent in the BR corpus are also of note. First, about 60 words per thousand (1 in 17 of running text) in the BR corpus are prepositions, being mainly to do with location (*above, below*, etc.) and *in* (mainly locational but occasionally temporal, e.g., 'in the morning'). While the preposition rate in the Spoken corpus is slightly lower (40 per thousand) for these prepositions, this pattern contrasts strongly with the appearance of prepositions in the Grades 3–9 corpus: first, the appearance rate of prepositions is higher in the Grades 3–9 texts (83 per thousand, or about one word in 12 of running text); second, about 60 per cent of prepositions in the Grades 3–9 corpus are *in* or *of*, and only 15 per cent are locational (*above, below* etc.).

Thus, the BR and Spoken corpuses are comparable in their presentation of 'place' as a contextualizing device and in their heavy reliance on *in*. The emergence of *of* (discussed in an earlier section), and a lower frequency of locating prepositions characterizes the Grades 3–9 corpus. This contrast is compatible with the frequency rates of locational and temporal deictic terms in the three corpuses. Locational deictic terms (*here, there*, etc.) are more prevalent than temporal terms in the Spoken and BR corpuses (by a ratio of about two to one), while temporal deictic terms (*now, then* etc.) are slightly more prevalent than locational terms in the Grades 3–9 corpus. Thus the books for the older students signal relative temporality and recontextualize through time as often as they do space, while the speech of the younger children, like the books written for them, realizes a more static temporal framework and more reference to physical location in the language. Thus as a literary form the BR books in this respect also may be seen to be transitional between conversational and textbook language.

CONCLUSION

In this chapter we have presented, using frequency analyses, some of the salient descriptive features of the vocabulary in the BR corpus, and compared some of these features with those of a corpus of the spoken language of 5-year-old children and with those of a corpus of school textbook language. We have shown that short words do a great deal of the work in the running text of BR books, but that many of these short words are not regular or easy to decode. We have also demonstrated that the vast majority of sentence types are declarative, with comparatively few exclamations and fewer still interrogatives. Thus, the extremely high incidence of reported conversations in these books consists to a large extent of the exchange of declarations.

We have argued that, in certain respects, the language use in the BR texts appears more comparable to the spoken language of young children than to that of school textbook language. For example, the predominant use of the present tense links the temporal dimension of the discourse closely to that mainly operating in speech, as does the reference to location within a present time-frame in the language of the books. In certain other respects, however, the BR texts can be seen as transitional in their language patterns between spoken language and the textbook language of school. At the most obvious level, the books include a great deal of reported talk; they also employ the 'conversational' pronouns *I* and *you* less than child speakers do but more than later school books do. The books, however, are not 'talk-written-down', a point we will develop further. The BR corpus does share characteristics with textbook language in that the term *the* replaces *I* as the most frequent word, there is more third person pronominal usage than is found in the Spoken corpus, and aspects of the frequency distributions of words, such as the proportion of very rare words, are more similar to the textbook corpus. In these ways we consider the language of these beginning reading books to share some features of both the oral and written language samples we have used for our comparisons.

We have attempted in this chapter to provide the background for the analyses of the BR books that appear in later chapters. These later chapters present more detailed examinations of the content and textual features of beginning school books. Many of these have been motivated by distinctive aspects of the word-frequency patterns in the books. We will pursue more fully the hypothesis that first school books serve a unique set of purposes related to transformations in the use of language to document and explore experience.

3

Constructing the Social World

INTRODUCTION: CHARACTERS AND ACTIVITIES

An important clue to the nature of the social world depicted in children's first school books is gained from an examination of the types of characters who most frequently appear as actors in the reading books — who they are and what they do. In this chapter we document the relative frequency of family members, boys and girls, animals and teachers, and we draw conclusions about the textual versions of the social world that the young reader is shown in early school reading materials. We also present data relating to the activities in which various characters in the books take part. That is, we address the question of whether or not, for example, mothers and fathers, boys and girls, children and adults, or people and animals engage in different activities. In addition, we attempt to document the emotional world that is portrayed in the books, by presenting the frequencies of expressions of emotive and evaluative language by the various characters. These portrayals derive their significance from the fact that many of the books appear to depict the everyday world of the child, and that this apparent everyday world is conveyed by the presence and activities of familiar character-types in the stories.

We view these contents as more than a reflection of young children's presumed natural interests. Rather, they provide the child-readers with a definition of what their identities, interests, attitudes and experiences are conventionally deemed to be. We elaborate on this idea of 'constituting' the child-reader more fully in chapter 6. The present chapter concludes with a brief discussion of the epistemological status of fantasy and everyday contents of the reading materials and the interesting interpretive puzzles this mixture presents to the reader. Some of the observations we make in this chapter could serve as resources for the teacher in drawing students' attention to how the social worlds of the texts are constructed — a project we outline more fully in chapter 8.

TABLE 3.1   Twenty most frequent common nouns referring to living creatures in the BR corpus

Rank	Terms	Frequency (per 1,000 words)
1	children	3.5
2	mother	3.5
3	father	3.0
4	cat	2.7
5	dog	2.7
6	man	2.2
7	pig	2.2
8	dad	1.9
9	fish	1.9
10	bear	1.8
11	boy	1.7
12	grandmother	1.6
13	daddy	1.5
14	boys	1.2
15	mum	1.1
16	mummy	1.1
17	baby	1.1
18	girl	1.1
19	horse	1.0
20	rabbit	1.0

We begin with a simple frequency count of the types of characters found in the beginning reading (BR) corpus. Table 3.1 presents the 20 most frequent common nouns referring to living creatures. A number of features of this table are noteworthy. First, seven of the 20 words describe roles in the immediate family, and six of these refer to parents. A very large portion of the text, then, seems to deal with events in the context of the child-characters' immediate family lives. Second, seven of the 20 terms apply to animals (five of the top ten). Many of these animal characters appear in fairy tales, in other fantasy animal stories and as domestic pets.

MOTHERS, FATHERS, GIRLS AND BOYS

A central proposition underlying this work is that the BR books display an apparent reflection of the child-readership's routine everyday activities, and that these textual versions of the child's everyday life become knowledge in the process of the child's becoming school-literate and, more broadly, of becoming a school child, and thus an 'educated' person. In that sense, the textbook version of children's everyday experiences that can be documented in such a transitional corpus of instructional materials assumes a particular importance in the introduction of the child to school-literacy.

In the previous chapter we documented some lexical aspects of the beginning reading books which we believe relate to this transitional function. Our attention is drawn here in particular to the uses of the terms *boy/s*, *girl/s*, *mother/s* and *father/s*. These categories, of course, entail both age relations and gender relations. These school books portray the activities of characters of different generations and sexes to a large degree in the non-school world of the child, thereby to some extent masking the organizational interest that the school has in a particular form of generation- and gender-dependent socialization. This makes even more powerful any systematic recastings of the child's 'natural' world, and attests to their force as a document of a school-endorsed version of how 'children' act in cross-generation and cross-gender interactions. The selection and elaborations of these category-referential terms (Sacks, 1974) may appear to be unremarkable within a common-sense view of children's experience. As we will show, however, description of the social world through this (or any other) set of categories is not a neutral activity, on a number of significant counts.

First, we deal with the simple issue of how frequently *boy/s*, *girl/s*, *mother/s* and *father/s* appear in the BR corpus. We take this step because, while *children* is the most frequent noun referring to living creatures in the corpus, the term *child* does not appear, and the terms *parent* and *parents* appear a total of only 11 times.

That is, kinship relational terms are heavily gender-marked.

It has been observed in previous research (e.g. Stewig and Higgs, 1973; Women on Words and Images, 1972) that males appear more frequently in children's literature. But several of these analyses have been somewhat impressionistic in their analytic method, and some have been conducted on award-winning children's books, a sample which may well display characteristics different from those found in school children's ordinary daily reading materials.

Comparing the frequency of *boy/s* and *girl/s* we find, consistent with other research, that *boy/s* appear more frequently than *girl/s* by a ratio of about three to two (total *boy/s* = 246; total *girl/s* = 168). (This ratio also remains relatively constant across all grade levels in the Grades 3–9 corpus referred to in chapter 2, even though the frequency rates drop as grade level increases.) A similar imbalance appears when male and female proper names are compared. There are approximately 2,000 proper names referring to males in the corpus and approximately 1,400 proper name uses referring to females. Thus proper name uses reinforce rather than compensate for the prevalence of the generic term *boy/s* over *girl/s*.

As noted, the words *children/'s* appear 294 times in this corpus, while the gender-free term *child* fails to make an appearance. That is, every time an individual child is described in these beginning reading books, the gender of that child is indicated either through the use of a generic term or through a proper name reference. Clearly, gender is made a very important personal characteristic in these books, and, with respect to children, boy characters are more prevalent than girl characters by a ratio of about three to two.

Over and above the issue of comparative prevalence, it has been asserted (e.g. Mercer, 1975) that boys are more likely to appear singly, that is, as individuals, in children's books than are girls. To test this we can compare the appearance rates of the singular and plural forms of *boy/s* and *girl/s*. It turns out, as predicted, that *boy* appears significantly more often than *boys* ($z = 2.87$, $p < 0.01$), while there is no significant difference between appearance rates for *girl* and *girls* in the corpus ($z < 1$). Thus, a girl is equally likely to appear singly or with other girls, while a boy is more likely to appear as a single character in these books. (This significant effect is also found when the Grades 3–9 corpus is examined.)

The imbalance of appearance rates favouring male child-characters is not reflected in the parental terms used in the books. There are 503 instances of words referring to mother (*mother, mum, mummy*) and 564 references to fathers, either in colloquial or formal terms. There are also 209 instances of *grandmother/s* and 63 instances of *grandfather/s*. Thus, at the parental level, females are about as well represented as males, and, at the grand-parental level, they are better represented.

Also of note is the replication in the beginning reading corpus of a finding reported for the older children's textbooks (the Grades 3–9 sample) — that is, preference for the informal terms *dad* or *daddy* for the male parent and preference for the formal term *mother* for the female parent. In the beginning reading corpus this association is significant (chi-square (1) = 18.6, p <0.01). That is, the mother-character is more likely to be referred to as *mother* while the father-character is more likely to be referred to as *dad* or *daddy*.

The researchers who compiled the Grades 3–9 sample do not offer any explanation for the imbalance they found in formality of reference to the parents (Carroll et al., 1971). We could take this result on face value to suggest that mothers are treated more formally and deferentially in the books and that their role and activities are more public than is the case for the fathers. In order to explore this observation further we examined in more detail the ways in which these various terms are used. To do this, we analysed their use in three contexts: first in the context of direct address, that is, when the child-character is addressing the parent-character face-to-face; second, as a referential device used by child-characters, in which the child is talking about the parent to another character; and third, as narrator-description, when the

TABLE 3.2 Percentages of formal and informal references to mother and father by category of use

| | Female parent | | | Male parent | | |
	mother	mum	*Total*	father	dad	*Total*
Address	10	2	12	5	5	10
Child-use	8	13	21	7	7	14
Narrator-use	43	24	67	36	40	76
Total	61	39	100	48	52	100

term is used by the narrator to refer to the parent.

In analysing the use of these terms in these three contexts, we can specify further how the preferences operate. Table 3.2 shows the percentages of parent terms used in the three contexts. It is clear from the table that uses of the terms *mother, father* and *dad* are distributed similarly in each of the three contexts. The term that is distributed differently across the three contexts is *mum* (Multidimensional Pearson chi-square (2) = 14.8, *p* <0.001). Writers of beginning reading books appear to employ the formal/informal distinction differently when referring to the male and female parents. Specifically, when child-characters address the mother face-to-face in these books, they are significantly more likely to use the formal term *mother* than the informal terms *mum* or *mummy*; but when talking about their mothers, the child-characters are more likely to describe her as *mum*; when the narrator is referring to the mother the term *mother* is significantly preferred. Thus the overall lower frequency of the term *mum* is accounted for by only two of the three categories of use that appear in the BR books.

In summary, the child-characters treat the female parent more formally in face-to-face addresses than they do the male parent, and the narrator refers to her in a similarly formal way. When child-characters are talking about the female parent there is a clear preference for such characters to use the informal term.

It may be that, when the narrator refers to the female parent, more attention is drawn to her public identity as a mother than to the kinship relation of the parent within the immediate family context. The more informal terms could be within-family descriptors (or even names) of particular individuals. Thus we might conclude that mothers, compared to fathers, are addressed by children and described by narrators in such a way as to mark more explicitly their public identity. Yet, when child-characters are talking to others about their mothers, they are more likely to use the informal, familiar term.

These ways of linguistically recasting the same character-type (by systematic variations of apparently equivalent terms) are likely to operate unnoticed in the text. None the less, methods of referring to characters are central to the textual representation of the social world in which these characters appear.

We now examine ways in which these four terms are described

and elaborated in the BR texts. It is not only the prevalence of certain character terms that builds the framework for the social world of the books, but also the ways in which those terms tend to be described and the activities in which the character-types take part.

First, we consider the activities undertaken by boy/s, girl/s, mother/s and father/s, in particular looking for verbs with which the various terms are uniquely associated: that is, of which verbs are male and female children, and male and female parents, uniquely subject or object? Initially, we compare uses of *boy/s* and *girl/s*. In this comparison it should be kept in mind that, in total, the terms *girl/s* are used only about two-thirds as often as *boy/s* in the BR sample. Any contrast in verb or adjective application should be viewed in the light of this imbalance in frequency of usage. It is also the case that many of the activities of boy and girl characters are introduced with the use of proper names rather than solely the generic terms — hence these analyses are not to be regarded as exhaustive.

TABLE 3.3 Verbs with differential relationships to *boy/s* and *girl/s* as subjects and objects

	Boy/s not *girl/s*	*Girl/s* not *boy/s*
Subject of sentence	answer hurt shout think work	—
Object of sentence	come to jump with like play with talk to walk with	hold on to kiss

For which verbs are *boy/s* and *girl/s* used differently as subjects and objects? That is, what do boys do and have done to them that is different from what girls do and have done to them in the BR books? The relevant verbs are shown in table 3.3. The first column shows the verbs for which *boy/s* only (including *he/they* when co-referring clearly to *boy/s*) are the subject (row 1). These gender-exclusive verbs cover a wide range of behaviours. We contend that it is partly through the differential allocation of these behaviours that concepts of 'boyness' and 'girlness' are constructed. In contrast, we see in the second column of table 3.3 that there are no verbs for which *girl/s* (including *she/they*) are the exclusive subject. Recall that fewer entries are expected in this column because of the lower frequencies of *girl/s* overall.

We can also ask, of which verbs are *boy/s* uniquely the object in contrast to *girl/s*, and vice versa? Table 3.3 contains these contrasts in the second row. Almost all of the verbs of which *boy/s* are exclusively the subject or object (left column) involve energetic interaction with others. In contrast, the activities uniquely done by, to and with *girl/s* (right column) clearly depict what we have called the 'cuddle factor' in action: *girl/s* are held on to and kissed; *boy/s* are not. This cuddle factor relates here to the portrayal of females as being associated with more emotional and less physically energetic activities.

We can extend this analysis by examining the adjectives with which *boy/s* and *girl/s* are described in the BR books. As noted earlier, the most frequent adjective overall in the corpus is *little*. Thus, we are led to examine the attachment of size-related terms to *boy/s* and *girl/s*. *Big* is hardly ever applied to *boy/s* or *girl/s* in the BR books (a total of nine times), while *little* is frequently applied (87 times). The word *little*, however, is not used to describe boys and girls with equal frequency. As shown in table 3.4, about one-half of the appearances of *girl* are accompanied by the adjective *little*, while only 30 per cent of appearances of *boy* are so described (chi-square (1) = 10.5, p <0.01). A similar, statistically significant distinction applies when singular and plural forms are combined. At 5 years of age there are no significant height or weight differences between boys and girls (Bayley, 1956). The more frequent elaboration of *girl/s* as *little* therefore could subtly construe female children as physically smaller. We suggest that it is the tenderness and/or the devaluation component of *little* that are related to its uneven application to *boy/s* and *girl/s*.

In addition, there are a number of adjectives applied uniquely

TABLE 3.4 Frequency of the words *boy* and *girl* described and not described as *little*

	boy	*girl*	*Total*
little	42	45	87
Not *little*	99	43	142
Total	141	88	

to either *boy/s* or *girl/s*. *Boy/s*, but never *girl/s*, are described as: *sad, kind, brave, tiny* and *naughty*. *Girl/s*, on the other hand, are exclusively associated with the following adjectives: *young, dancing* and *pretty*. So, in summary, there is gender-preferential use of the most frequent adjective, *little* and gender-exclusive use of the verbs *hold on to* and *kiss*, and the adjectives *young, dancing* and *pretty* in favour of *girl/s*. This fairly coherent picture further reinforces the view that a cuddle factor is at work in the BR books.

Similarly, we can analyze the elaborations of the terms referring to mother/s and father/s. It turns out that parents are very rarely described adjectivally, and rarely appear as the object of verbs other than *show* and *say to*. When looking at the verbs of which mothers and fathers (incorporating both formal and informal references) form the subjects, we find a pattern which reflects somewhat stereotyped notions of mothers' and fathers' behaviour. About half of the instances of mothers and fathers as subjects of verbs relate to the verb *say*; and a number of common activities are approximately equally engaged in by both categories of parent (*go, have, come, ask* and *look*). There are, however, a large number of verbs that are associated uniquely with either mothers or fathers. It is this unique association that presents in high relief the stereotyped nature of the various behaviours. For example, only fathers perform a number of activities related to male-stereotyped chores (*paint, pump, fix, drive* (car), *pull, start* (car), *water* (garden) and *light* (fire)). Also fathers, but never mothers, *milk* (cow), *shave, shout, let, draw* and *keep*. In contrast, there is a smaller set of verbs that uniquely describe mothers behaviours. This set is: *bake* (cake) *dress* (a child), *hug* (a child), *kiss* (a child), *pack* (bags), *pick* (flowers), *set* (the table), *splash* and *thank* (a teacher). With the possible exception of *splash* and *thank*, these gender-exclusive activities demonstrate first the cuddle factor, and second a fairly stereotyped presentation of the mothers' chores in the house. Mothers are more firmly located in emotion-related activities, through this set of verbs, while the only gender-exclusive verb of a vaguely emotional nature associated with fathers is the verb *pat* (the dog).

It is important to note that this description of mothers' and fathers' activities is more complete than the previous description of boys' and girls' activities, since parents almost never have proper names in these books. They are identified and addressed almost exclusively through parental terms.

We can thus discern a number of distinguishing attributes and activities that serve to circumscribe gender- and generation-related characteristics. Further, it needs to be kept in mind that these books are *school* books; thus, they assemble the school's version of gender- and generation-relations. They are significant elements in a constellation of sources informing young people not only of the aspects of their gender and age that are of general interest to the culture but also of those aspects specifically relevant to a child's place in the enterprise of schooling. A major parameter is gender: one gender group appears more often than the other, and, independently of this absolute difference, that same group's individuals appear proportionally more often as individuals than do those of the other group. Additionally, males and females engage in discernibly distinct subsets of behaviours, and are differently described.

Another, perhaps less immediately striking but equally prevalent parameter is generation: the books are written apparently from the point of view of the child-character in the nuclear family. We derive this observation from the prevalence of terms such as *mother, father, mum, dad* and *grandmother*, in contrast to the rare appearance of terms such as *son, daughter* and *grand child/ren* (which together appear a total of four times in the BR corpus). The term *children*, as we show in a later section, sometimes conveys kinship (parent–child), and sometimes generation (adult–child) and sometimes an institutional relation (teacher–children). The parent–characters perform manual and nurturing chores around the house along fairly stereotyped gender-based lines, but are never shown to engage in activities unrelated to children. Adult life is portrayed exclusively in its relation to child life. The caretaking chores are all that the parents are shown to do — the inference being that such activities are all a child would notice or need to know about adult life. The generational dimension of these reading books will be developed more fully in later chapters.

TEACHER-CHARACTERS

The argument developed so far is that the BR books serve in part to introduce children to the culture of literate-schooling. If this notion is warranted, then these books should provide implicit or explicit portrayals of the relationship between home and school life. We have argued that the structures and contents evident in the BR books underwrite a particular version of childhood and cross-age interaction that is compatible with the purposes of schooling, regardless of whether the stories happen to be set in or out of a school context. However, we would expect descriptions of teachers to highlight the transitional role the BR books may be seen to play in the transformation of children into students. Specifically, we might expect, given that the books portray mundane daily routines to children who are now attending school, that descriptions of the teacher would be prevalent and well elaborated. It happens, however, that the word *teacher* occurs only in 17 separate vignettes in the entire corpus, some of them only two or three lines long. In total, the word is used only 50 times in the corpus (twice referring to males). In 35 instances, the relationship between teachers and children is personalized by the prefacing of *teacher* with a pronoun (usually *my*). Sometimes the teacher makes an appearance merely to be named or identified in an accompanying picture (e.g., 'That's my teacher'). Additionally, the teacher is shown to engage in a number of activities, mainly helping and saying. Teacher helps in weighing, counting and writing; and is mainly liked, read to, talked to and shown things (a loose tooth, a sore knee and drawings completed at home).

The vignettes in which the term *teacher* appears are sufficiently few that they can be given close attention. A significant first point to be made is that examination of these vignettes shows that they are often in the immediate present tense, narrated by the un-identified 'I'. Hence, they are best read, not as stories relating events, but rather as expositions on the general attributes and activities of *teacher*, as in the following example:

Example 3.1

    My teacher.
    My teacher is at school.
    My teacher helps me at school.
    She is kind to me.
5   I am little and she is big.
    Sometimes we are naughty.
    My teacher is unhappy.
    She tells us off.
    Sometimes the children are very good.
10 My teacher is happy.
    She sings nursery rhymes to us.
    She helps us to measure.
    My teacher helps us to weigh and
    to count.
    I like reading to my teacher.

This is not a story but rather an exposition of the (unnamed) teacher's role and, more generally, the normative logic of classroom life. This logic is essentially a teacher's logic: terms of the discourse ('naughty', 'good', 'helps us') organize an adult construction of the classroom world. The teacher in this text is not an idiosyncratic, fictionalized character, but rather a generalized role-category that instantiates the attributes, uses and status of teachers *vis-à-vis* children. We can note in the example above the bald contrast of physical size in line 5 and the subsequent explication of the logic of teacher behaviour; lines 6–14 have the flavour of conditional logic about them. A genuine narrative would be structured, even in the narrative present tense, around particular people and events, as in 'Today Dan and I are being naughty. We are making a mess. Miss Johnson is unhappy. Now she tells us off ...'. The text of Example 3.1 is structured, instead, as descriptive exposition, with certain 'timeless' connections elaborated; it is read, therefore, more in the way of an exposition of some aspect of the workings of nature, such as 'How orange juice is made', or 'The structure and functions of leaves', serving thus to shape and naturalize an aspect of the child's daily experience.

This aspect of narrative practice will be developed further in chapter 4.

A second observation is that most of the vignettes in which *teacher* appears make explicit connections between home and school life. These connections take four major forms: first, child-characters express the intention to show the teacher things that are not related to the learning activities in school but rather to domestic details, for example:

Example 3.2

> She [mum] looked at my knee.
> She put something on it.
> Next day I walked to school with my friend.
> I showed my knee to my teacher.

Example 3.3

> I've got a loose tooth.
> I showed it to my teacher.
> Look it wobbles.
> My teacher said it will come out soon.
> I showed it to my mum.
> My mum said it will come out soon.

Such anecdotes construct a view of a teacher with interests in domestic topics similar to a mother's. The boundary between teachers' and mothers' roles is thus effectively blurred. School is presented as a social context in which domestic events of interest to the child are cared about.

A second way in which the social contexts of home and school are explicitly connected is the converse of the first. As noted, teachers are mainly 'read to' in the BR texts. In many of these instances, the parents are also displayed as proxy helpers in reading – an activity explicitly associated with schooling. The following illustrate this device:

Example 3.4

> I wanted to read to my mum and dad.
> I can read stories now.

My mum and dad said go to bed.
I think I will read to my teacher tomorrow.

Example 3.5

I can read.
I read to my teacher.
I read to my mum.

Example 3.6

"I want to read to you before I go to bed."
Jane says to Mummy. "I like to read to you,
and I like to read to my teacher."

So teachers and mothers are linked not only by a common interest in domestic events, but also by a common concern with one of the activities of schooling referred to in the BR books — hearing the child's reading.

A third way in which the books connect home and school is by the simple device of showing teachers as friends of the family. Teachers are invited home for tea, or are 'old friends'. The transition from parental care to teacher's care is thus shown to occur within a continuous social milieu. The inference is that similar expectations (specifically concerning child—adult relations) would be in place. Teachers are essentially the only friends that parents are shown to have in these books, and even then only rarely. In this sense, the adult social arena displayed to the child-reader is a highly restrictive one — a social system closed in by an interchangeable set of home—school features.

The interchangeability of home and school is, of course, not complete, either in terms of activities or personnel. A fourth position that teachers are shown to occupy in the BR texts is as custodians or 'gatekeepers' of who or what enters into school life. Parents may be shown to assist in this gate-keeping function. In one story, for example, a teacher is shown to pronounce on the suitability of certain animals the children want to bring to a 'Pet Day' at the school. In another, a pre-school child ('Jenny'), who is the younger sister of one of the school children ('Patrick'), insists on going to school, against the advice of Mother. Jenny breaks free on her tricycle, and, to the embarrassment of Patrick, appears at the classroom door. The story continues:

Example 3.7

> "Who can this be?" said the teacher.
> "Who can this be with little bare feet?
> Who can this be in a little pink petticoat?"
> The children looked at Patrick.
> Patrick went pink.
> "This is Jenny," he said to the teacher.
> The headmaster came in with Mother. . . .
> The headmaster put the tricycle in the car.
> Mother put Jenny in the car.
> "Come to school again when you are five,"
> said the teacher . . .
> [story continues]

This story can work only if the significance and comicality of a pre-schooler's attempt to be a school-child is assumed. The significance of Jenny's invasion into school territory is attested to by the appearance of the headmaster (who, along with Jenny, remains a strangely silent presence throughout the entire episode). The comicality of Jenny's precociousness is attested to by the teacher's theatrical rhetorical questions upon seeing Jenny, and by Patrick's highly public chagrin. Finally, when Jenny's attempt has come to its inevitable and silent conclusion, the teacher makes explicit the basis of Jenny's ineligibility for school. Age, a variable which to a great extent provides the organizational basis of school life, is thus given prime importance.

The social world of the child-characters in the BR books contains occasional mixtures of home and school. Domestic and academic interests are signified in both home and school; occasionally teachers visit homes and parents visit schools; and teacher and mother are often linked through parallel and adjacent utterances as illustrated in Example 3.5 above. We infer that the function of this mixing is to reconstitute the experience of home in ways that suit schools' purposes (specifically in the assembly of cross-age and cross-gender relations), and to point simultaneously to the natural, familiar quality of daily school life.

In other sections of this book we argue that the language of the BR books, regardless of the content of the stories, stands, at the levels of structure and dialogic interaction, at a transitional point between conversational and the schools' version of literate language use. In this section we have attempted to show how this transitionality is explicitly highlighted by a particular portrayal of the activities, attributes and status of the teacher-characters. In many respects, they are shown to be alternate versions of the parents. They are helpful in similar ways, interested in similar things and kind and likeable in a fashion similar to the parents. That is, the portrayal of teachers as pseudo-family members and the reciprocal portrayal of parents as pseudo-teachers entails a specific reconstruction of both social settings around the same set of generational relations.

THE EMOTIONAL WORLD

We have begun to document the general argument that these beginning school reading books show young children ways of being 'children' in that they portray particular ways of using language and interaction with parents, siblings, friends and teachers in everyday circumstances. We describe more extensively in this section aspects of the portrayal of 'childhood' and 'adulthood' that relate to the expression of emotion and evaluation.

One of the more important aspects of social behaviour is the way in which speakers' internal responses are expressed: one may or may not divulge one's feelings and values; one's internal responses may or may not be elaborated; and one's feelings and evaluations may or may not be used as explanations or justifications of behaviour. The argument here is that the patterns of usage of expressive words that we can delineate in a particular language corpus are an important element in the construction of its intended readership. When books written for young children reveal certain consistencies, the force is to present a definable version of school-literate childhood with respect to the expression of emotion and evaluation. Recall the Gedanken experiment described in chapter 1. Documenting the emotions and evaluations of the indigine characters in the books provided by the colonists would open one of the major windows on to the colonists' conceptions of indigenous culture, and on to some of the more subtle and implicit efforts of the colonists to represent and reshape that culture. Analogously, our goal here is to present some analyses of the patterns of usage of expressive words in the language of the BR books, and to distill from these patterns a picture of how the 'literate school child' expresses (or does not express) feelings and judgements. (The interested reader is referred to Freebody, Baker and Gay, 1987, for a more technical description of the findings we report here.)

Where certain expressive words and word families are found to be prevalent, we have analysed the ways in which they are used – for example, who utters them, about whom or what, and on what occasions. It needs to be emphasized that, on interpreting patterns of uses and particular instances of use, we, as readers, have needed to rely on our own linguistic and cultural resources to effect a reading of the utterances. These resources are similar, but of course not identical, to those available to young children themselves as readers of these books.

First, some general observations about the depiction of the emotional and evaluative words contained in the BR corpus. Initially we can note that words depicting positive emotion are more frequent in these books than words depicting negative emotion. The former category includes appearances of: *like, good, laugh, happy, brave, love*; the latter group contains, in order of frequency, *sad, bad, afraid, cry, not like, scared* and *unhappy*. Totalling these word uses we find that the ratio of positive to negative emotion thus depicted is about three to one (712 positive terms, 240 negative terms). Second, we observe that a large proportion of the words relating to negative emotions or evaluations are associated with animals in this corpus. One of the particular functions of these omnipresent animals seems to be to bear the brunt of the negative emotions expressed in the books. If we combined the four most common negative words (*sad, bad, afraid* and *cry*) we find that roughly two-thirds of the uses of these words are uttered by or applied to animals.

We can also delineate some gender- and generation-related differences in the use of expressive words. Our technique is to examine what category of character expresses the emotion or the evaluation, and also to whom or what the term is applied. We can thus determine whether or not certain categories of characters are more likely to express certain feelings or evaluations than others, and whether or not there are significant associations between the categories of character using the term and the person, object, or event to which it is applied.

For example, consider the use of the word *good* in the BR corpus. It turns out that when *good* is used as an adjective (a total of 99 times), as opposed to an isolated exclamation, there are significant differences among rates of use by different categories of characters, and significant associations between who uses the term and to whom or to what it is applied. While mothers and fathers are very frequent characters in these books, they rarely use *good* as a descriptor (13 times). Rather it is the children and the narrator who use *good* most frequently. Moreover, there is a significant association between mothers', fathers' and boys' uses of the term. Mothers are significantly more likely to use *good* to describe girls, fathers to describe boys, and boys to describe objects and events. We can see that, through the use of this positive expression, characters are 'attached' differentially to other characters and to various aspects of the environment in the stories: boys express this positive evaluation towards inanimate objects and activities that are conducted or proposed in the stories; parents apply this description almost exclusively to their same-sex children.

An additional point concerning the use of *good* is that it is the narrator who, more frequently than the characters in the stories, applies *good* to people. Thus the narrator can be seen to assume an evaluative role not often adopted by the characters. Conversely, the narrator describes objects and events as *good* significantly less often, apparently leaving that task to the children in the stories, especially the boys. We will argue more fully in chapter 4 that one property of the transitional role of the BR books is the unobtrusive but none the less organizationally critical introduction of the narrator's authoritative voice. The prevalence of the narrator's statements about 'goodness' of characters can be seen as an aspect of this early introduction of the narrator as an independent source of knowledge and evaluation.

Terms relating to 'badness' are not only significantly less frequent than terms referring to goodness in the corpus of BR books, but also are used in distinctive ways. It is only animals that describe human characters in the BR stories as *bad*. It is objects and events (e.g., toys, a fall) about which the word is generally used by human characters. The finding that only animals are given a warrant to describe children as *bad* reinforces and specifies the suggestion that young children's reading books are emotionally 'sanitized' (Hoffman, 1981). A general hypothesis is suggested:

when negative emotions are expressed, it is most often non-humans which express them. This may in part account for the prevalence of animals in the BR books.

As another example, we can consider the uses of the verb *to like* in the BR corpus. Through a similar analysis, we find a pattern closely resembling that relating to the use of *good*. In particular, parents express their likes very infrequently (about 4 per cent of uses) compared to children (about half of uses). This, in conjunction with the results for *good*, strongly suggests that the emotional and evaluative experiences of the child–characters are featured in these books more than the perceptions of the adults. While the adults appear very frequently and act as organizers and conversants in these books, their internal responses of an emotional or evaluative nature are virtually never represented. The centre of the emotional universe of these books is apparently the child–character.

Looking further at particular uses of the verb *to like* and associations among who uses the verb and about whom or what it is used, we find some notable gender and generational differences. In particular, girls are significantly more likely than boys to like animals, and less likely than boys to like objects and events. Moreover, about one-half of the boys' uses of the verb *to like* are applied to inanimate objects such as food and toys. That is, through expressions of liking, girls are attached to the animate world, in particular the world of pets, while boys are likewise attached to the world of objects and activities. It is noteworthy, moreover, that people express liking for other people a total of only 19 times out of the 281 character uses of the verb. Interpersonal liking is rarely expressed in the particular version of the social world constructed in these books. Rather it is used to relate boys and girls in distinct ways to different, non-human aspects of their environments.

We find also that interpersonal feelings expressed through the use of the term *love* and all its derivatives have quite a low appearance rate in the books (a total of only 22). Those who are described as loving are girls (7), children as a group (5), grandparents (3), unspecified 'I' (3), animals (2), a boy, Jack, and a teacher. Principal objects of the verb *love* are animals (5), activities (e.g., to 'play') (6), and grandparents. There are also two instances of children being loved and one each of a boy, a girl, a doll and an unspecified 'we'. In this corpus parents are never at any time associated with the use of *love*. Again, in spite of their prevalence in the corpus as a whole, parents nowhere express emotional attachment for any persons, animals, or events. Similarly, girls love more often, and, moreover, they love a greater variety of things than do boys. Girls are said to love dogs, children, grandparents, flowers, trees and a doll. Thus they love not only humans but also pets, nature and selected objects. There is only one instance of a male being said explicitly to love something. Here is that sentence: 'Jack loved his horse'. So there is a strong suggestion that girls are more deeply and more diversely loving and loved than are boys, again reinforcing our suggestion that the portrayal of girls in these young children's books is characterized by the cuddle factor.

The most explicit and unequivocal expressions of strong positive and negative feelings are laughter and crying. In the light of the under-representation of adults in expressing liking and goodness, it is noteworthy that they feature prominently as laughers. They laugh as frequently as any other group (mother and father about equally). The characters which laugh least are girls and animals. We find that boys and animals are most frequently the instigators or targets of laughter (80 out of 109 uses). Boys and pets seem to perform a clown-like function significantly more often than any other category of character. Parents and girls are very rarely laughed at (nine times in total), and the laughter directed at other adults is completely accounted for by the presence of professional clowns in the circus and at school. That girls are portrayed as both significantly more reserved, and as significantly less often the instigators of fun, is compatible with and reinforces the notion that the cuddle factor forms a central part of the representation of femininity in the BR books.

We consider now the systematic association between the sources and the occasions of laughter. The pattern of laughter of non-parental adults (e.g., teachers, busdrivers) in the BR books displays a number of notable features: first other adults laugh at boys and boys' activities significantly more than they do at others' activities. It has been hypothesized (see, e.g., Mercer, 1975) that school reading books place boys in an active role in extra-familial public life more so than they do girls. Our findings are compatible with such a hypothesis. Boys in these books attract non-parental adult attention and are rewarded with laughter substantially more often than are any other types of characters. Their laughter at other adults is also compatible with their greater involvement in the non-parental adult world.

We can examine similar patterns relating to the uses of negative emotional terms such as *cry*. Crying is a fairly intense experience, connoting despair and dependency. It is also a touch-stone for cultural constructions of maturity. Words relating to crying appear fairly infrequently in this corpus (25 times). Toys and animals account for almost half of all the crying done in these stories, and most instances of crying are stimulated by externally based experiences such as being lost, being hurt, or losing an object (17 instances in total). Internally based experiences such as being ill or tired, occur only as stimulants to the crying of babies; toys, animals, girls and princesses cry only because of externally based experiences.

The only case of crying as a result of the 'pangs of moral conscience' — a dereliction of duty — happens also to be the only case of a boy crying in the entire corpus. This occurs in a story about a boy who is put in charge of a herd of goats and instructed not to allow them to break through the fence into a nearby field of turnips. The boy falls asleep, the goats break through the fence and eat the turnips, and the boy cries. This contrasts with the types of reasons for crying that apply to all other characters in the corpus. So while crying is a rare event in particular for human characters in this corpus, there is a complete separation in the causes of crying for boys and girls.

REPRESENTING SOCIAL AND EMOTIONAL LIFE

It is important to note that the expression of emotion and evaluation is not a predominant feature of the BR books. The combined frequency of all these emotive and evaluative terms is far lower than might be expected. It is the rarity of these terms which can be seen as a notable aspect of these materials. The child—characters in these books are concerned less with the expression of feeling and evaluation than they are with the expression of more perceptual and pragmatic activities such as looking, seeing, acting, coming, going and saying. This can be read as relating to schooling's emphasis on strategic and material knowledge – another aspect of induction into the particular culture of school-literacy. Jerome Bruner lodged a complaint many years ago about the 'embarrassment of passion' evident in school life:

What is this 'life of the child' as seen by text writers and publishers? It is an image created out of an ideal of adjustment. . . . Its ideal is medio-centrism, reasonableness, above all, being nice. Such an ideal does not touch closely the deeper life of the child . . . [The children had learned] to be seductive in their recounting; they were not concerned with an honest accounting of the human condition. The books they had read were cute, there was no excitement in them, none to be extracted. (1959: 189)

We think it fair to conclude from our observations that the regime of blandness, niceness and cuteness applies with great force in beginning reading books. Bruner located the origin of the 'seductiveness' and 'cuteness' he observed in school students' classroom stories and accounts squarely in the school texts they read. In the case of beginning school reading books, an important and perhaps hidden dimension of this seductiveness is the recasting of the child's daily life into a highly constrained emotional framework.

   Following our observations earlier in the chapter on the portraits given of the lives of adult characters, we conclude that the representation of adult life is also highly constrained. The adult world is presented in curious and simplistic terms – an adult world divested of emotion, complexity and trouble. It is an idealized version of adult life that the books portray, no less than an idealized version of child life, as we will document more fully in chapter 6 below. Concerning the representation of adult life in these books written for children, we are reminded of the novelist Bawden's commentary on children's literature:

Remembering what I had enjoyed when I was young, I remembered what I had missed in children's books, too. The grown ups, apart from a wicked stepmother or uncle, were always flat, peripheral figures with no emotions and no function. The books offered to me in my childhood left out the adult world, and even when they didn't, entirely, they never presented adults as children really see them. Parents and teachers were usually shown as kind, loving, distant figures – [. . .] not only were they never beastly to children except in a stereotyped, fairy tale way, but they were never beastly to anyone. They were never the uncertain, awkward, quirkly, *dangerous* creatures that I knew adults to be. Since it was the adults who had written these books, it was reasonable to assume that they didn't want to give themselves away ... (1976: 8)

Such representations of adulthood are part of the texts' construction of their child-readership, an issue we develop further in the concluding section of this chapter. In many of our considerations of the contents of these books we are alerted to the problem of the 'fictionality' of the materials apparently describing everyday life. All of these fictional portrayals can describe only possible people in possible worlds.

INTERLEAVING FANTASY AND REALITY

In our analyses of the BR corpus, we have pointed out that most of the texts describe events apparently sampled from the everyday routine life of the reader. We have argued that the stories and expositions in first school books serve, among other things, to recast this everyday life in certain ways, and we will report analyses in later chapters that document other aspects of this recasting process. To conclude this chapter, we remark briefly upon a striking feature of these apparently everyday real descriptions that operates more subtly than the details we have summarized above. For any fictional text, the reader needs to determine what kind of world the world of the story is to be taken to represent (cf. Heap, 1985). This interpretive challenge is compounded where there is found to be mixing and blending of realistic and fantastic elements (as understood by adults). This is evident even in stories that appear to be set in the everyday world (see Baker and Freebody, 1988).

Consider the following examples:

Example 3.8

"Come, kittens," said Andy.
"Mew, mew," said the kittens.

Example 3.9

"Please will you hose me?"

said Mark.
Father hosed Helen and Mark.
"Please will you hose me?"
barked Boxer.
Father hosed Boxer too.

The imaginative capacities of child-readers are called upon in reading fiction of this sort. Part of the entertainment value of the materials entails playful excursions into a possible world of, for example, talking animals. Some of the texts unambiguously enter a possible world by displaying a fantasizing narrator ('I'm going to be a fat spider'). An interesting aspect of the everyday stories, however, is that some of them contain brief, unsignalled and unpredictable sorties into fantasy, often without any subsequent implications for the plot, as in the examples above.

The distinctions between these two examples illustrate the subtle variations in the strategies writers employ to effect these sorties. In 3.8 above, the actual sounds made by kittens ('mew') are approximated within the direct speech markers, while the narrator signals the fantastic nature of the kittens' communicative intentions ('said'). That is, the reported 'speech' of the kittens retains some fidelity with the sound-making capabilities of kittens. However, the narrator characterizes the kittens as 'saying' the words 'mew, mew', and the story proceeds as if they had communicated a linguistic message (Andy gets them milk and calls another pet). The narrator thus reworks an apparently real sound into a fantastic utterance. In 3.9 above, the opposite device is employed: Boxer's actual sound is not reported within the direct speech markers; rather the human interpretation is reported as the actual speech. The narrator however goes on, not to define Boxer's utterance as 'saying', but rather as 'barking'. This device embeds fantastic possibilities into the observable world of barking dogs, although the narrator remains faithful to realistic description by defining what Boxer did as 'barking', rather than by defining what Boxer did fantastically. These are options open to the narrator in characterizing any given event.

There are also instances in which the narrator mixes the realistic and the fantastic in the reported direct utterances of animal characters, as in 3.10 below:

Example 3.10

   "Meeow, I like fish,"
   said Mr. Whiskers.
   "I can have
   the big yellow fish with green spots."
   "No, no, no, Mr. Whiskers,"
   laughed Mother.

Mr Whiskers both meeows and verbalizes in the one reported utterance. In this case, the interleaving of fantasy and reality is more complex. It is not restricted either to the narrator's use of a speech act verb or to the reporting of animal verbalization, but combines both.

   Clearly such texts are intended partly to amuse the child-reader. Children, we assume, know that pets do not talk, except in stories for children or in other fantasies produced by adults for children. Therefore we must further assume that, in order both to interpret texts such as the above and to appreciate the intended playfulness of reading them, children need, at least implicitly, to collude in the adult construction of 'child-like playfulness'. At the same time, that playfulness arises only because of the obviously fantastic, unreal nature of the reported events. If the child-reader actually believed in the reality of these events, then the stories would lose their playful value (e.g., Boxer's question would be just another request, like Mark's). In this sense, the child-reader needs to know that, for example, talking animals are an element of (adult-defined) child culture that contrasts with a more 'realistic' adult culture, and to collude in this definition by playing the part of a child-reader. The playfulness arises out of playing the part of a child (interested in and susceptible to mixtures of fantasy and reality) for the purpose of interpreting and enjoying these texts.

   For the child-reader, such interpretations involve, not immersion in some actual child culture, but rather an appreciation of how adults view children. The paradox here, as identified by MacKay (1974b), is that the interpretive capabilities that children must use to participate in their own socialization are not acknowledged in contemporary constructions of children. We might conclude, then, that the mixture of reality and fantasy in stories apparently about recognizably ordinary people is a particularly powerful device for informing children about adults' definitions of what it is to be a child. This same point applies in a less blatant form to all of the texts which appear to describe some ordinary, everyday human world.

In this chapter we have attempted to point broadly to two issues: first, the issue of the ways in which the BR books present apparently ordinary people in their social worlds; and second, the issue of the work done by the narrator in the construction of those fictional worlds. In the next chapter, we turn our attention more directly to narrative practices evident in these books. We explore possible interpretive problems that may be presented to child-readers and ways in which narrative practice subtly builds a version of the school child.

4

The Work of the Author

A description of the work of the author in the beginning school reading books is central to an understanding of how these books serve as introductions to school-based literacy. These books are not typically presented or dealt with as authored works, that is, as works of literature in which the writer is personalized and located in a particular cultural milieu. In this respect they are similar to the textbooks children will encounter in many school subjects, where the informational content is given primary attention, rather than the unique talents, perspectives, or arguments of some particular authors. On the other hand, these books appear to be works of fiction, as stories to be enjoyed and discussed rather than information to be learned.

We will develop and document the proposition in this chapter that the stories in the BR books represent hybrid forms of texts whose function is ambiguous with respect to the information-entertainment dimension (cf. Brewer and Lichtenstein, 1982). Further we will argue that this peculiarity is best explained in terms of the transitional nature of the books; that is, they represent a bridge between recognizably oral-tradition stories and autonomous written expositions.

In what follows, when we refer to the narrator, our references are to narrative practices and not to the work of a particular author. We are aware that some of these books are children's books written essentially as literature, and are later selected for use in schools, while others are educational productions, sometimes of a collaborative nature. Certainly in the latter case these works are written specifically 'within ... assumptions about the nature and function of the pedagogical text, and the nature of the knowledges and competences to be taught by and through that text' (Luke, 1987b: 109–10). This draws attention to the fact that these books contain a special kind of narrative function, which we seek to describe in this chapter.

THE TEXTUALIZING PROCESS

In examining aspects of authorial practice in beginning school reading books, we draw attention to the ways the books are crafted — how they are constructed as texts to convey particular representations of the world. We therefore look at and beyond the surface features of their content, at and beyond their narrative or expository forms, and towards an examination of how they introduce the child-reader to aspects of literacy.

In talking or writing, our usual attitude is to treat language as a transparent medium for describing some topic. We typically do not treat the language through which we do this as opaque and thus available for analysis as a set of practices. Mulkay has observed that 'we construct the meaning of the world, we construct what we take that world to be, through our organized use of words and other symbolic resources' (1985: 73). Yet we deny the textuality; that is, we do not explicitly attend to the process of linguistic crafting through which accounts of events in the factual or fictional world come to be produced. Mulkay pointed out that all discourse may be viewed as the production of versions of the world through words — that is, through the 'selective and artful use of language'.

While students are instructed in the later years of school to view a particular subset of school texts — 'literature' — as crafted objects, they are typically given no parallel instruction with respect to informational texts. Apart from the possible interrogation of the correctness of some of the content of informational texts, students are not typically led to examine features of their construction or design. The school treats textbooks predominantly as repositories of knowledge, facts and information (cf. Luke et al., 1983) rather than as cultural products whose origins and methods are themselves to be investigated.

Our primary interest in this chapter is to explore aspects of textual construction and design in beginning school reading books.

We begin by presenting some examples of text in which different methods for representing spoken words on paper are adopted, showing different kinds of authorial presence and activity. To set the scene for our discussion of authorial practice in this chapter, consider the following textual methods in which an event and the talk constituting and accompanying it could be reported in written form. The first method is that of the diarist, writing a personal account of the event. In this case, character is narrator:

Example 4.1

I told Jack that Bumpity bumped into the toy-box and I couldn't get it open, could he help me. He said I can't open it so I said let's take it down to Father it's his old toy-box.

The second method is that of the conversational analyst, adopting an 'outsider' position:

Example 4.2

Jill   Oh, dea:ear — Bumpity bumped into the toy-box and I can't get it open Jack — can you help me? ((*frustrated*))
(*0.8*)
Jack   I can't open it — this is an old [toy-box
Jill   [Let's take
it down to father — it's his old toy-box — he'll know what to do with it.

This could be seen as a form of narration, in which some observer of the scene and the talk is both recounting and describing the spoken language of the named characters. Note the separated identifications of speakers and their utterances, the indication of emphasis through underlining, the timing of the pause, and the marking of the overlap ([). We might regard this reporting method as an elaborated form of a dramatist's script, at one end of a continuum of attempted fidelity to the details of the original oral form.

Consider now a method which 'regularizes' the conversational content and, in an unobtrusive way, introduces another voice into the scene — the narrator's:

Example 4.3

"Oh, dear!" said Jill.
2 "Bumpity bumped into the toy-box,
and I cannot get it open.
4 Jack, can you help me?"
Jack looked at the toy-box.
6 "I cannot open it," he said.
"This is an old toy-box."
8 "Let's take it down to father,"
said Jill.
10 "It is his old toy-box.
He will know what to do with it."

In this example taken from the BR corpus the narrator has a presence different from those in our first two examples. The narrator's contributions can be seen to be included within the text portraying the event. Note that there are few indications as to how to read the dialogue with respect to intonation and stress, and there are no interruptions or overlapping utterances marked. Also, speaker identification is not always straightforward. Who, for instance, uttered line 7? Who said lines 10 and 11? How might we know? That is, what resources do we bring to bear to read this apparently simple text? These resources are concerned not only with punctuation conventions such as commas or speech markers, but also with assumptions about continuity of topic across speeches, with what categories of characters are most likely to make certain types of contributions to conversation, and with the character-typing conventions that apply in particular genres.

Finally, consider the following account of the same event:

Example 4.4

Jill complained that her doll Bumpity had bumped into the toy-box. She inquired of Jack if he could assist her in opening it. After a little consideration and after examining the box, Jack declared that he was unable to open it, whereupon Jill suggested that her father would know, since it had been his, and that they should take it downstairs to him.

Here the narrator, outside of the scene, not only reports but selects, interprets and adds, not even displaying any particular need to use the original spoken words. The verbs change from the simple 'said' to the more literate 'complained', 'inquired' and 'suggested', through which the narrator not merely reports but characterizes the talk. These more complex speech act and mental state verbs are resources for literate discourse. They are verbs for talking about text (cf. Olson and Astington, 1986).

These four examples serve to illustrate possibilities for reporting talk on paper. This is one central dimension on which beginning school reading books vary. Texts of the type in examples 4.1 and 4.3 (first person accounts and the narrated story using direct speech) are found more often than type 4.4, where the characters' speeches are subsumed under the narrator's sentences, and which we see as closer to the expository form which predominates in the later years of school. Text of type 4.2, which is perhaps the most faithful to the details of the actual oral exchange, is not found.

A second, related dimension we attend to in characterizing beginning reading materials is the narrative-expository dimension: the balance of event-recounting story forms (as in example 4.3) and informational texts (as in example 4.4) within the corpus. A third related dimension on which texts vary is the use of first or third person forms in the design of the text. These three dimensions are pertinent to a discussion of how the texts are structured, how introductions to the authorship of written texts are provided, and how the possible readings of texts may be conveyed through these devices. These dimensions draw further attention to the point that many of these texts appear to draw on conventions of oral language to effect a transition to conventions of written prose.

Following the comparisons above of ways of reporting talk on paper, we will present for further comparison some examples of the kinds of texts children encounter in early school reading materials. We will develop from these a more extensive analysis of the three dimensions introduced above. Our discussion is organized around the predominant types of texts we find represented in early school reading materials (see Baker and Freebody, 1988). As an introduction to this discussion, we will first specify more fully our categories of 'expository', 'narrative' and 'experiential' texts.

Example 4.5

How Apple Juice is Made

Apples grow on trees in orchards.
The apples are picked when they
are ripe.
Ripe apples are taken to the
factory in big trucks.
In the factory, the
apples are washed many times, [etc.]

As background to a consideration of the school text as an apparently autonomous source of knowledge, we draw on the work of Olson (1977a, b, 1983), who has advanced the view that school texts detach knowledge from identifiable human sources such that assertions made within texts appear to have truth value independent of any particular expositor of that knowledge. This is the basis of Olson's claim that 'authority' resides in the construction of texts themselves. Example 4.5, taken from the BR corpus, illustrates the kind of text to which Olson's comments most forcefully apply. This text employs the passive voice not only to write out any identifiable source of the description, but also, in this case, to write out any reference to human agency involved in the procedures being described. The description is given in the present tense, not qualified by any modifiers, or located in any time or place. Rather, it is an example of a universal claim. The information in the text is presented as neutral fact, not opinion or observation belonging to some identifiable reporter or observer. This looks to be a precursor of the detached, autonomous, 'objective' text that comprises much of the reading material of the later years of school. Whether or not such texts are in themselves 'autonomous' or 'authoritative' is a question we address in chapter 7. In this chapter we are concerned with describing features of textual construction and design.

Olson (1977b: 77) has argued that the 'dominant means of instruction and communication in schools ... the language of formalized written prose' is a special language. It presents to readers 'distinctive pictures of reality or forms of knowledge' that differ from those available in and expressed through oral-conversational forms of language. Olson has further stated (1977b: 66) that the 'conflict' between native, oral language forms and the special language forms of school texts should be observable in the first school books children encounter. We are not convinced that this relation is best described as a conflict of languages, and have suggested that in a number of important respects the language of beginning school reading books attempts to capitalize upon oral-conversational language practices in preparing children for their eventual encounters with texts of the type shown in example 4.5. On the basis of our inspection of the BR corpus, we conclude that children do not observe a great deal of fully autonomous, informational text in their first encounters with written text at school. Rather, some interesting transitional forms predominate. These other forms may be seen to contain representations and reports of oral language in a way that Example 4.5 does not. We adopt the view that they prepare children to deal with text of the kind they will later encounter as the more standard 'language of textbooks'.

Far more prevalent in the BR corpus are texts that seek to describe, in story form, the everyday lives of child characters in the books, or seek to express, in a first person mode, experiences and observations of children in their everyday worlds. This is a characteristic also documented by Beck and others (1979) and Willows and others (1981) in their studies of the content of a variety of early reading programmes. Examples 4.6, 4.7 and 4.8 below illustrate these types of texts. First, consider the 'narrative' text, which describes episodes in the everyday lives of named characters:

Example 4.6

"There is a big grey horse.
I like him," said Jack.
"He is a good horse,"
said Grandmother.
"The man in red will ride him."
The man in red
stopped the horse.
Up he jumped and away he went.

"See the horse run!"
said Jack.
"See him jump!"

This kind of text bears a close structural resemblance to fairy tales, which also adopt a narrative, rather than an expository form. Further, such texts are characterized by the inclusion of reported speech: characters are not merely introduced and described, they are made to talk within the story itself. We have indicated earlier the very high frequency of the verb *said* in the BR corpus; we take this to indicate some prevalent features of authorial practice within the books.

Another frequently used form of authorial practice in the BR books is the first person account. In these texts, the author adopts the first person to convey sentiments and experiences, or observations and declarations. These first person accounts portray the feelings and thoughts of some (child) character who may be shown in an accompanying illustration. Example 4.7 is representative of this type of text.

Example 4.7

My Secret Place
    It's warm in here, in bed.
    My blanket's warm and my kitten's
    soft. I don't
    want to get up.
    I'm going to stay here, in bed.
    I can hear the radio in
    the kitchen.
    Mum's in there cooking breakfast.

Other first person accounts appear to convey a set of observations about the world, a commentary about some feature of the reader's world. In these instances, there may not be any indication of a specific source of the observation. Example 4.8 (quoted earlier) illustrates this observational type of text.

Example 4.8

My teacher is happy.
She sings nursery rhymes to us.

She helps us to measure.
My teacher helps us to weigh and
to count.
I like reading to my teacher.

In the remainder of this chapter, we address the significance of the use of these types of authorial practice for a number of themes which have been introduced in other sections. The authorial styles represented by examples 4.6, 4.7 and 4.8 above can be taken to be transitional to the style adopted in example 4.5 ('How Apple Juice is Made'). We observe particularly that each of the former mimics particular characteristics of oral language, including a subjective perspective ("I"), that are absent from example 4.5.

NARRATIVE TEXTS

We will comment in more detail first on the nature of example 4.6 (Jack and the big grey horse). This example is representative of a large proportion of the texts in the BR corpus. Here the author's voice is backgrounded to the speeches and activities of characters, such that if a child-reader were asked who is 'in' this story, the presence of Jack, Grandmother and the man in red would be remarked upon, while the author would not likely be named as a participant in the scene or in the text. The author's work here is essentially narration of the story line in which these other characters have parts. This narration can be seen, however, to penetrate the story in a manner which may be invisible to child-readers, but nevertheless critical for any reading of the text, and preparatory for an orientation to the kinds of instructional texts that are encountered later in school.

The narrative voice behind the scenes is recounting to the reader what occurred in some real or fictional world: what Grandmother and others said, what the horse did, and so on. Clearly, in order for there to be a report, someone must have observed or recorded the scene. That is, '(then I heard Jack say) "See the horse run!"', or someone must have had the scene described second-hand by someone else. But in the format that is employed in this kind of text, the presence or even idea of a reporter or recounter is backgrounded to the presence and activities of the characters who inhabit the story, as in standard narrative form. Through the use of narrative forms the reader is invited to enter the world of the story rather than to inspect the design of the texts. It is instructive to imagine a teacher or parent drawing attention in this kind of text to what the narrator did next or why the narrator did it, when there are named characters saying and doing things. It is these sayings and doings that are conventionally treated as comprising the story, though they are not the same doings which have led to the construction of the text or which comprise the totality of the text.

That these books are taken to be windows on a story world draws attention away from their textuality, and away from the practices and therefore the presence of the narrator as a speaker and observer. What is marked as a character's speech (e.g., 'There is a big grey horse') is to be read as someone's speech and observation, as an event in some real or imagined world; what is not so marked (e.g., 'said Jack') is to be read as no one's speech or observation, and thus not an event in any real or fictional world. It is to be taken as something autonomously known about the scene and the events.

The narrator as storyteller and recounter

In discussing narrative theory with reference to literary works, Banfield (1982) has presented a number of concepts that can be usefully applied to our discussion of the narratives in children's first school books. Banfield has provided some compelling observations about how 'narratorless sentences' (in Olson's terms, 'autonomous, authoritative text') can be produced.

The devices which provide for the production of autonomous text include, first, the use of the 'unanchored past of pure narration' – the simple past tense ('Jack said'), which is linguistically unmodified and not related to the 'present' of the reading of the narrative (compare this with the verb form 'Jack has said . . .', which connects the act of saying to some temporal point which might be inhabited by someone else). Banfield also commented that

in narration, the story is created by a descriptive language which is in some sense disembodied. It recounts the events which make up the story in a language where no first person need intervene . . . narration does not take place in the NOW of the events narrated. Nor is this narrator speaking to anyone. (1982: 178)

Narrative, then, as a literary form, can provide for treating the text as autonomous and authoritative. The use of narrative texts might appear to be a very indirect way of introducing children to the apparent autonomy and authority of expository texts. However Banfield pointed out how fictional statements come to be read as true within the fictional world:

the fictional narrative statement is immune to judgements of truth or falsity; in fiction, they are suspended. It is inappropriate to say that a fictional statement is false. Rather, it creates by fiat a fictional reality which can only be taken as fictionally true. [Any narrative sentence] must be taken as a fact within the fiction. (1982: 258)

Another option open to the narrator concerns how utterances are to be reported — directly or indirectly. We have observed that in the begining reading books, the narrator's preference appears to be strongly in favour of reported direct speech. Where the indirect form of reporting speech is employed ('Jack said that he could see the horse ...') or where thought is reported, it is assumed by the reader that what is being conveyed is the narrator's subjective representation of the character's thoughts or the gist of what was said. Where the narrator reports speech directly, it is as if these words are the words spoken — a claim to factuality of the same order as the narrative sentence. If indirect speech is a clue to 'fictionality' of a narrative, and conversely, direct speech a clue to 'factuality' (within the fiction), the particular form that is prevalent in the BR texts appears to be a variant of narrative that minimizes the interpretive work of the narrator. The narrator fades also as a result of the almost exclusive use of the verb *said*; use of verbs such as *thought* or *wondered* would draw more direct attention to the agency reporting the talk. Thus narrative devices in the BR corpus tend to convey "what was said" not "what was meant" (cf. Olson, 1982).

Further, such reported direct speech is an idealized form which 'confer[s] on the speech act a grammatical perfection it may not actually have had' (Banfield, 1982: 272). We examine in the next chapter how this speech is idealized in the case of beginning school reading books. Our point here is that choosing to report speech directly as distinct from indirectly conveys the sense of an actual record rather than the sense of a likely or possible rendition of what might have been said or thought — that is, rather than the sense of an interpreting agent in the assembling of the text. The textual features we have been describing suggest that these children's books are packaged as fiction but convey facts through these variations — expository text in narrative form.

These observations may guide our understanding of some of the ways in which 'narrative' text of the Jack-and-Grandmother variety can effect the child-reader's introduction to the knowledgeable but unobtrusive voice of the author. Through the fictionality of story forms the reader is discouraged from inquiring after the authority or competence of the text to convey what happened in some real or fictional world. Again it would be most unlikely within the spirit of the story form for some reader or listener to dispute either that Jack actually said what he reportedly said, or whether it was not Jack but Grandmother who said it.

In the BR books, the story line is typically carried largely through the activities, notably the speeches, of identified characters. The story is taken to be about those characters. It is the story rather than the text that is studied or enjoyed, and the features of the story, or ideas arising from the story, that are treated as exhaustively constraining children's comprehension and knowledge of the story.

Yet children's competence with written text can include their knowledge of how texts exemplifying these genres are worked — what the methods are for reading them. For example, we have described how the reader is acquainted with a method for hearing some segments of text as having been produced by someone (Jack, Grandmother, and so on), and for not hearing other bits of text as similarly socially produced. The use of markers around the reporting of characters' talk foregrounds the characters' talk, and backgrounds the narrator's activity (if these notations are conventionally interpreted). This order of children's knowledge about text rather than about stories is not typically part of reading instruction and remains largely implicit. This knowledge is of the same order as the reader's capacity to judge what epistemic status to assign to a text or to parts of it, and similarly rests on an unacknowledged awareness of what the author is doing to assemble the text. It is also one aspect of the paradox noted above in contexts of child—adult relations (MacKay, 1974a), that children (here as novice readers) must know how to do something they are not credited with being able to do in order to participate in the adults' agenda for learning how to do it.

Thus we can see that, while the activity of the man in red, and

Grandmother's comment, are events in the story, the narrator's activities are textual events, which do more or other than recount activities or fix events in the unanchored past of pure narration. We see the authorial voice in this kind of text, so prevalent in the beginning reading books, as having important scene-setting and choreographic functions. Many stories in the books are comprised largely of reported direct speech, and the conventions for interpreting these are among the more central that readers need to know how to apply. The issue of reading talk-on-paper is developed more fully in chapter 5. Here we examine further how the narrative voice encompasses and shapes characters' voices in narrative texts.

Example 4.9 below is similar in structure to example 4.6 (Jack and Grandmother). We will use it in conjunction with example 4.6 to extend our observations concerning narrative practices.

Example 4.9

> Pete said, "What can we do today, Mum?"
> "I have to work," said Mum.
> "Why don't you have a picnic?
> Ask Dean and Shirley to go with you.
> You can go to the park and take
> some sandwiches, apples and something to drink."
> "And cakes too?" said Pete.
> Pete went to Dean's place,
> but nobody was home.
> He went to Shirley's place,
> but nobody was there.
> Pete was disappointed.
> "I'll have to go by myself,"
> he said.

Where a text is comprised largely of reports of direct speech, the narrator plays what may appear to be a minor role in choreographing the talk. Text example 4.9 contains a number of turns at talk. The narrator identifies speakers with speeches and supplies contextual information. We note that this identification of speakers usually occurs after the speech has been reported or during its reporting. As illustrated in Example 4.9, speeches are often interrupted by the narrator's speaker-identification interjection (55 per cent of speaker identifications in the BR corpus are located within speeches). Reporting speech in oral conversation, we would typically begin with the identification of the speaker and then convey the words, for example, 'Mum said (that) she had to work'. In the case of indirect speech, the speaker identification that includes the verb (*said, wondered, asked*) is most likely to precede and not to follow the speech. With the quoting of speech directly on paper, the options are expanded, but we find in an inspection of the BR corpus that the most straightforward (but least literary) form, speaker identification followed by the speech, is the rarest (making up about 5 per cent of all forms of speaker identification in the BR corpus). Instead, the text has to be inspected, sometimes closely, to discover who the speaker is and when that speaker's turn is complete. We suggest that example 4.9 provides practical evidence for this. This makes the reader dependent on the narrator's interjections and requires that the reader look especially to the narrator's turns in between characters' turns, in order to make sense of the text as a story at all.

We have noted also that in these texts the narrator's speaker-identification interjections, and most of the narrator's scene-setting and scene-moving interjections, are in the unanchored past tense referred to above, while most of the characters' speeches are in the fictional present tense. It is the use of the direct speech form that allows this difference, for in the indirect speech mode we would typically require concordance of tense. The difference in tense increases the distance between narrator and character, and conveys the character as object of the narrator's observation, where indirect speech could convey a closer continuity of narrator and characters as in a hypothetical reconstruction of example 4.9:

> Pete asked his mum what they could do that day. Mum said that she had to work, and suggested that Pete have a picnic with Shirley and Dean. She said to go to the park ... etc.

This brings the narrator into the scene as participant observer (providing a running commentary, which invokes a listener), whereas the form in the original puts the narrator outside the scene being reported, and invokes a reader. In the original example 4.9, 'Pete was disappointed' is an instance of reporting an internal state, a device that draws attention to the narrator's interpretive work and omniscience, whereas, elsewhere in the example, the narrator adopts an outsider's position ('but nobody was home').

According to Brewer (1980: 232), the three main dimensions on which the narrative voice can vary are participation (as character in the story), visibility (drawing attention to itself), and access (to internal states of characters, to distant events, etc.). Participation and visibility correlate in that the narrator's presence in the story tends to entail visibility, but in this circumstance access to others' internal states is logically limited (Freebody, 1983). In the narrative texts in the BR books, what we find is typically a non-participant and low-visibility narrator. This should entail access to internal states of characters (the omniscient narrator), but, in the BR books, the non-participant, low-visibility narrator rarely conveys access to internal states or distant events. This is consistent with our observation of the preference for reporting direct speech. We find in the BR books a minimally intrusive narrator who adopts a reporter status.

The narrator as scene-assembler

The narrator's voice in texts of this kind has an additional function that we can describe as scene-setting. This entails more than imaginatively locating the story in some fictional but unspecified setting, and introducing the characters. It includes also the more fundamental work of making scenic announcements and relating them to what characters are doing and saying such that the talk and activities are made sensible within the scene, and the scene comes to serve as their context.

We observe the narrative voice setting the scenes in examples 4.6 and 4.9 not only in identifying speakers but in inserting time-passes segments (such as 'Up he jumped and away he went' or 'Pete went to Dean's place, but nobody was home'), that refer to previous activities or speeches of the characters, or provide for some next course of action or comment by a character. In an oral-conversational event, the topic and context are produced by the speakers. In the BR texts the narrator takes over some of the work of signalling the sense of what is going on. This sense, which the narrator's interjections assist, becomes the context for the interpretation of characters' speeches. For instance, 'I'll have to go by myself' in example 4.9 above, following the narrator's notations that nobody was home and that Pete was disappointed, is heard exactly as resignation rather than as, say, glee. The narrator's work serves as a clue to how to read Pete's utterance. Thus the sense of the character's speeches is made dependent on the scenic work of the author. The characters' speeches are referred back to those scenic practices in unobtrusive ways. This may be seen as an essential device, given the inability of the written language to carry prosodic (e.g., intonational) features of oral utterances.

Even more fundamentally, the author determines what categories of character will be described and how membership of those categories will be elaborated within the text. Every text organizes its content through a particular selection and arrangement of commonsense constructs or categories that shape the meaning of the text. The same scene can be described through the use of different referential terms, which would alter the sense of the story. For instance, in example 4.6, rather than Pete and Mum, the characters could be assembled as Lois and her son Pete. Thus, by reversing the direction in which their kinship relation is portrayed and supplying alternative identities, the scene could be restaged. The author is the contriver of the fictional scene, selecting both the identification categories and noticing for the reader what is observable in the scene. Changes in referential terms can serve to reorganize the identity and centrality of the characters, and thus subtly change the reading of the story.

EXPERIENTIAL TEXTS

Earlier we introduced examples 4.7 and 4.8 to illustrate a form of text found in the BR books that is distinct from the narrative, third person texts described above. These examples took the forms: 'It's warm in here, in bed. My blanket's warm and my kitten's soft ...' and 'My teacher is happy. She sings nursery rhymes to us ...'. In both examples the text is written in the first person without any explicit attribution of the statements to identified characters, that is, without the 'Jack said' device that characterizes narrative texts.

In this section we consider these texts in more detail, again attempting to show how they serve as transitional forms towards the fully autonomous school text. We see some differences among the kinds of texts that share the first person style. Text of the type illustrated by example 4.7 is presumably expressive of some particular individual's ongoing experience in the world ('I can hear the radio in the kitchen'), while text of the type illustrated by example 4.8 ('My teacher helps us to weigh and to count') we regard more as an observation and exposition about the world. There are further differences which we set out as we proceed to examine and compare such texts.

First we consider the 'experiential' text illustrated in example 4.7. Further lines from the same text are presented here:

Example 4.10

I'm going to slide down in my bed
and hide.
I'm taking my kitten too.
It's dark in here.
I can hear purring. My kitten's
soft and the bed's warm. [etc.]

Texts such as this are constructed differently from the narrative texts we discussed above. First, they are written not in the historical past but in the present progressive tense. Such texts do not have the quality of a story being recounted, but of an experience being lived. Where such text is accompanied by illustration of some character, as is typically found, we presume the text is meant to be read as conveying the experience of that character, as distinct from that of the reader or someone else, for example an author. Texts such as examples 4.7 and 4.10 appear to be highly direct, and possibly very straightforward, forms of putting thought on paper, and subjective consciousness into words. It appears to draw on children's oral language as used in their private thoughts to create a text which can be appreciated for its sympathy with the centrality of subjective experience.

The books do not always give explicit instruction that the character illustrated is the speaker of these sentences, or how to treat or enter into the 'I' voice of the text. To explore these points, we asked a large number of pre-school boys and girls to tell us stories based on the pictures contained in a set of

BR books. The children were read the beginning lines of such stories and were asked to continue telling the story in their own words. (The words were concealed after the first two pages which were read aloud to them). We found that, even though all of the stories used first person narration and the present tense (e.g., 'I am the wind'), the children almost universally switched to a third person recounting (e.g., 'It's making the trees blow around'). This change from first to third person occurred in 117 out of 119 instances of the children's storytelling, accompanied usually by a switch to the simple past tense (in 83 out of 119 instances). It is as if the first person, present tense mode is unfamiliar, uncomfortable or inappropriate. It could be that the children understood that a text cannot talk, or is not talk on paper, that there must be a distance in time between the event and the textual production to render a text writable. The children's resistance to first person present tense text of this kind might suggest that these children have come to view texts as being about the past (external) world, not expressions of present (internal) experience.

Nevertheless, beginning school books contain a considerable amount of such first person, 'experiential' text. Another kind of first person text which is found in the corpus is that which adopts the 'I' form to comment on some factual or routine feature of everyday life. We presented example 4.8 ('My teacher is happy . . .') as an instance of this. Another illustration of this kind of text is shown here as example 4.11:

Example 4.11

> We play doctors and nurses
> at school.
> My friend is the doctor.
> He's got a white coat.
> Some girls dress up
> as nurses.

In these examples, the narration takes on a different position with respect to the voices of characters. While in our earlier examples of narrative text the narrator assumes a position as 'puppeteer', identifying different story-characters and giving them voices and speeches, in these first person texts we see the author working as a hidden ventriloquist, giving a voice either to some child character ('I am going to slide down in my bed') or, where the object of the sentiment or observation is emphasized rather than the source of the sentiment, directly to the child reader, as in:

Example 4.12

> My teacher.
> My teacher is at school.
> My teacher helps me at school.
> She is kind to me.
> I am little and she is big.
> Sometimes we are naughty.
> My teacher is unhappy.

This text is unlike the 'sliding down in my bed' example above (which is event-based and expressive of an individual experience), and unlike the 'we play doctors and nurses at school' example (which has a sequential structure but is equally a report on activity in the world). The 'my teacher' text above provides normative comment rather than idiosyncratic observations on the world. It gives a description of the qualities of the category 'teacher' and of teacher—child relations. It is therefore more expository in nature than other first person texts, and in this way may also be viewed as a prelude to the introduction of more fully expository texts such as 'How Apple Juice is Made'.

We see then, that the ventriloquized, first person texts differ among themselves in several respects: in some, the text is individualistic, experiential and written to convey the here-and-now (the actual present) of the experience. These texts typically have an event-based, narrative structure, and describe idiosyncratic experiences — a particular character, or a particular set of circumstances. These characteristics provide for a reading of the text as a story. Other first person texts are written in an ever-present, describing states of affairs which hold across individual experiences and particular contexts, and states of affairs that are essentially routine if not banal. The verb tense adopted here is the simple present: 'My teacher reads to me ...' not 'My teacher is reading ...'. These texts have overall an expository flavour, although they can contain narrative segments.

It is the first person voice coupled with a present tense that allows for these variations. All of these first person texts are versions of direct speech or thought, ventriloquized talk-on-paper.

In some ways these texts appear to be more simple in structure than the narrative texts in that they lack the mediating voice of the narrator complicating the text. However, we can ask who is this 'I' speaking in the texts, and how does that voice refer or relate to the implied voice of the child-reader of the texts? We can also point to the complication that some of these texts represent or convey ongoing present experience in a way that complies with certain poetic and literary conventions or licences, but which is in fact logically impossible. The convention is that we pretend that the writing and saying are simultaneous, and that we attend to the saying rather than to the writing. This further conceals the textualizing process. We have reported above some evidence of children's resistance to sustaining the first person, present tense mode when recounting such stories, and suggested that this evidence supports the view that these apparently simple texts appearing to map oral language directly on to paper have some special qualities and peculiarities. One of the implications we point to here is that these texts serve as transitional to the fully autonomous, speakerless and characterless texts represented by example 4.5 ('How Apple Juice is Made') earlier in this chapter.

CONCLUSION

The 'conflict of languages' that Olson claimed could be found in these books may in part be made up of a number of inconsistencies and peculiarities in the way oral language events are written down within structures that are apparently narrative, or apparently experiential, and that involve different narrator—character—reader relations. These materials contain an intriguing mixture of textual practices which, we have argued, provide previews of the encounter with more fully expository texts in the later years of school.

We also suggest that these varieties of texts could be a major resource for drawing children's attention to 'textuality', not only to the content of the books. There is some research that bears directly on children's readiness to discuss the textualizing process.

Goldman (1985) has reported a series of studies that attempted to document children's and adults' inferential processes in reading. After reading single- and multiple-episode stories, children and adults showed no differences in their perceptions of why characters in the stories performed certain activities (a process Goldman termed 'text-internal' inferring). These inferences, Goldman argued, seem to be acquired 'through exposure to everyday events and to stories . . . [and] seem to require little in the way of formal instruction' (1985: 269). In contrast, those inferences that are based on a more abstract perception of the function of the story, in this case its purpose in transmitting 'rules of social conduct and the moral conventions and values of society' (a subset of what Goldman termed 'text-external' inferences) varied with age. Almost all of the middle and upper primary school children gave responses reflecting generalizations from the text to the social or moral purposes of the writer (as did the adults), while only one-quarter of the kindergarten to grade two children (age 5 to 7 years) produced such responses. Further, Goldman reported that about 60 per cent of these younger students appeared not to find questions about the more abstract purposes of the story meaningful. Goldman concluded that these text-external inferences, that is, perceptions *about* the story that are concerned with the writer—reader relationship, require more than simply exposure to the narrative form, and seem to call for more explicit and guided effort.

While our notion of textual awareness is more inclusive than that of Goldman's text-external inferences, her findings none the less suggest that young children's initial approach to stories is to treat them as given and uncrafted, in which the content of the text is exhaustively contained in the actions, speeches and intentions of the characters. Wells' study of parent—child story-reading sessions (1985b) and the classroom interaction data we report in chapter 7 remove any need to regard this initial approach of children as a 'natural' strategy. It is clear that the sources of the invisibility of the textualizing process are in the oral conventions adults use when they read and discuss stories with children, as well as in the camouflaging practices of the narrator that we have described in this chapter.

We have drawn attention here to the authorial agency behind the words on the page even though this agency is not explicitly marked in the text. Children are not invited by the text to view the narrator as agent or to view narrative work as a textualizing process at this point in their school careers. In this sense, children are shown, by negative inference, what questions not to ask of informational texts they encounter later in school.

As a conclusion to our discussion of the preparatory function of the BR books, we present two examples from the early pages of a social studies and a history textbook written for upper primary and lower secondary students. These texts exemplify points further along the continuum towards expository text, whose beginnings we have described in this chapter. Example 4.13 is taken from the introduction to a book on earth in space (Beddis, 1982: 8).

Example 4.13

> For thousand of years, men and women knew little about the world, other than their immediate surroundings. They thought the earth was flat, and they could not understand the movements of the moon, sun and stars. ... Several centuries ago a number of brilliant astronomers and mathematicians worked out the truth.

Example 4.14 (quoted earlier) is taken from the early part of a book on the early European discoveries of Australia (Murdoch, 1974: 7).

Example 4.14

> Everyone recognises Captain James Cook as Australia's greatest discoverer-hero, and indeed he was. But he was not Australia's only hero, nor was he the earliest ...

We see here examples of the substantial claims to authority made by school textbook writers, authority to speak from a privileged epistemological vantage point about a level of factuality beyond everyday human understanding. This vantage point is explicitly worked into the text of example 4.13, in which everyday understanding is relegated to the status of 'thought', and 'truth' is achieved through the almost occult 'workings out' of 'brilliant' members of an intellectual elite (in which, as well, the writer is implicitly placed as a transmitter of these 'truths'). Similarly, in example 4.14, we see clearly marked the separation of the commonsense understandings of 'everyone' from the factuality made available in the text. In this way, the writer has implicitly negated the status of popular, 'common' knowledge in the official content and conduct of (school) history.

The authorial practices in the BR books can be seen to lead towards a relation between reader and text in which the text contains knowledge to be learned by the reader, and in which attention is deflected from the textualizing process. The basis for this type of relation, we argue, is partly the expository nature of the narrative styles adopted in the BR books. In this additional sense, the texts provide for a transition from the conventions of oral language towards the conventions of written prose (especially the conventions of the essay-text). This transition serves to recast the conventional oral language itself in a direction that suits the particular literacy-instructional purposes of schooling. This notion is further developed in the next chapter in which we examine the kinds of apparently oral language used by the characters in the books, and the relation of this to the building of the concept of school-literacy.

5

Talk-on-Paper: The Representation of Conversation

We have argued that a central feature in the characterization of the BR books as transitional from the conventions of oral language to the conventions of written prose is the extent to which the books contain talk-on-paper.

In this chapter we describe how people talk with each other in these books, focusing not on lexical or syntactic content but rather on conversational practices. The analyses we report apply to conversations in those school reading books that present apparent portrayals of everyday family and school life, since it is these that draw most explicitly on the child-reader's oral language knowledge as part of the method of introducing children to literacy. Below are some examples that typify the conversational exchanges found in the BR corpus:

Example 5.1

Andrew ran to meet his father.
"Daddy," he said, "my cousin Sue
is coming today, but it is raining."
Andrew's father took him to the window.
"Look at the sky, Andrew,"
he said. "This is a storm.
Soon the storm will stop and
there will be no more rain."
The storm did stop soon and
there was no more rain.

Example 5.2

Elizabeth went up to the well.
She looked into the water.

"I wish I could be an elf,"
she said.
"With long funny ears and
little red whiskers!" said Jack.
All the children laughed.
Everyone made a wish at the well.
"Do you want to play now?"
asked Miss Brown.
"I wish we could," said Jack.

Example 5.3

Jill got the big yellow basket.
Mother cut the lunch.
Ken and Jill put the lunch
into the basket.
"Pamela is awake now," said Jill.
"May I go and get her?"
"Yes," said mother.
Pamela saw the big yellow basket.
She went to play with it.
"Come away from the basket,"
said mother.
"Come and get dressed.'

We begin with some observations related to the analyses presented in chapter 4 on narrative practices. This will serve to outline some general points about characters' speeches before we undertake detailed analyses of specific sequences of conversation.

First, in most of our narrative text examples in this and other chapters, the characters' commentaries are concerned predominantly with the pragmatics of what is occurring in the here-and-now of the scene. Characters rarely speak about the past or about some distant event or person. They comment mainly on what they are currently doing or about to do, drawing attention to some observable features of the immediate fictional environment.

The topic that characters talk about is the scene itself. Many of their statements are routine declarations or announcements: 'It is raining'; 'Pamela is awake now'. In one sense, the characters talk like on-the-spot reporters, describing what they see or are doing, while the narrator frames and incorporates the characters' reports. In ordinary conversation, such explicit identification of what is visible or obvious to everyone on the scene might appear puzzling. The texts in the BR corpus present an exaggerated, almost pica-resque, version of this potentially problematic way of talking. However, 'there are occasions in which interactants announce their behaviors in the course of performing them, probably for persons outside of the episode ... preserv[ing] the action for the record' (Twer, 1972: 344). In this additional sense, characters seem to speak as though there is an audience beyond the fictive audience in the story. This sometimes occurs through explication of what in ordinary conversation might be assumed, for example, 'My cousin Sue is coming' rather than 'Sue is coming' — informa-tion the reader needs but that the fictional Daddy probably already has. Characters are continually reporting to each other what the scene is about, such that the consciousness of characters is conveyed as consciousness of the scene itself. This feature of conversational portrayals can be observed in many of the examples presented in this chapter.

Second, conversational turns are usually short, and therefore the narrator frequently reasserts a presence (Luke, 1987a: 102). Because characters' speeches are so short in these books, this reassertion might be seen to be more frequent in BR texts. Yet the reassertions are relatively light-handed in that to a large extent all they do is the work of identifying characters in between speeches or supplying brief scene-setting or scene-moving interjections. The brevity and scene-specific nature of both characters' speeches and narrator's interjections restrict the world of the story to the pragmatics of the here-and-now scene. Neither characters' speeches nor narrator's interjections draw attention away from the im-mediate fictional scene, and thus together comprise 'high redun-dance messages' (Luke, 1987a: 103). From a reader's point of view, the imaginative boundaries of the story are limited. It could be for reasons such as this that teachers may have difficulty in finding much to discuss about the text itself, and may rather adopt the practice of pursuing lexical or pictorial details. These and other aspects of the use of these texts in early reading instruction are discussed more fully in chapter 7.

Third, characters often respond to each others' turns whether or not specific questions have been put. Characters 'talk to a topic' rather than 'topically' (cf. Wells, 1981: 29) — that is, there are few digressions from the common agenda. A large number of question—answer sequences assist with this focusing on the topic. Together with the observation that the speeches are well formed, uninterrupted utterances conveying clear messages, these features suggest that the oral world is idealized as literate in its nature, a point more fully developed later in this chapter.

The first and most obvious question we may ask about such conversational exchanges is whether anyone, anywhere, actually talks like this — that is, is there a recognizable speech community portrayed here? We take the view that these are idealized conversational exchanges. It is the case that most written narrative minimizes the complexity of actual oral interaction. In the case of the BR books, however, it is also that the conversations perform much of the work of characterization and plot line, and portray a curiously constructed version of human interaction and of the social world in which it occurs. Our second question, then, is how the representation of conversation in the BR books relates to the larger project of introducing children to school-literacy.

Our main objective in this chapter is to give detailed consideration to the conversational practices of child and adult speakers in the BR texts, focusing mainly on question—answer sequences, and treating the participants as if they were members of a hypothetical speech community. Our second objective is to compare our descriptions of talk within the texts with the findings of research on child—adult talk at home and at school. This will provide grounds for estimating the extent to which these books can be said to reflect oral language practices that occur in young children's interactions, and to assess whether the books present a model of language practice that, in specific, identifiable ways, does not match children's oral language experiences.

Also, in conducting our analyses we have encountered particular difficulties in making sense of some of the conversations, and we wonder whether for many children a source of difficulty lies here too. To our knowledge, this issue has not been addressed before. Attention has been given to vocabulary, sentence length and to the use of pictures as indices of readability (see Klare, 1975), but not to this aspect of the organization of these texts. That is, in the case of the BR texts, the problem of reading is to a large extent a problem of reading talk-on-paper.

A third objective relates to our interest in the portrayals of children, child—adult relations and family life provided in the texts. The way conversation is conducted between speakers in the texts contributes significantly to the images of children and adults which the books provide. The details of this contribution have rarely been examined. The issue of who talks, to whom and how often, is a critical one in the study of these reading books. Characters who get turns at talk, in these texts as well as in ordinary conversation, have a presence in the story that is more immediate than, say, those who receive only mention or description by the narrator — they are made to speak for themselves. In the school scenes, for example, where we presume a classroom full of children, only those who have turns at talk are named and thereby become characters in the story. Giving the person a turn at talk is a narrator's way of bringing that person into the story and thus to the imaginal attention of the reader. Given that the organization of these texts seems to be based largely on a distribution of turns at talk interspersed with brief scene-setting or scene-moving interjections by the narrator, the turns at talk carry much of the story line. Hence, getting turns at talk marks a character's presence in the story and thus in the world it is supposed to represent.

Cultural images of children and adults are built subtly into the texts through the representations of how people talk to each other. This is yet another possible source of children's difficulties with the texts, especially as the books are largely stories about children and their conversational interactions with others, and the books are written as if from the perspective of children, as we pointed out in chapter 3. In this chapter, we detail the bases for the claim that the images of children, adults and families are made available to the reader in part through the ways in which talk is represented.

QUESTION—ANSWER SEQUENCES

In presenting our analyses of the representation of oral conversation in the BR corpus, we attend first to question—answer sequences. These analyses are followed by an examination of how questions, answers and other conversational units are integrated into the texts.

Part of our interest is in the ways in which conversational interactions in children's first school books compare with descriptions of naturally occurring home and school talk between children and adults. In this regard, we consider question–answer sequences to be especially salient for a number of reasons. First, the large number of question–answer sequences in the BR corpus allows for some study of how two or more characters are shown to interact through language. Second, previous research on child–adult conversation has paid considerable attention to various aspects of question–answer sequences as a category of linked initiation–response exchanges. There is therefore comparative material available concerning this aspect of conservation. Third, such sequences have also been shown to be important for language learning in the home (Wells, 1981), and fundamental to the organization of instructional classroom talk (e.g., MacLure and French, 1981; Mehan, 1979; Walker, 1981).

Textual representations of question–answer sequences can be viewed as displaying a particular version of coherent and 'literate' discourse, and can be seen to index important aspects of social relationships between speakers, in our case especially between children and adults. As Edwards (1981: 303) has stated, 'forms of social relationship are signalled, and are reproduced or modified or challenged, *in the act of speaking*'.

We have located more than 1,700 conversational turns (i.e., speeches separately attributed to individual children or adults by the narrators) in the texts. The corpus also contains conversations among animals, between animals and children, and among people in fairy tales and similar sources. These are not included in the analyses described here. We have attended only to narrated conversations in everyday contemporary settings in the books – mainly home and school scenes and stories. We have also included only those in which the text provides quotation marks to identify the separation of speeches and speakers, due to the considerable interpretive difficulty associated with those few narratives in which this punctuation was not used.

With the constraints above applied, we have located some 300 instances of questions being asked or answered in the corpus. We have used as the criterion for selection of a question that the utterance be expressed in interrogative form – although we appreciate that in naturally occurring conversation utterances in non-interrogative forms can be heard and treated as questions or requests (cf. Schegloff, 1984). We also recognize that there are types of utterances other than questions that strongly invite a response or second part to form a conversational pair (as in the Andrew—Daddy exchange in example 5.1 above). This amounts to an acknowledgement that we are inspecting only a portion of potentially interesting pairs of utterances in the corpus, and that some of the work we do with our particular selection is relevant to a wider range of conversational couplets outside that selection. In this chapter we examine 290 instances of question—answer sequences that were readily discernible as discrete pairs.

A point that refers both to our methodology and to the child-reader's task in interpreting text is that in undertaking identification of question—answer pairs we have had to practise certain techniques of reading. We occasionally note the various linguistic and format clues and the kinds of cultural knowledge that any reader would use to read adjacent utterances in this way. It is the case that pairs of this kind are more readily identifiable than some other two-part exchanges, due to the use of markers in the punctuation, sometimes the use of address terms and usually the adjacency of the pairs. None the less, we have noted difficulties that could be encountered by the child-reader on the basis of having encountered some of these difficulties ourselves, even given these textual markers. Similarly, the identification of the speaker or recipient of a question or answer is not always straightforward. We examine this problem in reading such texts in our analyses of longer stretches of conversation later in this chapter.

To identify possible differences in the content, structure and context of the textual representations of question—answer pairs, and with a practical interest in subdividing the varieties of cases observed, we developed a typology of question—answer sequences comprised of 'information', 'request' and 'permission' sequences.

In information sequences, the questioner is heard genuinely not to know something and the question is put to find out. The sequence is deemed to be complete when the answer is provided:

Example 5.4

"Where are you going?" asked Dan.
"I am going away," said Jack. "I am going to my house."

Example 5.5

"Will he let us help him milk?" she says.
"Yes," says Peter, "he likes us to help him with
his work."

In the second category are *request sequences*, which in some
cases we see as intermediate between information and permission
questions. Speakers use this question form to ask others to engage
in an activity.

Example 5.6

"Can we see some more of the farm?" asks Peter.
"Yes," says Pam, "come on, then, let us go for a
walk."

Example 5.7

"Father," said Jill. "Can you come up here?"
"Yes I can," said Father. "I can come up and play
with you. We can have fun."

In the third type of sequence, *permission sequences*, the speaker
requests approval to engage in an activity or to be given something.

Example 5.8

"May we come again soon?" asked Robin.
"We shall see," said Miss Brown.

Example 5.9

"Can we have some apples, please?" says Peter.
"Yes," says Mummy. "Apples do you good."

The task of classifying sequences into the categories of the
typology also involves interpretive problems. Not surprisingly,
the request category contains more of the ambiguous cases than
the others since the ambiguity often pivots on the word *can*. It
should also be noted that the information, request and permission
notions are applicable to sequences, that is, to the two-part ex-

change. None the less, after we have classified sequences as, say, permission sequences, we then proceed to talk about the question turns in them as permission questions. But the form of words of the question alone does not always decide the classification. It is often only with the second part, the response, that we have clear grounds for our decision.

While our discussion of the three categories of questions involves some analysis unique to each category, we ask repeatedly some parallel questions. Who initiates the sequence, and who completes it? How are the turns within the sequence typically constructed? Besides describing individual utterances in this way, we ask how the two parts of the sequences might be connected. In each section we comment on the contribution of childhood and of family life in the books. Having treated each category of question separately, we briefly discuss some more lengthy passages, describing how these question—answer sequences are woven together with other kinds of conversational moves and with the narrator's contributions to form a story.

Information sequences

In this category we have placed those question—answer pairs in which one speaker asks for information on some state of affairs from some other speaker/s. Questions in which information is sought and provided are the most numerous in the BR books (204). Some exemplary exchanges classified under the heading of 'information' sequences are presented below.

Example 5.10

> "Hello, Jack," said Robin. "Is this your ball?"
> "No," said Jack. "It is Jill's ball. Your little
> dog ran away with it."

Example 5.11

> "Oh, Ginger," said Mother. "Where did you find
> him?"
> "I did not find him," said Ginger. "He came to
> see me. He looked in and he liked me. Now we are
> friends."

Example 5.12

Mummy says, "Can you see the train?"
"Yes," says Jane. "I can see it down there. It
looks like a toy train."

We ask first who initiates information question—answer sequences in the home- and school-located exchanges portrayed in the BR books. Table 5.1 shows the distribution of question–initiations across the 204 instances of information sequences. As we are describing two-part sequences, our interest is in who asks the question, not who initiates the entire stretch of talk in which the sequence is found.

A number of overall aspects of table 5.1 are noteworthy: the children portrayed in these texts ask significantly more of the questions than do the adults (64 versus 36 per cent); children ask a larger proportion of the questions set in the home context than they do of those set in school (68 versus 56 per cent). In the school scenes, children ask considerably more than the research on actual classroom lessons would predict. For example, Mehan (1979: 80) found that students initiate less than 18 per cent of sequences in lessons. McHoul (1978: 208) estimates that 80 per cent of lesson talk is teacher talk. However, it is not formal lessons but the planning and doing of other activities such as a

TABLE 5.1 Participants in information sequences in home and school contexts

		At home	*At school*	*Total*
	To adult/s	31	13	44
Initiated	To child/ren	53	14	67
by child/ren	To other or unclear	13	7	20
	Total	97	34	131
	To adult/s	6	2	8
Initiated	To child/ren	31	24	55
by adult/s	To other or unclear	9	1	10
	Total	46	27	73
Grand totals		143	61	204

play, or a class excursion, which is portrayed in the books. Much of the classroom talk appears to be organizational talk rather than instructional talk. It is the special events of classroom life rather than routine lessons that are described in the children's first school books.

Most of the adults' questions are to children (75 per cent). Only occasionally do mother, father, teacher, bus driver, grandmother, or farm helper ask questions of each other. Children's questions are directed significantly more often to other children than to adults in the home context. Overall, approximately half of these sequences involve cross-generational talk, with a significantly larger proportion of it occurring in the school context.

This gives an initial indication of how representations of conversation in the texts give speaking roles to children and adults. While on the one hand, the adults appear to be onlookers and supervisors in a 'child-centred' world (children's play, children's trips, etc.), we note that a central place is given to the representation of talking with adults. In this sense adult characters are not backgrounded, but are central figures in the communication that goes on. Their presence and perspective is continually sought and portrayed. In these books the children are continually dealing with the adults in ways, we suggest, that endorse the conventional roles and responsibilities of adults as well as the conventional interests of children.

The questions in the corpus are usually answered in the next turn at talk, with very few questions left unresolved or unanswered. In this sense, therefore, the books portray a language community and a culture in which questions achieve immediate response, a characteristic that reflects the special conditions of formal classroom talk and not of conversational conventions in all situations. For example, Phillips (1983) has shown that in child-organized problem-solving talk, questions may not receive immediate answers. The books portray strict adherence to conversational maxims of the cooperative principle (Grice, 1975) – a principle that, as we pointed out in chapter 1, reflects literate conversational practice.

Table 5.1 serves as a reliable guide to the speakers of the second-part turns. On very few occasions, the narrator supplies the resolution without having another character speak. There are some 'open' queries framed to invite self-selection to answer, as in 'Who will help me?' and in which some participant in the scene can self-select as answerer. The majority of questions in this (information) category, however, are seen as being addressed to children (60 per cent) or answered by children (62 per cent).

About half of these questions seek a *yes* or *no* answer to establish some point of fact (as in example 5.13 below), while about half are *when, where, why, what* and *how* questions, which require further content to be supplied by the answerer (as in example 5.14 below):

Example 5.13

"Is big brown bear in it?" asked Father. "I like him."
"Oh yes," said Jack. "He plays with the bunny and the mouse."

Example 5.14

"When will our bus be here?"
asked one of the girls.
"Very soon," said Miss Brown.
"Now, is everyone here?"
"I do not see Peter," said Elizabeth.

The initiation turn poses the query fairly succinctly. The narrator rarely gives a speaker two turns in a row, and speakers do not hold the floor for very long. The answer turn typically contains a more-than-minimal response, sometimes explaining or elaborating the answer. We note also that answer turns usually contain complete sentences ('I did not find him' rather than 'I didn't' in example 5.11). Often, some of the words in the initiation turn are incorporated into the answer. We suggest that this use of sentences, and the frequent incorporation of some of the words of the question into the answer, endorses a classroom model of asking and answering questions.

A number of *yes/no* information sequences occur in school or classroom scenes. Many of these questions seem to be framed to establish what is about to happen or could happen (e.g. 'Are you/we going to ...?', 'Would you like to come/have/tell us ...?'). Along with a number of questions inquiring where some character is, these question sequences describe a process of locating, assembling and organizing people for activities. This could be read as depicting classroom life realistically, as an instance of the management of large groups of people for collective activity.

Information questions are the most numerous in the corpus, and convey a speech community that uses questions and answers to structure cross-generational talk. In addition to 'is it the case that ...' questions, speakers also ask open questions, of which *wh-* questions are a major subset. The nature of the *wh-* questions in the everyday texts is summarized in table 5.2.

TABLE 5.2 Distribution of *wh-*questions in school and home contexts

	School	*Home*
Where	10	33
What	8	27
When	1	1
Who	3	6
Which	—	1
Why	—	3
Other	4	3

We see that questions beginning *where* and *what* predominate within this category within both the home and school settings. Many of the *where* questions concern where some person or object is, has been, or is going. Missing children or objects figure in a number of stories. The prevalence of *what* questions also indicates the insertion of puzzles into the stories, as in 'What is in the box?' or 'What is that on the road?'.

Table 5.2 offers a clue to the depiction of the intellectual world displayed in these texts. It seems that there is relatively little concern among the speakers with when things happened, but somewhat more about when things will happen. Nor is there much interest in reasons for events (three instances of *why* in the question–answer materials). *Why* talk may occur in the actual teacher's use of the book in the reading class, if the teacher makes causes and motives points of discussion. However, characters in the stories are not shown to concern themselves overly with understanding or explaining the world. Rather, they are made to remark on it as it happens, and seem to live in a perpetual present with half an eye to the short-term future.

The predominance of information questions portrays children and adults as people in an interactive search for factual knowledge, adopting positions as either novices or experts. Moreover, it is knowledge about the here-and-now of the fictional scene that is taken to be the immediate field of quasi-pedagogical inquiry. This point is compatible with our more general observation concerning the transformation and reduction of child—adult relations to suit the interests of schooling.

Request sequences

This category includes those sequences that contain a request for assistance, favours, or specific action by the listener. Wootton's (1981a, b, c) work on address terms and request sequences involving 4-year-old children and their parents is relevant to our analysis of request sequences and to our discussion of permission routines in the next section. In our request sequences, we read speakers to be seeking to involve other/s in some activity, while in our permission category, we read speakers (almost always children) to be asking that they be allowed to do something. We have noted enough of these latter, which to us are especially expressive of child—adult relations in the texts, to warrant treating them as a category in themselves. Also, Wootton's materials contain exclusively children's requests to parents (our permission category is largely this), while our materials contain a proportion of sequences involving the reverse, as well as within-generation request sequences. Additionally some of our sequences are sited in school settings.

We have located 21 request sequences in the corpus, only two of which appear in school scenes. Hence, we will not distinguish in this section between school and home scenes. The three question forms we found in this category are: (*a*) 'can you (come, help, etc.)' — 11 instances; (*b*) 'can we (have, come, look), etc.' — five instances; and (*c*) 'will you (tell, get, etc.)' — five instances). As noted, some of the instances we have put into this category appear to be intermediate between information sequences and permission sequences, as in example 5.15.

Example 5.15

> "I like milking time. Can we come again?" asked
> Sue.
> Andrew said, "We will come every morning."

In this example, we hear Sue making a suggestion in the form of a request (i.e., the sense of 'let's') rather than asking about permissibility or approval. This category also includes five cases of 'will you ...' initiations, such as:

Example 5.16

> "Will you tell us some more stories about Rinaldo?"
> asked Robin.
> "Next Saturday we may have another story about
> him," said Miss Long. "Now it's time for the other
> surprise."

There are also 11 instances of 'can you come/help ...' routines, such as 5.7 above. Of the 21 initiations, 18 are by children, two by parents and one by the family dog. Thirteen are requests directed to adults, seven to children and one indeterminate. Of the 21 sequences, 12 are cross-generational. Most of the initiations (18/21) receive a positive response. In four of the sequences, the request is 'answered' by a descriptive sentence from the narrator, as in:

Example 5.17

> "Please will you hose me?"
> said Helen.
> "Please will you hose me?"
> said Mark.
> Father hosed Helen and Mark.
> "Please will you hose me?"
> barked Boxer.
> Father hosed Boxer too.

In most sequences, the request is answered by a speaker, as in:

Example 5.18

"Will you tell us something about it?" asked Susan.
"It is a place where there are trees and birds and
animals," said Miss Brown.

but usually with a *yes* term included in initial position, and some
additional comments, as in:

Example 5.19

"Mother," said Jack. "I cannot take my green fish.
It is too big. Can you come and help me?"
Mother laughed. "Yes, Jack," she said. "Here is a
big box for you."

The *yes* term is included in ten of the 14 grantings done verbally
by the second speaker, while *no* term is avoided in two of the
three non-grantings. This parallels Wootton's (1981b: 61–2) finding that 'granting tokens' (*yes* or the equivalent) are stated, usually
in initial position, while *no* terms are omitted: 'refusals of requests
are frequently softened, delayed, and accompanied by accounts'
(see 5.16 above for an example). Thus this aspect of natural
conversation seems preserved in request sequences in the BR
corpus.

In most of these request sequences, children are asking another
person to help or attend to them in some way. They do this far
more often than do adults in these books. Still, in the context of
our concern with the images of childhood and child–adult relations
available in the texts, and even combined with the larger category
of permission sequences discussed in the next section, they are
not numerous compared with information sequences. It would
therefore be inappropriate to suggest that the primary model of
childhood presented in these texts is a simplistic dependency
model. However, these sequences of request and permission occur
often enough to impute the presence of such a model as part of
the portrayal of childhood. We will return later to this discussion
of how childhood is constituted in the texts.

The most frequent type of routine within the category of request
sequences is the one we have called the 'can you come/help'
routine. There are ten of these routines, all in home scenes, six

of them put by children to adults, three by children to other
children and one mother—father exchange. Examples 5.19 and
5.20 illustrate this type. In all of the ten instances, the request was
granted.

These are interesting as the only sequences within this category
in which an address term is contained in the initiation turn,
usually in the first position, as in 5.20:

Example 5.20

> "Jill! Jill!" said Jack. "Can you come and help
> me?"
> "Yes," said Jill. "The pets can play here. I can
> come with you."

Eight of the ten routines, and eight out of 21 (38 per cent) of the
request sequences, contain an address term in the first turn. We
note that address terms are relatively rare in information sequences,
and we will show later that they are about as frequent in permission sequences as in request sequences. About 30 per cent of
answers in request sequences also contain an address term.

First-position address terms are understood as devices for securing attention and for directing the hearer to take careful note
of what follows (Wootton, 1981a: 153). In these textual representations the narrator's voice (e.g., 'said Jack') usually occurs in
between the address term and the request proper, such that the
'pause' so effected in the speech might mimic the speaker's check
on whether the listener is attending or can hear. Hence the splitting
of speeches with the narrator's speaker-identification suits the
interactional contours of the exchange. The listener, over the
period of the pause for the narrator's contribution, is assumed to
have become ready for the request proper.

It is also the case that children sometimes place address terms
in the first position, as summons or notification to listen, and
sometimes in final position, where they behave like question tags
to keep conversation going (Wootton, 1981a: 143—4). It is rare in
this corpus for an address term to appear other than in first
position. This could be taken to suggest that (child) speakers in
the books do not face the kinds of conversational problems for
which, for example, the final-position address term can be seen to

be a solution. It seems that the compacted format of the exchanges prevents the representation of an almost infinite set of conversational practices that characterize real child—adult talk, and in this presents a curiously distorted view of the child as speaker. Children may find these representations of talk artificial.

In detailing ways in which the texts represent child—adult talk, we are attempting to show fine points of contrast or similarity with specific findings from naturalistic research in and out of classrooms. We are also suggesting the possible significance of these for the overall model of child—adult talk which comprises much of the content of the books.

The organization of the answers generally indicates that the attention was secured and the request heard. While we hear these requests essentially as requests for action (*come, help*), most respondents supply a more than minimal verbal answer about their agreement — a kind of verbal reflection on agreement.

Example 5.21

"Mother! Can you come in here?" called Father.
"Jack and I have a surprise for you."
"Yes, Father, I can come now," said Mother.

In most cases, the words in the answer turn recycle those in the initiation turn. Thus the two speakers are made to share the same vocabulary, to take into account the precise wording of the initiator's talk. This is reminiscent of teachers' requests that students answer questions in complete sentences, incorporating the vocabulary of the question (Mehan, 1974). We will note in chapter 7 a similar device in which teachers often incorporate, and elaborate upon, students' answers in their reception of those answers. This recycling of vocabulary may result in part from a need to repeat a limited number of words for purposes related to early reading instruction. None the less, as we elaborate in the next section, the conversational turn supplied by the initiator to the respondent is used by the respondent to do more than provide a minimal answer to the query. Through such devices, a community of speakers, children and adults is fashioned, and a common language constructed. In these respects both children and adults are shown to talk like teachers and students.

Speakers in these reading materials seem to attend carefully and consistently to each other. Answers always seem to display an understanding of what the question was about. Questioners appear to have few problems in gaining the attention of others. In contrast, it has been shown that in child–adult talk children may have to employ specific opening routines to gain attention and generate conversations (Sacks, 1974: 231; Schegloff, 1968: 1091). Speakers appear to be producing compact, streamlined versions of real-life talk, in which the interactional work takes very few turns. Imagine the expansion of example 5.19 above to incorporate the observations of Sacks and Schegloff on children's problems in securing adult attention:

> "Mother," said Jack.
> "What is it, Jack?" said Mother.
> "I cannot take my ..."

Hesitations, interruptions and mishearings never occur between speakers in these books. Nor do speakers employ the variety of artful conversational practices that have been documented in the conversation-analytic literature (see for example the papers in Atkinson and Heritage, 1984). The textual representation of talk is a simplified textbook version of ordinary conversation, in which utterances express whole thoughts in grammatically well formed sentences. The statements follow each other through repetition or clear pronomial reference to preceding statements. We suggest, then, that the number of turns it takes to accomplish a given interaction is reduced in textbook talk, but that each turn is packed with material which might comprise several turns in ordinary talk. The strong implication is that the earliest school texts introduce and underwrite a model of not only literate but formal instructional talk, in the guise of representing natural oral conversation.

Permission sequences

Permission sequences are those that typically take the form of a *can/may I/we* first part, which is usually a request to proceed with some action, followed, almost always immediately in the text by a *yes* or *no* opening by the next speaker, plus some continuation of the topic within the turn. Examples are shown in 5.22 and 5.23:

Example 5.22

"Can we go to the hospital for them?" said
Timothy.
"Yes," said Father, "we will go for them in the
car. Susan, you get ready. I will look after
Timothy."

Example 5.23

"Father," said Jill. "May I come down and play?"
"No, Jill," said Father. "You have red spots."

Not surprisingly, the overwhelming majority of sequences we describe as permission sequences contain a query addressed by a child to an adult. Table 5.3 presents the distribution of permission seeking in the home and other non-school scenes. In the school scenes, we have located an additional 18 instances of such questions, all from child speakers to the teacher. As this section proceeds we will provide comparative figures for the home and school materials.

TABLE 5.3   Sources and recipients of permission questions in non-school settings

	No. of questions	
By children to mother	15	
father	14	
grandmother	10	
Total to grand/parents		39
to other adults	2	
Total to adults		41
to other non-adults	4	
Total asked by children		45
By others	2	
Total permission questions		47

We note that no permission questions are asked of children by adults, although we can imagine that this does occur in family life. Only two permission questions are found in child–child talk, of the 'may I join you (in this play)' type. From other sources (Corsaro, 1979, 1981) we might expect that this under-represents the prevalence of the problem of access in actual play settings. However it appears that entry into play with other children is not usually attempted through 'direct, verbal access strategies' which Corsaro (1979: 323) suggested are more 'adult-like'. He also pointed out that in attempting access, 'the probability of being ignored or receiving a negative response is much higher than that of receiving a positive response'. Thus it appears that this is an additional interactional problem within child culture that is not represented in these texts that appear to be about children and their world.

TABLE 5.4   Forms of permission questions in home and school settings

	Home settings	School settings
May/Can I	19	6
May/Can we	15	12
May/Can he/she	6	–

In 40 instances of children seeking permission from adults in the home materials, and for the additional 18 instances in the school materials, the forms in which the requests are cast are summarized in table 5.4. The speakers of the *may/can we* queries are almost always identified as individual children (14/15 in the home and 11/12 in the school). In school scenes, the preference for the *we* form, which we interpret as introducing questions about what the class may or may not do, indicates that the children in school are shown to fashion themselves into a cohort, a community of interests, through this method of framing questions. Child speakers ask questions on behalf of some collectivity of children more often than for themselves as individuals, while in the home materials the children are more likely to speak as individuals or for other individuals. Appeals on behalf of another individual do not appear at all in the school materials. In the school scenes, the preference for the *we* form marks the characters' representations of themselves as student members of the classroom community. Where *we* is used in the home materials, we find a similar fashioning of a cohort, typically of siblings in relation to parents. In the home materials, the preference for the *I* form could be accounted for in part by the absence of other child participants in the conversational setting. (This could apply to 13 of the 19 instances.)

An additional aspect of the form of the question part of the sequences we are examining is that, in about 40 per cent of home scene permission questions, children name their adult listener usually in the first part of their turn, as in example 5.23 above. However, we find no instances of the teacher being addressed by name in the permission sequence itself. Thus a model of permission seeking in school is described in which the addressee can be assumed, while at home one often has a choice of parents. However, in some of the home sequences only one parent is present, but is still named in the query. In the corpus as a whole, address terms occur considerably more frequently in home scenes, accounted for largely by request and permission sequences.

It is interesting that, while address terms are used in a number of permission rituals, *please* is rarely used. The addition of *please* could indicate that the decision could be grounded on personal whim or revisable upon persistent pleading (e.g., 'Please will you hose me?'). The notable absence of *please*, given other formalities in these sequences, suggests that the adult's decision is based on rational grounds not open to revision. This conveys a sense of rule-boundedness in adult behaviour that constructs teachers and parents as exercising the Weberian notion of rational-legal authority (see Freund, 1969: 229). This speculation supports further our view that these conversational materials, even when portraying non-school talk, are underwritten by a model of school-literate language practice.

We now turn to some observations on the nature of the adult responses to chidren's permission seeking turns, keeping in mind that the BR books portray not only a version of child culture but also a reciprocal version of adult culture. Table 5.5 presented below shows the balance of positive and negative answers to children's permission seeking attempts in the BR books. In table 5.5 are included cases where the sense of the response is 'yes' or 'no' even though the word *yes* or *no* may not be used. This classification problem arose especially in the school materials, as in:

Example 5.24

"Can we go for one more swim?" they said.
Miss Pennyfeather said, "I want to go for a swim
myself, but it is too cold. Look, here is a boat.
The water will be in the pool for one more day. We
cannot swim, but we can sail boats. Tomorrow we
will have a boat day. Remember to bring your boats
tomorrow."

Also in the school materials, we find questions (presumably)
addressed to the teacher which are not directly answered, as in:

Example 5.25

"What are we going to do now?" asked Peter. "May
we eat now?"
"We are going to take a walk," said Miss Brown.
"We are going to look for some of the things on our
plan."

Miss Brown is heard here to have chosen to respond to Peter's
information question in preference to his permission question.
   In addition, one equivocal answer by a mother is the only
instance in the corpus of a challenge from a child:

Example 5.26

Max ran to his mom and said, "I am six and I am
big. Can I get a gun and caps?"
"Not yet, Max," said Mom.
"Why not?" asked Max.
"Run into the den, Max," said Mom.
"It is not fun to go into the den," said Max. "Can
I get a cap gun?"
But Mom said, "No, go into the den."

Apart from example 5.26, we find no indication of bargaining
or challenging from children over adults' decisions throughout
the corpus. In this respect it is instructive to note Wootton's
summary of permission seeking in child—parent talk:

requests are handled quickly by most parents, in one or two turns ... in standard grantings, though it is not the case for nongranting sequences. In the latter, there is greater variability in length, some sequences being terminated relatively abruptly, others extending through many pages of transcript. A feature of many of these nongranting sequences is that children continue to make various appeals against the initial parental line on the issue, and in some cases of course, they win concessions. (1981b: 72)

With the exception of Max in example 5.26 above our child characters seem satisfied with 'you have red spots' (5.23 above) or other rationales to be presented later, and do not engage in further negotiation. It is interesting, however, that Mom's 'not yet' in 5.26 is unique in the corpus, and is an example of a weaker refusal than a *no*. This would seem to be a type of non-granting which could invite further discussion (perhaps more than would a *no*) in the otherwise clearcut world of permission seeking in these books.

TABLE 5.5   Positive and negative answers to children's permission seeking

	'Yes'	'No'	*Equivocal/other*
Home			
Father	9	4	—
Mother	11	2	1
Grandmother	9	1	—
Other adults	2	—	—
School			
Teacher	10	3	2
Total	41	10	3

Children's permission questions result in positive answers much more often than in negative ones, the best chance of success lying with Grandmother. It should also be noted that many of the children's permission requests are framed, or more often placed, in such a way that a negative response would cast the adult as a rather mean and somewhat churlish character, as in example 5.27. This sequence is preceded by Grandmother and the children making toy puppets and talking about their activity.

Example 5.27

"Grandmother," said Jack, "May I make a little
puppet too?"
"Yes, you may," said Grandmother. "Look in the box."

It is the children who ask adults for permission in these books.
At the most general level, we have seen that adults tend to
respond favourably. However, there are other aspects of the
adults' responses to these invitations to exercise authority that
inform the model of family life displayed in the conversational
exchanges. We can see from the examples shown already that a
format of the type ' "Yes/No, (Child)," said Adult. "Further
talk." ' is most common. Minimal answers, for example 'yes' or
'no' alone, are rare. The permission seeking move often occasions
further speech by the adult in which (i) the child's identity
(name) is acknowledged; (ii) the child's words are recycled in the
follow-up to the *yes* or *no*; (iii) the child's topic is pursued or
elaborated; and/or (iv) a reason is given for the answer. The 38
complete sequences found in the home and 14 complete sequences
in the school materials are summarized in table 5.6, showing the
percentages containing the various components.

TABLE 5.6   Occurrence of various components in adults' answers to
permission questions in home and school contexts (per cent)

	Home	*School*
'Yes/No'	97	70
Child's name	32	7
Echo	50	42
Elaboration	66	42
Rationale	11	14

We characterize the components of the responses in the following
ways:

'Yes/No':   A clear decision is announced at the beginning of the
response. In the school materials there are a further three instances
where the sense of the answer 'yes' or 'no' is inferrable from the
context and content of the response, as in Example 5.24 above.

Child's name   The inclusion of the child's name could be interpreted as evidence that the adult is attuned closely to the particular
child who put forward the request. The answer is given back
explicitly to that individual. However, teachers' answers to questions from individual children are almost always designed in such
a way that the answers could be heard to be addressed to the
whole class. Individual children are identified by name in doing
the asking (question turn), but the absence of this naming term in
the teacher's answer suggests that the query has been heard by the
teacher as being put on behalf of the group (effectively, 'May
we'), and that the answer is designed such that all children could
be the recipients. The organization of the class as a cohort is
achieved partly through such design features of teacher talk (cf.
Payne and Hustler, 1980).

Echo: We mean here that some portion of the child's wording in
the query is worked into the answer. The adult models a response,
usually early in this part of the turn, on the child's choice of
words. We consider examples 5.24, 5.25 and 5.27 above to contain
this recycling of the child's wording, and would treat this as
possible confirmation of having listened carefully to the precise
vocabulary used by the child and finding it suitable as a basis for
the adult's choice of words.

Elaboration: By this term we mean that new material relevant to
the topic initiated by the child is introduced in the adult's response.
There is only one example that we would describe as containing a
topic change by an adult during the answer turn in a permission
sequence. This is Mom's 'go into the den' in Example 5.26. We
comment further on what can be seen to be done in elaboration
components below.

Rationale: In example 5.23 above, we read Father's 'You have
red spots' as a reason for having just said 'no'; we hear no echo or
continuation of the topic in that statement. Rationales will also be
discussed further below.

Using our sketch of five possible terms in the answer turn, we
have examined each question—answer pair. For example, we find
three terms in the answer turn in example 5.28:

Example 5.28

> "Mother," called Jack. "May I take a bowl for Mr.
> Whiskers? He likes the red bowl."
> "Yes," said Mother. "Take the red bowl. Take the
> little bed, too."

'Take the red bowl' is the echo term constructed out of words from both parts of the child's query in this case. The subsequent utterance we see as the elaboration term.

Table 5.7 is a summary of the organization of adult answers based on the criterion of how many different terms are used in the answer. It appears that adults in the home materials build in rather more components more often than do teachers. As the elaboration and rationale terms tend to be the lengthiest terms in these responses, it is worth noting that ten of the 15 two-term responses in the home materials contain one or both of these, and that 16 of the 18 three-term responses contain one or both.

TABLE 5.7   Number of components in adults' responses to permission questions in home and school contexts

No. of terms	Home	School
1	2	5
2	15	5
3	18	4
4	3	—

We find then that in home scenes, the adults' (usually the parents') responses to permission queries are typically constructed so as to (i) indicate a clear decision initially, (ii) acknowledge the child by name (12/38) and/or the child's choice of words (19/38), (iii) offer new material in a elaboration and/or rationale as part of the response (29/38).

In observing these features of adult answers, we are reminded of the point made by Wells and Montgomery (1981: 229) that adult speech which encourages language development 'contains a larger number of acknowledgements of the child's contributions and a larger number of directives and utterances related to the child's current activity or to the joint activity of child and adult'. In this respect the parent-characters in these books have been assigned some highly preferred qualities – they speak as literate parents. We suggest also that this has relevance as a model of how children should answer teachers' questions, as we develop further and summarize below.

If the representation of conversational interaction in these texts can be seen as providing a model for turn design within permission sequences, the texts can thereby be seen as a source of language socialization. They show how permission requests can be framed by children, and offer an image of family life in which parents respond in a way that acknowledges the child by name or the child's use of language. The texts also demonstrate how permission exchanges constructed in these ways usually amount to the request being successful. By seeking permission every so often, the children are portrayed as dependent on adult decision-making, and at the same time, children are assigning to parents and other adults the conventional position as persons who are (to be) approached in this way by children. Initiating the permission routine fashions an opportunity for the adult to exercise a conventionalized responsibility for children. Thus we find a clear underwriting of a model of social relations between children and adults. The participation of parents in question–answer sequences, in conjunction with their unemotional and unevaluative style referred to in chapter 3, suggests that it is formal and organizational aspects of parenting which are emphasized, thus connecting parenting and teaching as complementary activities.

To develop this point, we now look at what parents do in their turns when they opt for adding the elaboration or rationale terms to their answer turn. We can read these routines as instances of children handing to the adult an opportunity to exercise authority, and as instances of adults taking the opportunity to add something which is elaborative of the status implied in having been asked to decide in the first place. There are 25 elaborative terms in our home materials. In 15 of these, the term contains some reference to what will be done next by the child or the adult, for example, 'Make the big spot red and the little spot green' (Father to Jill's 'May I help' make the puppet?), or 'Take the yellow bowl and go down for some apples. You and I can make something good to eat' (Grandmother to Jack's 'May I help?'). In 12 of these the adult uses the imperative form. In 17 of the elaborations the adult's comment can be heard as organizational, for example, 'He can sleep with you, Bill', 'Swim where I can see you', 'Now you can come and help me', 'Here is something for the mouse'. The elaborations develop both the topic and the parents' rights to pronounce and organize. Additionally there are a few cases where the opportunity is fashioned out of this conversational option to make a further 'adult' judgement, as in 'Milk is good for you', or 'Dan can play in the shed but he cannot jump and run', which might also be heard as examples of making a *yes* answer an accountable matter: 'why I said yes'. Wootton (1981b: 72) claimed that in ordinary talk it is refusals and not grantings which are made accountable matters. Again we see this as contributing to a portrayal of adults as rational in that they accompany both their refusals *and* grantings with explanations. This constructs the child-recipients as interested in the logic behind the permission as well as in the permission itself.

In refusals, the rationales are all pronouncements about a state of affairs which should, once made available to the child, count as adequate and reasonable grounds for saying 'no'. The 'fact' produced in explanation is presumably knowledge to which either the child would not have had prior access or has been inattentive. The child is retrospectively shown to have been unaware of some obvious aspect of the environment. Besides the sequence in Example 5.23 we have three other home sequences which we find to contain a rationale:

Example 5.29

"I like the one called Bumpity," said Jack.
"May we have it again?"
"No," said Grandmother. "It is time for you to go now."

Example 5.30

"Can we go fishing?" said Michael.
"No, the sausages are ready," said Father.
"You can go fishing tomorrow."

Example 5.31

"Father," said Jill.

"May Sandy come up here and play?"
"No, Jill," said Father. "Sandy is too big."

Our general point is that children invite displays of adult competence from adults by initiating permission routines. Adults use those occasions to demonstrate decision-making skills, knowledge and logic, to provide what the child has sought, to confirm the adult identity acknowledged by having been asked, and to endorse the act of asking. Hence a particular version of the permission seeker's identity as child *vis-à-vis* adult is constituted.

CONVERSATION IN STORIES

The study of question–answer pairs provides us with considerable detail about how characters' turns at talk are constructed. We now describe how these turns are embedded into longer stretches of talk and narration. Here our attention is given not to formal story grammars (see Luke, 1988a for an application of such grammars to initial basal readers), but rather to the interleaving of talk and narration.

Example 5.32 below illustrates the nature of the turn-taking system in which question–answer sequences occur:

Example 5.32

"Robin," said Miss Brown, "Have you something for show-and-tell time?"
"Yes," said Robin. "It is in this big box. Susan, can you guess what it is?"
"Is it a toy?" asked Susan.
"Yes," said Robin.
"Is it a toy car?" asked Jill.
"No," said Robin, "but it runs just like a car."
"We cannot guess," said Jack. "Tell us what it is."
Robin took a toy bus out of the box.
"When we lived on the farm, we went to the show," said Robin. "We went on a big blue bus. It looked just like this one."
"We like your bus," said Miss Brown. "Someday we

shall all go for a ride on a bus."
"Peter has something for show-and-tell time," said
Jack.
Peter said, "I have a magic hat at school ..."

In this example we see Robin taking over from Miss Brown
and having every second turn from then on in the way teachers
usually do in instructional talk. After Miss Brown's contribution,
Jack nominates Peter as next speaker. It is usually the teacher's
prerogative to nominate next speaker (Edwards, 1980, 1981;
McHoul, 1978; Mehan, 1979). We note, then, the portrayal of
conversational initiatives taken by the children here, not only as
questioners, but as distributors of turns to each other. We note
also that Jill and Jack self-select as next speaker in this passage.
Events of this nature are rare in instructional talk in classrooms.
The talk in the books is, however, orderly, and its 'sense of
formality' (McHoul, 1978) rests primarily on the discreteness of
the turns, the narrator's insertions, the complete-sentence rule
and various other features of the sort we have discussed above.
   Our point concerning implicit socialization into classroom talk
through the orderliness and formality of represented talk can be
developed further by observing some aspects of the structure of
example 5.33 below, another sequence from the BR corpus. In the
immediately preceding segment (not shown here), a classroom
scene is described in which students announce their desires and
intentions for things to do on a classroom outing. Their announcements are cast in 'I want to ...' and 'I am going to ...' terms,
and follow each other with no intervening turns taken by the
teacher. The episode continues:

Example 5.33

   "Girls and boys," said Miss Brown,
   "please do not all talk at once.
   I did not hear what you said."
   One at a time the children talked
   about things they wanted to do.
   This time Miss Brown did hear
   what they said.
   She put it down on the plan.
   "May we take a ball, please?"
   asked Robin.

"Yes," said Miss Brown.
"We may have time to play."
"May we take something to eat with us?"
asked Jack.
Miss Brown laughed, "Yes, you may."
[story continues]

This episode provides good illustration and a unique explication of our point that the texts provide implicit acculturation into conventions of classroom discourse. The topic and the moral of this story segment seems to be about organizing classroom talk. 'One speaker at a time', made explicit here, is just one of the many conventions which appear to be operative in the speech community portrayed in the books.

The changes in the children's speeches that occur after Miss Brown's request for orderly talk can be noted as follows: first, Miss Brown now has every second turn, as in instructional talk. Miss Brown is now made the recipient of the children's speeches — the children are heard to address their contributions to her. Second, the child speakers change from an 'I want' to a 'may we' format. In this, the conversation changes from statements to question—answer sequences, from individual announcements to collective requests.

The narrator's scene-setting and scene-moving interjections assist in how the talk of the children should be heard. The narrator announces prospectively that the children will now follow the rule and that Miss Brown will hear them as doing so. 'Miss Brown laughed' in the last line is another scenic practice by the narrator which provides for hearing the children's speeches as now properly done.

Although this story is in a school setting and although rules for talking are made explicit here, implicit conventions for child—adult talk can also be seen in most of our other examples. We suggested that these books are as much about learning to talk for school as they are about learning to read in school, in that the 'child as speaker' assembled in these texts approximates a theoretically derivable 'ideal pupil'.

In examining example 5.34 below, we will comment further on some aspects of how narration and talk are combined, and show some possible difficulties in reading such texts. Here we attend to the reader's practices as distinct from the narrator's practices to show some of the complexities involved in reading talk-on-paper:

Example 5.34

> At the Camp
> "Who will help me
> with the tent?"
> said Father.
> "I will," said Michael.
> 5 "Penny and Brian
> will help me make the beds,"
> said Mother.
> The tent is up.
> The beds are ready.
> 10 "Can we go fishing?"
> said Michael.
> "No, the sausages are ready,"
> said Father.
> "You can go fishing tomorrow."
> 15 "Is tea ready?"
> said Father.
> "Yes," said Mother.
> "Where is Brian?"
> "Here he is with Bimbo,"
> 20 said Father.

Consider, for example, the apparently simple problem of deciding who are asking and answering questions in this text. We have observed that the identification of lines 1–4 as a question–answer pair is not settled conclusively until the reader arrives at line 7. In the first few lines, we can read 'I will' as the answer to the first question only after having scanned the two lines following. These lines (5 and 6) could have been a continuation of the first answer, but it is in line 7 that we can decide they are not. The problem here turns on the narrator's device of identifying speakers after their turn has begun. We have pointed earlier to this feature of speaker identification. A similar problem occurs later in the text: who says 'Where is Brian?' (18) and how it is decided? Retrospectively, and by inference, we (and probably the child-reader) attribute that utterance to Mother on the basis of punctuation and genre clues. It must be in the second part of Mother's speech, because (*a*) if Father (next speaker) asked and answered his own question, we might not have quotation marks between 'Brian' and 'here' (there is one instance in the corpus where a speaker answers his own question); (*b*) writers of these texts seems to prefer two-part answers and utterances split by 'said Mother' or equivalent; (*c*) answerers in our corpus usually do more than *yes* or *no* with their answer slot; (*d*) speakers are almost always identified somewhere, so it must be Mother or Father, who are the immediate speakers in this episode. Ignoring the clues that arise out of familiarity with these texts, anyone on the scene could have said the lines 'Where is Brian?' and 'You can go fishing tomorrow' (line 14).

Additional to the problem of speaker identification and the identification of question—answer pairs is the work child-readers must do to make the answer to a question sensible as an answer. The second question—answer sequence in the story (lines 10—14) starts the next round of talk after the narrator has announced the results of the first round of talk. There is an implied connection between going fishing and sausages being ready which requires the importation of a good deal of cultural knowledge. We can well imagine a teacher asking 'Why couldn't they go fishing today?', inviting the children to use the text as a basis for inference (Heap, 1985), to find or produce a connection between these items. Unpredictably, Father then asks in the third question—answer sequence (lines 15—17) whether tea is ready. Hence the need to distinguish between sausages being ready and tea being ready, that is, tea is more than and inclusive of sausages. Although turns at talk are typically well formed and complete utterances, there is still a considerable amount of inferential work to be done to make the utterances cohere into a story.

The final question—answer pair (lines 18—20) overlaps with the second part of Mother's turn in lines 17—18. Mother's one turn here includes both a response and an initiation. Wells (1981: 31) suggested that such 'linking' devices often accompany topical continuity, but here Mother uses her turn to conclude one topic and open another. Following stylistic rules that arise from familiarity with this corpus, we might have expected instead a continuation such as 'Tea is ready now'. We would also have expected line 15 to be said by someone other than Father. It is rare for a speaker to have two turns in a row. We see then, how closely the text must be read to work out who said what to whom, and how dependent we are on the narrator, on punctuation and on culturally based inferences to cope with both regular and irregular formats.

The task of reading is further complicated by the observation that the utterances and conversations which make up the story could be assembled differently. If we were to extract Michael's 'I will' from its position, and enter it somewhere else in this dialogue (two possible spots are easily recognizable), Mother's first turn could be heard as a response, but not an answer, to Father's first turn. In its present position, it is not clear (to us) to whom Mother's remark is addressed. It is not tied through adjacent position to Father's first query, though it repeats the 'help me' phrase. It could have come before Father's first turn. The conversational episodes within our example have been put into a particular sequence of conversational turns which comprises the story line. Indeed we could mix up the sequence of these turns at talk in various ways and still ask children to make sense of them to show the various resources readers might bring to bear in making the story sensible (cf. McHoul, 1982).

We make these points to emphasize our claim that the reading of conversation is a complex task in which understanding the arrangement and coherence of utterances within a story or episode requires identification of adjacency pairs such as question–answer sequences, and a preparation for announcements (such as Mother's) whose interactional target cannot be found without calling into play considerable textual and cultural resources.

The child's ability to bracket pairs of utterances into question–answer sequences (or other adjacency pairs) is crucial to the understanding and discussion of the story as any experienced reader (e.g., a teacher) would be able to do. We have attempted to show how the representation of talk could variously clarify or confuse the child's grasp of the sequence and logic of this talk-on-paper.

Analyses such as these are critical, given that in the comprehension aspects of reading lessons the principal concern seems to be with the understanding of what is going on among the characters rather than with the decoding of words (as we discuss in chapter 7). It seems to us that the representations of conversational interaction in the texts do not reflect how children talk with each other and with adults in everyday life. Therefore, to assume that children can recognize and follow these representations easily is unwarranted. The force of this point increases when the density of reported conversation in early reading books is recognized. Putting conversation on paper reshapes the conversation, giving it a format and logic that are not identical to ordinary speech exchanges, such that the textual representation of conversation is transitional between conventions of oral conversation and conventions of written school materials. Children are asked to read and follow representations of possible oral conversations that are lodged in the language conventions and culture of the school and of the literate world. This is both a powerful source of socialization into school-literacy and a possible source of reading difficulty.

CONCLUSION

In the entire collection of question—answer pairs, and as illustrated in the examples above, children ask most of the questions. In these texts, child-characters frequently initiate talk with each other and with adult-characters; they do not wait until they are spoken to. Through their question initiations they formulate problems, pursue their curiosity, make suggestions and seek help, organize their environment and approach others, and ask permission (thus recognizing their dependency). We do not, overall, see that this reflects the reactive speaker roles which have been noted for children in instructional talk in classrooms (i.e., teacher initiates, children respond, teacher selects next speaker). Children in the texts have a more active part in the generation of sequences of talk. This heightened conversational activity is formal in nature, undertaken, however, in a highly constrained and artificial cultural domain.

On all other dimensions of represented direct speech, however, we have found evidence of parallels between the textual representation of talk and the 'literate' oral forms that characterize instructional talk. First, chidren talk more with adults than they do with other children in the BR books. An introduction to literacy through these texts therefore includes the linguistic engagement of children in the texts with adults in the texts, as shown by examining the conversational patterns. The children and the adults in the texts talk the same way, and they talk the 'special language' of BR books that we see as transitional to the 'special language' of later school textbooks as described by Olson (1977b: 76).

On the point of what 'child' is constructed in these texts, we have focused here on the model of the child as conversationalist, and have shown specific points of contrast between the textual portrayal and details available from naturalistic research. Differences between the child-speaker as constructed by the texts and the child-reader's experience of verbal interaction as studied in real-life settings have been reviewed in this chapter. We noted that the number of speaker turns in conversational sequences seems to be reduced in comparison with naturally occurring home talk, and that speakers make maximal use of their turns. This parallels Mehan's point that in classrooms most children have few turns, and once children get the floor, they need to use their chance to display competence in form and content (1979: 137−9). We also observed that answers in question−answer pairs are designed to correspond closely to the questions: the answer comes immediately, incorporates words from the question, and is expressed in complete sentences. Text-characters ask and answer questions in ways that accommodate the 'form' requirements of classroom questioning. Further, Romaine (1984), in describing Michaels' study (1981) of children's acquisition of oral conventions for classroom purposes, pointed out that when children are relating events and experiences to the teacher or class, 'the school narratives expected by the teacher are book-like in that details have to be fully lexicalized and explicit and are in certain respects far removed from the narratives of everyday life' (1984: 177). We could take this to suggest that children are (implicitly) requested to talk in a way that prepares them for an acquaintance with written language. This complements our point that the BR texts represent talk in a way that suits oral language practices in the classroom.

With respect to the nature of the dialogue portrayed, we noted that speakers talk as if they were closely attending and highly attuned to each other: questions are answered immediately in the next turn of talk; conversational tasks are accomplished economically and tidily; there are few irrelevances, interruptions or hesitations. Speakers seem to face few conversational problems such as getting attention, opening a conversation, or having co-speakers go off the topic. We have presented the only instance in the BR corpus (example 5.33) where talk is itself made a topic or a problem.

The characterization of talk in these books conveys little of the conversational politics that accompany child status in our culture (cf. Corsaro, 1979; Maynard, 1986; Speier, 1976). Such problems instead are submerged in an apparently problem-free, cooperative conversational world. This is not compatible with Speier's observations of adult conversational dominance over children in actual interactions (1976). Even in school scenes in the BR books, children do much of the asking of questions, and everywhere adults are benevolent, attentive and prepared to follow children's choices of topic and activity. The texts combine this image of the 'child-centred' family with due recognition of conventional roles and responsibilities of parents. The kind of adult constructed in the books matches the kind of child produced there. Both are literate, rational versions who talk a form of secondary orality. Our observations about the kind of speech community portrayed in the books and about the textual methods for putting talk on paper, reported here and in chapter 4, are attempts to illuminate the practices and problems of drawing apparently on oral conventions of language to effect a transition to written conventions, and, at the same time, to transform the oral.

6

Characterizing Children

We have continually pointed out that particular images are constructed of children as characters in and as readers of these books. We view this as especially important in that guidelines for how children should conceive of themselves as children and as members of the school world can be found embedded within the texts. Some of the textual methods that appear to suggest a relation between the child-character and the child-reader (see also Baker and Freebody, 1988), and some methods for seeing the category 'child' used tacitly as fundamental topic and as fundamental resource are described and illustrated more fully in this chapter. These books may be viewed as texts that contain an adult theory of childhood that cannot be separated from the pedagogy they are designed to service. Further, introduction to school-literacy cannot be separated from acculturation into a particular version of social order, as we illustrate below in our analysis of the categories of discourse that appear in the books.

The study of how 'childhood' itself is built and used as a category within these books makes explicit one of the most pervasive tacit features both of these materials themselves and of school culture generally — that is, the extent to which the practices of schooling rely on assumptions concerning the age-related distribution of capacities, qualities and interests, and on preferences for authority relations based on particular commonsense constructs of 'child' and 'adult'. It is important to recall Jenks's view that

the idea of childhood is not a natural but a social construct; as such its status is constituted in particular socially located forms of discourse. Whether the child is being considered in the commonsense world or in the disciplined world of specialisms, the meaningfulness of the child as a social being derives from its place, its purpose, within the theory. Social theory is not merely descriptive and certainly never disinterested ... the child is constituted purposively within theory; that is, the child is assembled intentionally to serve the purposes of supporting and perpetuating the fundamental grounds and versions of man, action, order, language and rationality within particular theories. (1982: 23)

We propose, as an adaptation of Jenks's position, that early school reading books contain a form of social theory, and that this is theorizing about the nature and position of childhood within the adult-defined social world. Such theory is embedded in the textual methods used in the books, which encompass the presence and activities of child and adult characters in the books, the presence and activities of the narrator, and, by inference, practical reasoning required of the child-reader.

Since these books appear to be representing the everyday lives of children, they invite tacit acceptance by child-readers of the particular cultural images of childhood they contain. Young readers whose identities as children differ from the images embedded in the texts (perhaps most children) may have various difficulties in relating seriously to these books. For all children there may exist the practical problem of knowing how to treat these images while taking part in reading instruction based on them, in such a way as to appear to be concurring with the school-endorsed portrayals in the texts. The significance of the discussion in this chapter for the practical work of teaching and learning to read in school lies in our attempt to identify some features of the cultural images of childhood that the books contain, and that, by inference, schools endorse.

VOCABULARY USE

In this first section, we set out those aspects of vocabulary frequency that indicate, for the corpus overall, elements that are made significant in the social world of childhood portrayed in the books, and the perspective from which such a world is apparently constructed. In subsequent sections of this chapter we examine in some detail examples of how these vocabulary items are used in context.

Animal characters

As an initial observation, children are repeatedly shown to be interested in and attached to animals. As we noted in chapter 3, animals appear extremely frequently. Indeed, the total number of animals in the corpus as a whole approaches the total number of references to humans of all categories. Since it is unlikely that in their everyday lives children encounter almost as many animals as they do people, this emphasis must be accounted for on the basis of the kind of material the writers of these books, and the culture generally, deem to be interesting or relevant to child-readers.

Fairy stories containing speaking animals have been considered a significant part of child culture for some time, though we would point out that these are said to have originated as stories for adults as well (Jackson, 1982: 45), and that they later became revised and defined as literature for children. The selection or production of certain kinds of text for particular categories of people is ultimately a matter of conveying an identity to the readership itself. The inclusion of both 'fantasy' and 'everyday' stories in beginning school books describes the child as familiar with and receptive to both worlds. Child-readers are expected to treat as plausible (or to appear to treat as plausible) the idea that animal characters can talk, just as they are elsewhere expected to treat as plausible the idea that these books describe a fictional everyday life. The interleaving of fantasy and reality elements in the BR books often occurs around the activities of animal characters. In one respect this is part of the textual description of the readership of the books. Both animal and human stories may be seen to invite comparison with the social life and the psychological world of the 5- to 6-year-old reader of the books. In another respect part of the interpretive challenge of the books is the mixing and blending of fantasy and reality in both human and animal stories, as we pointed out in the conclusion to chapter 3.

Further, within this context, there appears to be a particular kind of activity assigned to animal characters. In everyday human stories, animals appear often as family pets, and they are treated as sources of fun and surprise; they are often motivated by human-like objectives, particularly in interaction with other family members. But animals occur more often in fairy stories, where they bear the brunt of negative emotion in the texts (humanized objects such as toys do most of the remainder). For example, almost half of all crying, and over half of all sadness is assigned to animals, as we pointed out in chapter 3. These allegorical descriptions of animals as participants in human-like worlds are part of contemporary constructions of childhood.

Human society

Human society in the BR books is conveyed primarily through activity in a few key sites: the home, the school and some other territories visited with adults or where adults are encountered (e.g., shops, a farm, the beach). Children are sometimes shown going to or from these locations, but are rarely shown to be away from the adult gaze. The world of the family is the central arena for many of the stories in these books.

Generation and kinship   The high frequency of parents as characters in the BR corpus indicates the prevalence of generational and kinship markers in the books. By contrast, the kinship relationship sibling is not underscored through explicit use of *sister* and *brother* terms, even though some of the pairs of child-characters in the books are siblings. Further, the pairs and groups of children who figure as characters in the books are shown to be of similar age. There are very few older siblings or friends. Other possible kinship relations are rarely mentioned. Same-generation *friend/s* and *pal/s*, and next-generation *teacher/s* are other relational terms marking the members and the boundaries of child-life in the books.

Thus of all the possible kinship relations that could be salient to children within cultures or within varieties of family life, we conclude that the books portray the child as a member of a family comprising three discrete generational bands: the child generation, the parental generation and to a lesser extent the grandparental generation. A portrayal of a conventional family structure consisting of two parents and two or three young children is found frequently in these materials.

Also, central to our general argument that everyday life is presented as if from the child-reader's perspective, the kinship and other relational terms are almost all terms which describe a relationship from the child-characters' position within the family. There are few referential terms such as *daughter* (4) or *son* (0). Further, the narrator often refers to the parents as 'Mummy' or

'Father', thus using the terms as appellations in the same way that child-characters might. Thus the membership categorization device, 'family' (to be discussed below), is worked in a particular direction, from the child-character's position. These categorical terms convey a child's gaze on the world, and delineate an apparent perspective on the scenes in the stories.

Children   From a word count alone, it is not possible to tell whether the sense of *children* to be read from its use in context is as a term referring to kinship or to age or to some other possible occasioned meaning. This may be stated as the problem of determining from which membership categorization device the category *children* has been drawn (Sacks, 1974). *Children* could be heard as meaning a kinship relation within the device 'family' (children—parents) or it may be heard as being a general 'stage of life' description (children—adults) or a more specific instance of child—adult relations (e.g., children—teacher, or children—bus-driver). Although the prevalence of parental terms noted earlier suggests that the occasioned meaning of *children* would usually be as a category in the device 'family', it appears upon inspection of all the instances of the use of this word, that slightly more than half of the appearances occur in school and other non-familial settings. For example, 'One day a boy and a girl come to her house. She puts a spell on them. But the children are clever. They learn a spell to make the witch into a mouse.' In this example, *children* does not invoke a familial relation, but is heard as a superordinate for 'a boy and a girl', themselves age-referential terms without familial reference on this occasion.

In the remaining cases, *children* can be heard to be referring to membership in a family. In these family life stories, references are usually to 'the children', not 'his, her or their children', such that age and generational position, not kinship, is emphasized, for example, 'Daddy comes in the car to take the children home.' Such hearings of the term rely on the tacit use of membership categorization devices by the reader, a point to be developed below.

Additionally, as in these examples, *children* is almost always used as a category-referential term (98 per cent) rather than as an address term (2 per cent). The narrator uses this term far more (93 per cent of instances) than do speakers within the texts (7 per

cent). The term always occurs in the plural (the word *child* does
not appear) and collective membership of this category is, in
about 8 per cent of cases, further marked through the use of
devices such as 'all the children laughed/liked/wanted . . .'. Most
of these 8 per cent occur in school scenes. Our main point here is
that the occasioned hearing of *children* in these texts is as an age
status and as a social category over and above possible kinship
uses. This suggests that categories of age relations are clearly
marked as basic terms of the social organization of the world as
presented in the texts; the texts provide for self-definition by
child-readers as members of this special cultural community of
'children'. In the light of this analysis, such provision may be
argued to be the most fundamental way in which conventional
uses of the social category 'children' and the centrality of this
category to their social identity are made available to child-readers.
No matter what the story context, and in preference to other
possible categorical identities (e.g., son, student, bus passenger),
the social category and identity is typically age-marked: if not
children, then *boy/s* and *girl/s*.

Gender   Recall that *boy* and *boys* appear more often than *girl* or
girls and that the gender-neutral singular term *child* never appears,
indicating that gender is always attributed to individual child-
characters, just as it is almost always attributed to individual
parent-characters (*parent/s* occurs only 11 times in all). One issue
here is that of an imbalance in references to male and female
characters, as has been addressed in studies of children's books
for some time. Another issue is that gender is made so salient. A
third issue is the problem of how gender-linked attributes and
activities are worked into the texts.

We have already mentioned, for instance, the prevalence of the
adjective *little*, and its proportionally more frequent application
to *girl/s* than to *boy/s*. In the texts themselves, *little* and *big* are
applied to a variety of nouns, but are also marked as opposites on
a number of occasions, as in:

Example 6.1

Big children and little children.
The baby is little. My teacher is big.
I can make funny little bears. Can you make a big bear?

Thus child-readers are shown the centrality of this pair of opposites in describing the world. The repeated attribution of littleness not only to children but to a myriad of animals and objects (more than 100 different categories) suggests that the world of childhood in the books is described heavily through a reference to the dimension of size, which becomes an integral part of the description of social relations in the books. The repeated use of these adjectives serves to emphasize non-adult status (i.e., a social as well as a physical descriptor). Thus the prevalence of the little—big dimension in these first school books suggests this to be a salient notion in the school culture, paralleling its role in parent culture.

Also, when we consider the preference for the application of *little* to *girl/s*, we can view this textual feature as a contribution to the construction of gender in the texts. As noted, fully one-half of the appearances of *girl* are accompanied by the adjective *little*, while for *boy* the proportion is one-third. The repeated association of particular nouns and adjectives or particular nouns and verbs, in adult-produced discourse shows children the culturally endorsed notions of what terms go together; thus linguistic categories become social categories (Garnica, 1979; Sacks, 1974). In our materials, we see that 'littleness' becomes a descriptor of girlness and girlness becomes a category of membership to which 'littleness' is often attached, and indeed these terms become reciprocally elaborative within the language community described in the books. We have not located any other adjective-noun pair that is both so frequent and so closely co-related.

It appears that animals are another category with which *little* is associated. About 22 per cent of the appearances of *pig*, about 19 per cent of the appearances of *kitten*, and about 39 per cent of the appearances of *mouse*, are accompanied by the adjective *little*. Altogether, we estimate that about 40 per cent of the instances of *little* are applied to various categories of animals or pets. Since we have seen that this adjective also applies frequently to girls, and since we see that the rate of description of particular animals as *little* also does not correspond to the objective size of these animals, it seems that *little* is applied not as a literal description of size, but a description of relationship, carrying a connotation that we termed earlier the 'cuddle factor.'

Gender relations in childhood   The social categories that are used in the texts and the activities or attributes that describe those categories are fundamental to the unique composition of the social world of the BR books (see Freebody and Baker, 1987, for a detailed discussion of gender dimensions in these books). Gender relations in childhood are conveyed through a variety of aspects of the portrayal of the relationship and interactions of boy and girl characters. For purposes of elaborating these portrayals as they occur across a series of texts, we have examined one set of stories about 'Peter and Jane'. These stories nicely illustrate how the device of having one female and one male character can offer a description of gender relations in childhood. (The following excerpts, examples 6.2–6.8, are taken from Ladybird Key Words Reading Scheme, 1964.) We do not intend that this series be treated as exceptional in this regard; however, it comprises some 3,600 lines of text in our corpus (about 20 per cent), and thus provides for analyses that extend across many episodes.

Conversational exchanges: The manner in which Jane and Peter converse with one another is one of the most central and complex dimensions of their relationship that may be seen to contribute to gender-typing in the stories. Much of the conversation between these two child-characters is reciprocal in that a turn taken by one is followed immediately by a turn taken by the other. They attend to one another very closely and take interest in what the other has said. They do things together a great deal. They are constructed as an interactional pair, as indicated by the relatively few occasions on which either is presented alone by the narrator. Therefore, reading their relationship as a gender relationship, over and above a sibling, friendship or peer relationship, requires that we attend to some subtle features other than turn-taking and amount of speech. As illustration of these points, consider the following segment.

Example 6.2

"We have to jump this," says
Peter. "Come after me. I know how
to do it. Come after me, but keep
out of the water."
Jane says, "Mummy said that

we must keep out of the water."
     "I know she said so," says Peter,
"but we are not going in the water.
I know how to do this."
     Peter jumps again. "You can do
it, Jane," he says.
     Then Jane jumps. She says, "Yes,
I can do it. Look at me, Peter. I can
do it."

It is difficult, even from a superficial look at this segment, not to
read it as conveying Peter's initiative and leadership on this occasion. Jane's 'Mummy said' speech could be heard as the voice of
conscience or of Mummy's authority, or it might be heard as
reflecting and reformulating Peter's initial warning to keep out of
the water. Certainly Peter and Jane are expressing different perspectives on the activity.

In the following example, it is Peter's interest and aspirations
that form the basis of the episode, while Jane acts in a supportive
role:

Example 6.3

     "I want to have a boat like this, one
day," says Peter.
     "You can have a big boat like this
when you are a man," says Jane.
     She puts a hat on Peter. It is Tom's
hat.
     "There you are," she says. "You look
like a man now."

In contrast, there are other occasions on which Jane is given the
central attention by Peter, and still other occasions on which Jane
appears to be the leading member of the interactional pair:

Example 6.4

     "Come and see this, Peter," says
Jane. "Do come and look at this. It
is the farm cat. Look what she has."

"What fun," says Peter. "Will she
let us play with her?"
"We will get her some milk,"
says Jane.

There are many possible approaches to analysing in more detail
the conversations involving consistently paired characters such as
Jane and Peter in ways that could be taken as documentation of
the embedded dimension of gender in their relationship. Also, it
is not single episodes of talk such as our selected illustrations
here, but the accumulation of all the instances of conversational
interaction involving the pair that underwrites the gender-typing
in the texts. Therefore, we have undertaken some analyses which
supply clues to how the relationship is marked linguistically within
the text.

Introducing the characters: First, the narrator's introductions of
characters as members of categories are central to an adequate
interpretation of the story. In these stories, Peter and Jane are
given approximately equal mention by the narrator and approximately equal numbers and lengths of turns at talk. The
child-characters are sometimes referred to by the narrator as 'the
children' (46/212), 'the two children' (17/212), or, very rarely,
'the brother and sister' (8/212), and once, 'Peter and his sister'.
However, we find that the narrator most frequently (138/212)
uses the device of introducing both children by name within the
same sentence ('Peter and Jane like to draw'; 'Jane likes the dog
and Peter likes the dog'), or within an adjacent pair of sentences
('I like Peter. I like Jane.'). We find that in these 'paired' mentions,
Peter is introduced first almost three times as often as is Jane (101
versus 37). This is a possible form of 'couple talk' such as adults
use in personal references, which may indicate the speaker or
hearer's closer relationship with the partner mentioned first, and
may also vary with the context of use. In addition, we note that
in this series the narrator's 15 other references to other pairs or
groups of children always present the male term first. This is
reversed with regard to parental pairs, where there is a clear
narrator preference for mentioning the female parent first by a
ratio of three to one.

The use of *big—little*: In these stories there is a distribution of narrator and character uses of *big* and *little* which confirms our analysis of the differential application of these adjectives to the words *boy/s* and *girl/s*. The narrator uses *big* in descriptions of what Peter, Daddy and other males are doing about seven times as often as the word *big* appears in a sentence referring to activities or interests of Jane or other female characters. Peter himself uses the word *big* about three times as often as Jane does. The word *little* occurs less often within this series, and is more often used in sentences about or by Jane or other female characters than about or by Peter or other male characters, by a ratio of about two to one.

The *big/little* contrast occurs in many contexts. Example 6.3 above and Examples 6.5 and 6.7 below illustrate some of the narrative and conversational contexts of these words.

Example 6.5

"Let us make a little play house
with this," says Jane.
"Yes," says Peter. "It will be fun.
There will be no danger."
Then he says, "We will not make
a little house, we will make a big
one to play in. Then you and I, and
the dog can get in it."
"Good." says Jane.

Pronomial uses: An inspection of pronomial uses within conversational exchanges exclusively between Peter and Jane shows that both use the collective forms *we/us/our* about twice as much as they use the second person *you* form. Their uses of the singular first persons forms (*I/me/my*), however, exceeds the totals for the collective *we/us/our* and the second person (*you*) forms combined (see table 6.1). Further, Peter uses the *I* form significantly more often than does Jane, while Jane uses the word *you* to refer to Peter more often than Peter uses *you* to refer to Jane (chi-square $(1)=4.52$, $p<0.05$). Jane and Peter both talk more about Peter.

The contexts of the use of pronomial references by Jane and Peter in conversation with each other need also to be considered. Our observations apply to examples 6.2 to 6.8:

TABLE 6.1   Pronoun uses by Peter and Jane in conversation with each
other

	Peter	Jane
I	90	66
You	24	34
me/my	27	15
us/our	22	26
we	35	24

Example 6.6

Peter wants to make a car to
play with. He wants to make a
car like Daddy's.
Jane looks on. "It is good," she
says. "We can have fun with it."
"I want to make it red," says Peter.
"Yes," says Jane. "Make it red.
You and I like red."

Example 6.7

"What do you want to do?" says
Jane to Peter.
"I want to play with my boat on
the water," he says.
"Come on, then," says Jane. "Let
us go and get the boats and play."
Peter gets his toy boat. His boat is
a big one. Jane gets her boat. Her
boat is a little one.

Example 6.8

"I can read what it says there"
said Jane. "It says DANGER, MEN AT WORK."
"We can all read it," says her brother.

Some of the subtleties of the politics of conversational interactions between men and women may be conveyed in these Jane

and Peter sequences. We have approached this through the index of pronomial usage, although many other routes are also possible. Examples 6.2 to 6.8, when examined for pronomial content, show proportions of pronomial usages that correspond generally to our calculations for the whole of the conversational interaction between Peter and Jane as shown in table 6.1. In these seven examples Peter uses *I* seven times, Jane four times; Peter uses *me* twice, Jane once; Jane uses *you* six times to Peter's two; Peter uses *we* five times to Jane's three. On this index, at least, the examples appear to be broadly representative of their conversational practices with each other.

Assuming this representativeness, we can observe the kinds of conversational work done by Jane and Peter partly through pronomial usage, partly through uses of key terms such as *big* and *little*, and partly through the activities accomplished through their utterances. It is usually Peter who states preferences or announces courses of action, as in examples 6.2, 6.3, 6.6 and 6.7; he redefines an initiation or a comment of Jane's in examples 6.5 and 6.8. Statements or actions of concurrence or deference usually come from Jane, as in examples 6.2, 6.3, 6.5, 6.6 and 6.7. These sequences are compatible with Fishman's (1978) conclusion of a 'division of labour in conversation' with 'routine maintenance work' done by women, and with Pauwels's summary that in talk 'women display a more cooperative, collaborative style whereas men interpret conversations as a competitive speech act' (1984).

A number of exchanges, such as in examples 6.5, 6.7 and 6.8, lead us to speculate that some of the girls' comments on events appear to function as topic openers, inviting or perhaps requiring the boys to provide specific nominations for their joint activities. While these specifications serve the pragmatic purpose of organizing the children's fictional activities, they may also be seen to display the organization of the public form of the children's relationship.

Relying on word frequencies and on some examples of text in this section, we have identified some of the features of these texts that can be seen to contribute to a particular social constitution of the child-characters in the books and implicitly the child-reader of the books. The interests, qualities and social relations of child-characters in the books seem to be heavily marked as age- and gender-bound. We build on these observations in the next two sections of the chapter, in which we explore textual methods in more detail.

The 'membership categorization device', introduced and briefly illustrated above, is a method that speakers and hearers use to decide the situated meaning of ambiguous terms, to select and interpret descriptors in order to invoke particular contexts of meaning, and to account for actions and events. Uses of these devices include attaching particular activities or attributes (*little*, *big*) to categories within a set or collection of categories (*girl*, *boy*). Our analysis of the connection between *little* and *girl* above is an example of how an attribute can be bound to a category through frequency of repetition.

We have also considered the prior question of which particular membership devices are invoked in the texts by the use of categories from within those devices. We found for example that the term *children* could be heard as a kinship term (children—parents), as an age-status term (children—adults), or as an institutional term (children—teacher) when examined in context. We also indicated that the devices 'generation' and 'gender' (collecting the categories 'boy', 'girl', 'father', 'mother') are central in describing the social identities made relevant to child-readers of the books.

The membership categories through which the social world is assembled and is to be understood and accounted for, and the categories which announce those identities and relationships that should be taken to be salient for the child-reader permeate the texts. Further, these pervasive categories underpin the logic of the stories in ways that are implicit and non-negotiable. The categories set up a basis for interpreting what activity then goes on among characters, themselves identified as members of categories. The categories are not directly available for inspection as apparent features of the texts themselves.

The segment of text we present below illustrates our comments so far, and provides for a discussion of how membership categorization devices are used in reading the text:

Example 6.9

Here We Go
    The big day came.
Miss Brown and the children were ready
for the bus ride.
Three mothers had come to help.
5   "Will there be room for everyone?"
asked Susan.
    "Yes, Susan," said Miss Brown.
"There will be room for all of us.
It is a big bus."
10   "When will our bus be here?"
asked one of the girls.
    "Very soon," said Miss Brown.
"Now, is everyone here?"
    "I do not see Peter," said Elizabeth.
15   "He was here," said Jill
"but I do not see him now!"
    All at once Jack called out,
"Here comes our bus.
Here it comes."
20   "Oh dear," said Susan.
"I know Peter wants to come with us.
What are we going to do?"
    The bus stopped at the school.
[story continues]

In this segment, we see that three categories of characters are
introduced in the first four lines, and that each category is linked
to some activity (waiting, helping). To show how membership
categorization devices are used in reading the text, we can point
to an initial problem of how to read *the children* in line 2:
specifically, from which membership categorization device the
term is drawn in this instance. We note that 'Miss Brown and the
children' is presented as one collection while 'three mothers' is
introduced separately. This is an indication that the situated meaning of *children* here refers to their collective relation to Miss
Brown, not to the mothers. Hearing *the children* as 'school children'
further relies on identifying 'Miss Brown' as a teacher.
The conversational sequence in lines 5 to 16 can be read as a

conversational display of the social relation 'Miss Brown and the children' introduced in line 2. Thus Susan, for example, is heard unproblematically to be speaking as one of the children and not as one of the mothers. There is, however, no explicit directive to hear Susan as a child-character in the text; that she is heard that way attests to the reader's implicit 'membership categorization' work that is guided by the narrator's organization of categories as described above. A picture in the book might serve as an additional clue, but unless speech bubbles are used, even the text and the picture together cannot assure that Susan is a child-character. A further clue for the reader familiar with this genre is that mother-characters never have first names like 'Susan'. They are called 'Mother' or 'Mummy' by the narrator and by the characters. The characters continue to develop the categories they represent by speaking in particular ways. In this example, the child-characters, through their conversational turns, show their readiness for the bus trip by asking questions about the trip. They develop the sense that it is their 'big day' and they provide Miss Brown with conversational turns that allow her to display qualities of the category 'teacher' as one who can answer the children's questions (cf. Davies, 1983, on student's conversational contributions to the identity 'teacher').

Similar interpretive work applies to reading the category 'mothers' in this text. Technically, the three mothers could be the mothers of the children who are assembled, and could be the mothers of children not yet present, or possibly mothers of none of the children in this story. How do we identify these 'three mothers' as some of the mothers of some of the children in this story and not a random collection of mothers unrelated to another random collection of children? The device that effects the intersection of the sets 'mothers and children generally' and 'children in this story' is 'Miss Brown and the children', in that the mothers present are heard to have a collective relation to the school class rather than individual relations to particular children. Any reader has to infer such connections among the characters who occupy the categories 'mother', 'teacher' and 'children'. The reader needs to adopt the logic and conventions of the text to read the text. In this way the child-reader is guided towards using the author's logic and rationality.

In such texts, category identifications by the narrator provide for how subsequent speeches are to be heard. These category identifications remain a non-negotiable feature of the text. What characters do and say are available as topics of instructional talk, but the salience, relevance and significance of the membership categories themselves are unlikely to be topicalized. The texts serve largely to elaborate categories such as 'children', 'teacher' and 'mother' – that is, to attach activities in the forms of interests, speeches and perspectives to particular categories of characters that are repeatedly worked into the stories. These repeated workings effectively present a theory of social organization: the world is made up of 'teachers' (who do and say certain things), 'children' (with their own discernible patterns of activity) and so on. Indeed, one major achievement of such stories seems to be not so much the production of entertaining discourse, but rather the identification of particular kinds of speeches with categories of characters. That is, the talk offers exposition concerning the categories of characters in the story (and by implication in the reader's social world) as much as information that significantly advances the plot.

In the next example we again see how the narrator's use of *children* continually signals the social definition which the child-characters' actions and interactions serve to elaborate. Child-readers of these books are invited in this way to see what 'children' say and do. They are both constituted as 'children' and shown how to display the qualities of 'children' as assembled here.

Example 6.10

At the Pet Shop

One Saturday Susan, Peter and Robin went
to the pet shop. They wanted to see Mr. Best
and all the pets. When the children got to
the pet shop, they looked in the window.
5   Peter said, "Look at this."
The children saw the words Out to Lunch.
"We should come back at one o'clock,"
said Susan.
"We should wait for Mr. Best," said Robin.
10   Just then the children heard a voice say,
"Come in, come in, come in."

[story continues]

While it may on the one hand appear reasonable that *children* be used as a collective noun in these texts, we can consider whether in materials written for adult readership, the word *adults* would appear with such frequency. This would indicate that, in the adult culture that produces these books, childhood is remarkable as a primary social definition, while adulthood (independent of parenthood or teacherhood) is not. In texts written for adults, other individual and group characteristics serve to locate people in social space. In the BR texts, the child status of the readership, we believe, is continually underscored through a variety of textual practices such as those we have reviewed, and we see this deriving from an adult cultural perspective. Children of the age of the readership of these books, to our knowledge, do not use the term *children* as a collective, referential noun to nearly this extent. For example, in a corpus of the oral language of 5½-year-old children comprising 18 children and a total of more than 60,000 words (Hart, 1974) the words *children* and *child* do not appear; the colloquial *kid(s)* occurs nine times. Similarly, the term *children* is 200 times more frequent in the BR books than in the much larger Spoken language corpus described in chapter 2. *Children* is a word used largely by adults to describe non-adults.

Jackson (1982: 26−7) has pointed out that 'a great deal of effort is spent keeping children childish' in contemporary culture. We have shown that the BR books make a special contribution to that effort by continual reference to child status and by making the social world of the books turn upon that status.

The selection of categorical references is largely the work of the narrator, not the speakers themselves. The characters in the books display qualities of the categories to which they have been assigned. The selection of relevant categories through which people's actions and statements are to be interpreted is both central to the acquisition of a 'sense of social structure' (Cicourel, 1974) and basic to the sense-making methods that comprise the social organization of everyday life. The quiet, behind-the-scenes definitional work of the narrator looks to be a powerful source and expression of adult culture in that it delineates a relatively unchallengeable interpretive framework for the actions and speeches that ostensibly comprise the story line.

The narrator establishes 'children' as a central interpretive category as well as a primary social identity of some of the characters. We have seen that, as characters speak in the texts, their attributes and perspectives in relation to other categories of characters are described. Another major aspect of the narrator's work is to represent the social world as if from the perspective of child-characters. We take it that the actions and speeches of child-characters in the books, which express various sentiments and observations, are actions and speeches that child-readers should be able to recognize as plausible. We consider that this is a powerful device for assembling the child-reader socially, emotionally and cognitively. This membership categorization work is at the basis of the versions of language, rationality and order that these books portray to their child-readership.

CONCLUSION

We have developed the contention in this chapter that materials such as these do not merely describe; they also construct images which become part of every child's encounters with adult views of how 'children' speak, act and perceive the world. We have also gone beyond a description of the child-characters in the books or of the social worlds those characters inhabit, to examine some of the textual devices that occasion the use of practical reasonings based on tacit assumptions about language, rationality and social order. This is where and how the child as reader is constituted in the image of the (adult-produced) text. Thus these texts are, in complex and subtle ways, part of the culture's organization of age relations, not only a reflection of that process.

Recall Walter Ong's remark that our growing awareness of literacy has led us to 'revise our understanding of human identity' (1982: 1). Analagously, children's first school books, in explicit and implicit ways, propound a version of childhood — in effect a theory of how children think, act and talk, and of their position in the social world. This invites, and possibly requires, children to revise their own identities at least for purposes of successfully engaging in school reading instruction and in using the discourse of the books to talk (indirectly) about themselves. The 'theory' developed in the books, even though it may remain unexplicated, is none the less relied upon as a resource in the production and use of instructional reading materials.

Returning to the concerns presented at the beginning of this chapter, we may wonder whether the images of childhood produced in the texts correspond to children's own constructions of who they are, of how the social world is assembled by and around them, and of the nature of their relations with other children, adults and animals. Our analyses of the assembly of versions of 'childhood' in the BR books explicitly raises this question of correspondence. This question is not applied only to those children who may be in a cultural minority in English-speaking Western schools: it refers to all children, since the analyses point beyond more familiar concerns with gender or class stereotypes to show how the category 'children' is a fundamental one in the construction and interpretation of the texts. The question applies to successful socialization of children into students, and to reading difficulties that might arise when children encounter adult elaborations of the category in which they as readers are deemed to belong.

7

Lessons in the Culture of School-literacy

To develop a more complete picture of the processes of introducing literacy, we need to go beyond an analysis of the textual materials themselves towards a description of how the texts are used in the classroom. In this chapter, therefore, we address the issue of how beginning reading texts might be worked into reading/comprehension lessons in the early years of schooling. We are interested here in how teachers orient children to the nature and status of written text. We illustrate our major points by close attention to some transcripts of lessons in which early reading books are used, and we attempt to document the kinds of strategies teachers and students might employ in working with such texts, focusing to a large extent on teachers' questions, students' answers and interjections and teachers' responses to students' utterances.

This work is intended to supplement other studies of the use of texts in early literacy instruction, for example the research conducted by Beck (1984). This research pointed to a number of types of teacher practices that Beck viewed as potential impediments to student learning. Among the practices examined were: misleading 'direction-setting' activities (scene-setting by the teacher which provides too little, too much, or too confused a background to the story); apparently unsystematic shifts of activity during the reading lesson; and problematic post-reading questions (comprehension/discussion sessions which, again, appear to offer too little, too much, or too tenuous a connection to the significant interpretive problems presented by the text). This research forms a background for considering in more detail the ways in which teachers' questions may be interpreted by students and the ways in which, in turn, teachers work with students' responses in literacy instruction. In this chapter, we supplement such work by studying some examples of teacher—student interaction during early reading activities, and we treat episodes of teacher—student exchanges as integrated events. Our analyses draw on the work of analysts such as Heap (1982, 1985, 1986) and Green, Harker and Golden (1987) who have studied participation in classroom reading activities.

Heap (1982, 1985) has documented aspects of the social organization of reading activities, focusing on the discourse between teacher and students, and pointing out that the text may be used in reading lessons as a source of information or as a basis for inference. We develop this perspective on reading lessons to look specifically at teacher questioning, which we take to provide essential documentation of presumptions both about teachers' relations to the content and methods of a text, and about students' relations to teachers and to texts. Classroom discourse about and around text is viewed here as coded information for students concerning how to read and how to treat texts and teachers within the context of the classroom.

A further theoretical extension developed in this chapter concerns the role of early literacy instruction in establishing the groundwork for the later use of informational school texts. In this respect the work reported here expands upon the observations we made in chapter 4 about the authorial practices that provide for textual authority and that presage the structure of informational texts encountered in later schooling.

We need to stress that our discussion is based on only a small set of lesson examples; these data are intended as supplementary to the analyses of the books. It should be noted that teachers differ in their questioning strategies, even when the same text is being discussed, and that this places different kinds of performance demands on students (cf. Green et al., 1987). Such variations also offer different descriptions of the text itself and of orientations to text. By giving detailed attention to some actual instances of reading instruction, we attempt to provide descriptions of practices that may also apply more generally. Our analyses have uncovered details of conversational methods that are recognizable in other studies of instructional talk, and there appear to be some common and recurring features as well as some variations. Our analyses of the lessons, therefore, should by no means be taken to be exhaustive, nor should our observations and remarks be taken to apply to all cases. Rather, the examples should be read as pointing to some of the problems that might arise for teachers and students in the use of texts, and for speculating about how books are used to build relations between student, teacher and text in early literacy instruction.

We begin by examining the pattern of questions and directives or hints that one teacher gave in a reading/comprehension lesson to 6-year-old students in their second year of schooling. The teacher first read alone from a 'Big Book' (entitled *One Cold Wet Night*), then had the students as a group read the story with her. The teacher proceeded to ask a total of 79 questions in the 12 minute period that followed the completion of the joint reading of the book. Table 7.1 includes a categorization of these questions, an example of each type, and the number that fell into each category in this particular lesson.

TABLE 7.1   Question types used by one teacher in a reading/ comprehension lesson

Question type	Example	Number
Picture-related	'What can you see in the picture that tells you …?'	29
Student's background	'Who has a rain hat like that at home?'	15
Alternative vocabulary	'What's another word we could use there?'	14
Student's preferences in story	'If you had the chance to be one of the characters in our story, which one would you choose?'	13
Inferences from the story	'Why do you think he wanted to get into the bed?'	7
Explicit memory for the story	'Who came in after the dog?'	1
Total		79

We may infer from table 7.1 that the teacher's main emphasis in this particular lesson was to indicate the importance of interpreting pictures and of using background knowledge and alternative vocabulary to expand upon the reading of the story. We observe that the teacher asked very few questions that appear to focus directly on the linguistic content of the book. Issues that immediately arise here are, to what extent and how do such excursions into picture understanding, background and vocabulary elaborate the story or the text? Do they lead the students further away from an understanding of the particular story at hand? Many of the questions concerning information in the pictures seem to be episodically rather than thematically directed. A search for thematic development in the lesson suggests that the questions produced an idiosyncratic and serendipitous reading of the picture at hand, rather than a coherent sequence that advances the particular plot line of the story or illuminates aspects of the plot line so far.

Example 7.1

T   ... do you think he's pretty well equipped to go out in
     the rain?
Ss No, no
S   Yes
Ss [No/
Ss [Yes/
T   /have a look see what sorts of things he's got on
S   Yes?
T   Who can tell me some of the things he's got on. Jacky?
S   He's got a, rainhat on?
T   A big rainhat, See th− how the rainhat comes down
     right down over his back? Does anyone have a rainhat
     like that at home?
Ss yeah[(   )
T   [I wonder why they come right down there?
Ss ohh!
T   Who can tell me, Danny?
D   So the rain doesn't go down [your back.
T   [So the rain doesn't go
     down your back, very good ...

In this lesson the teacher also gave a surprisingly large number of clues or directives as to how her questions could be answered. She explicitly pointed to various sources of possible and acceptable answers to her questions − a form of talk we may think of as 'metacognitive commentary'. Associated with her 79 questions

TABLE 7.2   Teacher's accompanying directives as to the source of answers

Type of directive	Example	Number
Looking at picture	'Just have a look at the picture . . . forget the words for a moment'	19
In the teacher's mind	'I'm wondering what other words we could use . . . One I'm thinking of . . .'	9
General thinking	'Now just have a think about our story . . . Thinking caps on . . .'	8
Reading	'It said in the book . . .'	2
Other books	'Think about the story we read yesterday . . .'	1
Remembering	'Remember what it said in our story . . .'	1
Total		40

were 40 of these commentary statements relating to how the answers could be produced or where the source of an acceptable answer may lie. Table 7.2 contains a summary of these directives.

From table 7.2 we can see, as we would have guessed from the distribution of question forms shown in table 7.1, that the commentary the teacher gave as to where the answers may be found reflects the importance of pictures in this lesson. In particular the pictures have to be inspected, elaborated and interpreted – they have to be 'read', not just viewed. Of the 19 directives pointing to the pictures, almost all were followed by interpretive questions extending rather than simply describing the information shown in the picture.

Example 7.2

   T Let's forget the words for the moment, what can you see in the picture that tells you he might be

   Ss   (   )

   T unhappy? Carl, can you tell us?

```
Ss   (                                      )
T    What can you see in the picture that tells you he might
     be unhappy? In this picture here?
S                                    (                    )
T    What can we see there, that might give you a clue?
Ss                                   (h h h)
T    Caroline? (4.0) Lindel. (4.0)
S                                      ohh!
T    Yeah, his hands, but what does that mean?
```

We can also note that about one-fifth of the directives offered by this teacher in this particular lesson explicitly signalled the importance of what the teacher herself was thinking. In a sense the evaluation of all utterances in one way or another (even by ignoring) indicates to the student that all of the right answers are in the teacher's mind to begin with and that particular aspects of the picture, of their background knowledge, or of their preferences need to be evaluated in terms of the teacher's particular interpretation of what is interesting in and important about this story:

Example 7.3

```
T    ... why's he trying to hide?
S    He wants to /
S              /He wants to stay //in
T                             //Probably two reasons
     I can think of. Why let me see, Danny?
D    He wants to stay, stay in.
T    And he wants to hide to stay there and what could be
     the other reasons?
S    Uh!
S    (        )
S    frightened
```

One way in which the teacher signalled that she had an answer in mind is through the persistent elaboration of students' responses to her questions. In this strategy, the teacher paraphrased the students' acceptable answers into more complete or otherwise more acceptable language. Some of these can be seen as minor elaborations, as in examples 7.4 to 7.6:

Example 7.4

    T   ... who can tell me what a giant weta might be.
        Try looking there's another picture of one.
    S   Oh!
    T   Tom?
    T   A grasshopper?
    T   A grasshopper [yes a big grasshopper.
    S   [New Zealand one.

Example 7.5

    T   ... maybe some of the animals that normally live in?
    S   Barns
    T   Barns or sheds, yes.

Example 7.6

    T   ... How do you know it's night from this picture?
    S   Uh! 'cause he's ahh!
    S   Lamp?
    T   Yes he's got a big lamp, hasn't he.

Other paraphrases, however, reformulated the students' answers
more substantially, as in examples 7.7 and 7.8. (Example 7.17
below shows further illustration of the teacher's method of receiving and elaborating student's answers.)

Example 7.7

    T   Have a look here what, what does this tell you?
    S   p.j.'s
    S   p–
    T   He's still got his p.j.'s on hasn't he so ...

Example 7.8

    T   ... what happens to him that's so uh so good do you
        think?
    S   'Cause he, he gets to stay in the bed.
    T   He gets to stay in the bed.
    S   Yeah an' he gets the farmer, like, the farmer//
                                              // Right
    T   he gets to stay in the warm of the bed ...

In example 7.8, it is the implications for warmth versus cold that the teacher signalled to be the preferred hearing of 'good' in the original question, not merely that the animal gets its way over the farmer. These reformulations are ways of setting the reading of the text around selected details construed in particular ways.

We will develop further the argument that strategies such as these serve to present a problem to the student that goes beyond an unmediated understanding of the text (or the accompanying pictures), but that rather points towards the production of responses as close as possible to the teacher's preferred interpretive statements about the text. One further indication of this point is found in the observation that a number of students' answers to teachers' questions were themselves uttered with interrogative intonation (as in examples 7.1 and 7.4 above). Regardless of the student's understanding of the text, then, the further problem remains of whether the teacher will accept the answer as it is expressed by the student.

There are a number of ways of interpreting findings such as these. One is to argue that the teacher can be seen as modelling a version of the reading/comprehension process, in this case heavily reliant upon the use of pictures, background knowledge and preferences. That is, the student may infer that in reading one interprets pictures, uses personal background and preferences and thinks of alternative vocabulary in the course of reading a story. This argument runs that the students will then apply these modelled strategies when reading by themselves (see Bereiter, 1986).

A second way of interpreting these findings involves a different perspective on classroom talk. Instead of being seen as models of a cognitive process of reading, the teacher's questions and evaluations can be viewed as providing guidelines to the student on how to produce right answers in question–answer sequences in classrooms. From this point of view, the central features of classroom discourse are the teacher's ownership of knowledge (Edwards, 1980, 1981) and the production of right answers (MacLure and French, 1980) organized around the teacher's assumed competence to pose appropriate questions. The students' task, we infer, is to use the pictures, memory of the story, or understandings from their own background to guess what the teacher is thinking of. A critical point is that the students may well be given very few, or ambiguous, clues as to what particular interpretation of a question the teacher intended.

With respect to the modelling argument, it is difficult in many classroom transcripts to see clear evidence of teacher talk that indicates the explicit modelling of cognitive process. Nor is there evidence that the teacher models the process of production of right answers. That is, the interpretive path to the right answer itself may not be made explicit. The right answer is sought and then evaluated positively by the teacher, but the process of arriving at the right answer, as the teacher has construed it, is generally not specified by any explicit work on the part of the teacher. We illustrate this point in a later section.

Our introductory examples, taken from a single lesson, have provided a basis for some observations about possible features of reading-instructional talk. These features are presented as illustrations of the kinds of devices that teachers may use (for a variety of pedagogical reasons) in text-based teaching. In the next sections of the chapter, we present a number of additional examples of classroom discourse, in order to extend our analyses of how beginning reading books are used, and to raise some further issues relating to the texts as well as to discourse about the texts. We do not view these practices as independent of the materials with which teachers work. We have shown that the texts provide for particular kinds of readings, that the texts variously invite parallels to be drawn between child-readers and text-characters. All of these features of the texts themselves, some of them subtle, are characteristics with which teachers work in sometimes unexplicated ways.

INSTRUCTIONAL PRACTICES

Learning to read in school involves learning to adapt to a particular context of teacher–student relations within which text is studied. In the very early years of school, this may involve talk about pictures rather than print. This talk can 'set the text' in four respects: it can settle the issue of how a particular story should be read; it can thereby establish that textual interpretation is a closed affair; it can demonstrate the kind of discourse about texts that can occur in conditions of teacher–student interaction; and it can serve to illustrate the differential identity and status of teachers and students.

We provide below a number of further examples of teacher questioning and student answering from oral reading and comprehension phases of reading lessons in the early years of school to illustrate these points. In particular, we attend to how teachers refer to texts either as sources of information or bases for inference, and we treat these referrals as displays of teacher knowledge and teacher authority, and as containing constitutions of the child-reader in relation to teacher and to text.

The running metatextual commentary

Luke, de Castell and Luke (1983) have pointed to the 'running metatextual commentary' that teachers provide as mediators of the relation between students and texts. This comprises the questions teachers ask, their receptions of student answers, the features of the text that are pointed to and the contexts teachers establish and invoke in the course of discussing the text. Some general features of this metatextual commentary are outlined and illustrated in this section. Example 7.9 below is drawn from a teacher-made audiotape that is designed to guide an individual kindergarten student's reading of a book. We can see in this example a repertoire of practices that can also be observed in our transcripts of group reading lessons. (In example 7.9, a line space indicates a clear pause.)

Example 7.9

Carefully turn over the page from the outside edge.

Here's Mrs. Wishy-Washy. She doesn't really look very happy, does she? You can tell because her hands are on her hips. And she isn't smiling.

Let's read page number 8.

Point to the number 8.

That's right.

The first word is ALONG. Point to it. Read it with me now.

ALONG CAME MRS. WISHY WASHY. Dear she has a funny look on her face now.

JUST LOOK AT YOU   SHE SCREAMED.

She's definitely not very happy. But I wonder what she's going to do about it.

Let's find out. Turn over the page.

This tape-recorded reading lesson contains illustrations of the teacher directing both observations of and internal responses to the pictures and the text. The teacher's running commentary provides for exactly what the student is to attend to and how the student is to respond. It provides interpretations to be used in elaborating the story (e.g. 'hands on hips' indicates 'not happy') — an illustration of Heap's point that teaching reading looks much like teaching cultural conventions (1985: 267). The teacher's directives and comments comprise a particular construction of the story in these ways. The teacher is effectively announcing what there is of interest and note in the text.

The running metatextual commentary builds an emotional component into the reading of the story, particularly anticipation ('I wonder what . . . Let's find out'). It also builds in an imagined discourse between teacher and child-reader, in which the child is assumed to be following directions and in which the teacher asks the questions and leads the 'wondering'. This commentary offers a description of how a child-reader could be responding to the story — in this sense, the teacher's construction of the child's 'mind'.

In this example, we can see how the teacher assumes an interpretive posture between the story and the child, inserting comments into the reading of the story, and fragmenting the story at selected points with calls for internal responses from the child-reader. These insertions comprise the teacher's metacommentary, which is a feature of reading instruction throughout school life. Such metacommentary does not appear merely to parallel the text, but, at this very early point in reading instruction, to penetrate and shape the text. Thus it is a metacommentary not only on the text itself but on the social relations in which school learning from text will occur.

Teacher-made tapes are especially informative instances of

reading-instructional discourse, since they are produced in a simulated and idealized rather than an actual interactive setting. The child-listeners are described in their physical absence, for a future engagement. In an interesting way, this parallels the production of written text, in which writer and reader are spatially and temporally separated. Given that the audience is not present at the production, the problem of conversational cooperation in building either a reading of the story or a description of the relation between teacher and student knowledge does not arise. At the same time, as we have shown, the teacher-made tape introduces the teacher's metacommentary that shapes and sets the text, and to which child-readers need to be sensitive.

The teacher–text partnership

A teacher–text partnership is built through various teacher practices that can be observed in lessons such as in our examples here. Luke, de Castell and Luke have proposed a similar notion in their point that 'text and teacher can be seen to co-constitute a domain of knowledge, and to co-constitute one authoritative identity' (1983: 124). This is, in our view, a product of instructional practices. First, we can observe some practices that demonstrate to students the teacher's privileged knowledge of the text.

Example 7.10:

(Year one)

```
1  T  ((commences reading)) What sort of train is that?
        ((points to text))
2  S  Big?
3  S  Little?
4  S  Steam
5  T  How do we know it's steam Jody?
6  T  'Cause of the smoke.
7  T  Yes. The smoke here ((points to picture)).
```

The teacher's first question and the students' attempts to produce a correct answer illustrate the teacher's use of implicit frames of reference in describing the story. The problem for the students here appears to be to grasp the teacher's meaning of 'sort', and to display that understanding through the production of a word which the teacher can then hear as satisfying the tacit presumption of the question − in this case, apparently, that the question was not about size but about how the train is powered. MacLure and French (1980) have shown such categorization problems in other questioning and answering exchanges in classrooms.

The students' answers in example 7.10 stand as evidence of the absence of any principled way of determining the meaning that the teacher attaches to 'sort' on this occasion. The teacher's eventual concurrence with 'steam' does not resolve this problem, for there is no way to determine that 'steam' is the only possible 'correct' answer. We do not know that Jody located 'steam' in any principled way, although the teacher's responses in lines 5 and 7 suggest that she did: that is, that the smoke in the picture is an obvious and sufficient clue to describing the train 'correctly' as 'steam'. Just what the students are to have attended to in the picture to arrive at this answer is only retrospectively made available to them by the teacher. This may apply to Jody as well as any other correct answerer. Jody might have noticed the smoke only after the second question was put, and might have tried 'steam' on other grounds. (Also, the teacher might have found the smoke only after Jody's answer.)

Here Jody is not only being told that her answer is correct, but that she must have found it correctly. That is, correct answers are retrievable from the text through the use of correct procedures. The teacher is offering a reading of the text that will stand as the correct reading not only for all practical purposes, but because it is shown to be constructed using the correct interpretive procedures. The teacher implies that this way of reading the text is provided by the text itself, retrievable through correct attention to detail, such as that implicitly attributed to Jody in this instance, and presumably eventually available to all students. This process is a construction of the text and of Jody's competence both of which are further linked to the teacher's competence to ask about and pronounce upon the content and methods of the text.

Also significant for our present interests is that in this instance we have an illustration of how a teacher takes a proposition (the train is a steam train), produced through the question−answer format, and locates the proposition *in* the text − 'Yes. The smoke here.' The teacher has used an answer to support and legitimize the text as a source of knowledge. The correctness of the answer established by reference to the text also legitimizes the question itself. The question is shown to have been a competent one by having an answer to it available in the text. It is a form of self-authorization using the text as resource. The teacher has connected first an acceptable answer and second her pronouncement of acceptability to the text itself. She thus shows her prior and privileged knowledge of the text.

The question—answer—evaluation format of reading comprehension lessons presumes that the teacher can know or does know all of the answers. More fundamentally, it is presumed that the teacher does know or can know all of the appropriate questions. The pragmatics of classroom participation by students involves minimally an appearance of trust in these presumptions.

Example 7.11

(Same lesson, shortly after the preceding segment)

1 T Why is it [the train] getting slower and slower, and slower?
2 S Because it's a real steep hill and the carriages might fall off?
3 T It's a very, very steep hill, yes. ((*resumes reading*))
4 S He must be strong.
5 T Yes, he must be! ((*resumes reading*)) Who knows why they have tunnels for trains to go through?
6 S To keep them out of the rain.
7 T Does rain hurt trains? Jack?
8 T To go through big hills.
9 S Yes, that's right. If you have a big hill like that ((*continues to explain*))

In this further segment, the teacher extended questioning beyond inference from the text (line 1) to extra-textual considerations (line 5). Discussion about the text shaded into discussion about the world outside the text. The question in line 5 came to count as part of the lesson about the text, as shown in lines 7 and 9 where the teacher commented on the acceptability of the students' attempts to explain the presence of tunnels, but drawing here not on the text as source, but on her own cultural knowledge as source. This method of relating the text to everyday life through consult-the-text questions alongside consult-your-commonsense-knowledge questions also displays the teacher as arbiter in both realms of knowledge, able to cross the boundaries with ease. However, whether a question is to be answered from the text or from outside it is to be decided on each occasion of a question being put.

In line 7, the teacher supplied an interpretation of how one student must have arrived at a wrong answer. It is the teacher who provided an implicit formulation of what the student's reasoning procedures must have been ('Does rain hurt trains?'), and of whether the student's method and cultural logic attributed to it was right or wrong.

Heap has pointed out that students need to 'sort out what kind of possible world the . . . story is to be taken to represent' (1985: 264). The relevant possible world to be invoked can vary from question to question. In the steam train story, the train has human-like qualities but the notion of 'hurt' was disqualified in line 7 of the lesson. The student was shown to have selected what was announced to be the wrong frame of reference for this question. Another student's comment, 'He must be strong!' had, however, been endorsed earlier by the teacher (lines 4–5). Note also the shift from 'it' to 'he' in references to the train in lines 1 to 5. This shift was initiated by a student, and acknowledged by the teacher. The teacher then reasserted the everyday world later in lines 5 and 7. It appears that both teacher and students can alternate between invoking the world of fiction or the world of fact from the same text. It appears to be the teacher who accepts or rejects frames of reference used by students. This potential for shifting frames of reference may apply more to the kinds of fictional texts used in early reading instruction than to expository texts.

The construction of teacher questions is a construction of the nature of the text itself. Teacher questions may indicate that the answer lies 'in the text'; alternatively, teacher questions may carry the implication that the answer lies in bringing the student's knowledge or experience to the text. We suggest that this is not strictly inference from the text, but inference to the text, where it is the text and not the student's knowledge that is to be made coherent and plausible (cf. McHoul, 1982). We propose further that it is describable also as inference to the teacher's discourse, where it is the teacher's questions that are to be made coherent and plausible. This is addressed in more detail below.

Where an answer lies in the text, or can be inferred from the text, the teacher is presumed to know the text in a privileged way, in order to pronounce on the adequacy of the answer. Where an answer lies in conjoining some extra-textual knowledge to the textual clues, the teacher is further presumed to know how to accomplish such a connection between everyday knowledge and textual knowledge.

This theory of reading text (that the text contains the answer, one has to learn how to look), concretized through the questioning and answering routine, places the teacher in a position of mediation between student and text. It is the teacher who describes the text in her questions, correct answers to which constitute students' competence. The text is given a particular shape by the nature of the teacher's questioning. While students may discover that not all of the teacher's clues are equally salient, these subtleties do not discount students' reliance on teachers' utterances as the foundation for their sense of knowing the text, and for their sense of knowing how to read.

The partnership of teacher and text is indicated also in the practice of answering from within the text:

Example 7.12

(Year one)

T   ... if you look at this picture you can see something else
    with the alligator?
S   Hippopotamus ((*whispered*))
T   What other animals are [they? A bit hard to tell when
S   [Hippopotamuses?
T   they're dressed up in clothes, isn't it. Andrew?
S   (   ) See um there's a hippopotamus there?
T   Umhm. And what do you think the other one is? Daniel?
S   (   )
T   Bill?
B   A hippopotamus?
T   Possibly, we'll find out when we open the story. Let's

start now. ((*12 seconds whispering and giggling*))
SMALL HIPPO AND BIG RHINO, you were right,
LIVED DEEP IN THE FOREST ...

The children who offered 'hippopotamus' were praised from within the teacher's reading of the text ('you were right'). The teacher was apparently deferring to the text as the source of the answer, but also evaluating the answer from within the text.

The student—teacher—text relation

The 'wait and see' practice   Other instructional practices serve to describe the relations between students and teacher, students and text. We examine in this section two such practices we have observed in our transcript materials. In the next example (taken from the same lesson as example 7.12 above), the teacher twice suspended discussion of a puzzle and referred the students to the text as the source of the solution:

Example 7.13

(Year one)

T	Who is the stranger? Andrew?
A	Crocodile
T	Think about the name of the [story, it is an ...
S	[Alligator
T + S	All:li:ga:tor.
T	Yes alligators and crocodiles look a lot alike, don't they Daniel?
S	[Yeah my, my sister's got an alligator
S	[Yeah
S	[Only only only some have got small beaks and some have got long beaks
S	[but there's a diff-
T	[We'll have to have a look at that and find out what the difference is later.
S	There's a difference in 'em.
T	Mmmhmm. Do you know the difference?
S	Umm one can swim and one can't.

T   We'll   have   to   find   out,   won't   we?   THE
       ALLIGATOR DIDN'T ANSWER ...

Further, what the students are 'allowed to know' about the text
at any point in the reading of the story is established by the
teacher (cf. Heap, 1982). In our next example, the teacher controlled
the public reading in a way that disqualified a student who already
knew the story from displaying that knowledge. The formal
lesson was conducted as a demonstration that students do not
know until taught.

Example 7.14

(Year one)

T   The story's about Arthur. Let's have a look at the
S   (   ) my brother has this
T   picture. What do you think this story's going to be
    about? Mike?
M   Um I was just going to s-
T   You've read the story, have you ['cause your brother's
M   [Yeah
T   got it. Well, if you haven't read it. Now if you keep
    making that noise I think (you're going to spoil our
    story). Have a look at the picture and tell me what
    the story is about. Brett?
B   It's about this dog call Arthur.
T   Yes, about a dog called Arthur. And if you look
    closely, he's a bit of a strange dog ...

Mike's prior knowledge of the story was apparently at odds
with the teacher's preferred methods of teaching the text (see
Hammersley, 1977 on teacher strategies for controlling lesson
topic, timing and student participation). Mike could not participate
at this point in the lesson since the teaching methods presupposed
that students adopt a stance of not yet knowing, and pretend to
be imagining. Mike cooperated here, and withdrew from participation. Very soon after this opening sequence, other children
remarked that they had 'had' this story before. They suggested it
was not the 'news' the teacher's discourse constructed it as being.
The teacher's responses ('have you, well you haven't had it in our

class', 'maybe you had it in library or something like that', 'I'm sure it's a story that you've enjoyed if you have had it') again indicated that the students' knowledge of the story had to be publicly discovered with the teacher, under the teacher's questioning. Cazden (1981: 135) has commented on such constraints on what can be known about a text 'within the limits of and the terms of a convention, a game'.

The 'imagine and consult' practice   In a number of these examples, we find teachers introducing puzzles to be solved by consulting the text. The students are deemed not to know the answers to the puzzles until the text is consulted. This is a form of control over what the students are officially constituted as knowing and not knowing. In examples 7.12, 7.13 and 7.14 presented above, the students' observations about the cover illustration were treated as possibilities (e.g., "What do you think the other one is?"); the actuality (truth) to be decided from the text ("Possibly, we'll find out when we open the story"). This practice appears to cast students' observations and their everyday knowledge as hypotheses or guesses, while the text is made to be the authoritative confirming source. The text must be consulted for the teacher to find a student's guess right or wrong. The practice of eliciting and constructing students' offerings as merely possibilities, and the textual source as the actuality, appears to imbue the text with the final authority on these matters. This evidences the teacher's construction of the relation between student and text.

The same possible—actual distinction is found in another segment of the Arthur lesson (see also example 7.14 above):

Example 7.15

(Year one)

T   ... SO THAT NIGHT WHEN ALL WAS QUIET,
       ARTHUR PRACTISED BEING A RABBIT. How
       could you practise being a rabbit? Sam?
S   Start jumping?
T   Mmm? What else might a rabbit do?
       ((*17.0 seconds whispering*))
       There's something that y— a rabbit mi— uh to practise
       being a rabbit you might like jumping what's a—

another thing that might make you feel like a rabbit?

S Carrots! ((*whispered*))

T Yes, Kim?

S Eat carrots ((*whispered*))

T Right, and that's exactly what he did. Look here. HE PRACTISED EATING CARROTS . . .

((*later in the same lesson*))

T . . . HE PRACTISED. I wonder what he practised if he was trying to be a snake? Barry?

B He practised sliveling.

T Wiggling, yes. Peter?

P [by doing sss [sss

T [Yes [Yes

Ss ((*much hissing*))

S Um, going up things.

Ss ((*more hissing*))

T Umhmm. Let's see what the story says. HE PRACTISED HISSING, AND SLITHERING, like Barry said, AND SLIDING, AND LOOKING COOL. That means just lying about, not in a rush, just taking things easy. HE PRACTISED VERY HARD UNTIL HE WAS SURE HE COULD BE A

T+Ss Snake

The teacher invited the students to guess, to imagine and to hypothesize, but suspended her explicit resolution until the text was consulted for the answer. That is, she pretended that she did not know whether a student's answer was correct until they had read the text, almost as if the praise comes from the text itself. In this correctness of some students' answers during the oral reading of the text, almost as if the praise came from the text itself. In this case the text itself and the teacher's running commentary on the students' reading of the text combine as a unified basis for the evaluation of the students' capacity to 'imagine' or 'guess' correctly.

The examples above show that in early reading instruction it is the students' abilities to imagine, infer, or guess that are being called upon. Such instructional sequences appear to be methods for training students to hypothesize, to participate in anticipation routines and to acknowledge the text—teacher nexus as the arbiter of their competence and as the source of actual knowledge. The students are being asked what might be the case and what they think (that is, to offer possibilities), while the teacher announces from the text what is the case. Right answers and actuals are made equivalent through the teacher's evaluative comments. This is a concrete demonstration of teacher self-authorization in which the text serves primarily as a resource for describing the differential status of teacher and student, and for linking this difference in status to the public activity of reading. It is a demonstration of the reliance students must place on the teacher's pronouncements of the adequacy of their guesses, while the text is not treated as a possibility but as an actuality.

These procedures also work to turn fiction into fact. They reconstitute a story, anticipated through students' imaginations, into factual events — what really did happen ('What else might a rabbit do?' — 'Right, and that's exactly what he did'). These practices mirror some of the narrative practices we pointed out in chapter 4, particularly in the ways in which they establish the status of the text as a factual record.

Such practices offer constructions of the child-reader at the same time as they offer constructions of the text. Students are cast as inhabitants of the world of possible knowledge until they are taught. Texts are made to contain actual knowledge — 'facts' of occasion, of sequence, of personality, and so on. These facts are conversationally produced after and as evaluations of students' guesses, imaginings and inferences in fictional realms. These instructional practices may underwrite those attitudes to text which Olson (1977a, b) has described and which we outlined in chapter 2.

Further, the question—answer sequences that comprise these practices also convey a construction of the nature of the readership, in the invoking of particular kinds of relations between child-reader and text-characters. The texts offer variations here, in that they present many possible worlds inhabited by diverse kinds of characters, many of them child-characters and many of them humanized animal-characters. Through the organization of discourse about the texts, teachers may suggest and imply continuities between child-reader and text-characters in a variety of ways. For example, in the Arthur extracts given above, the teacher invites the children to suggest how they might practise being a rabbit, snake and so on. Arthur's problem is made to be their problem, or put another way, they are asked to imagine having his problem. Another example comes from one of the teacher-made audiotapes:

COME AND EAT SAID MOTHER DUCK AND, GOBBLE, GOBBLE, GOBBLE, THEY DID.

Look, children, they're diving with their heads under the water to find food. You don't find your food that way do you?

Such invitations to compare oneself with the text-characters in these ways assist in the maintenance of child−adult relations in the classroom by constituting the child-readers, but not the teacher, as possible inhabitants of the fictional world. The test of whether a constitution of childhood is embedded in questioning routines is whether we would ask such questions of adults. It is partly in the nature of the reading materials as described in chapter 3 and elsewhere, combined with the teacher's commonsense constructions of childhood conveyed through classroom discourse, that childhood, as a social identity and status, is appropriated and further accomplished in and for early schooling.

We presume that these instructional practices are employed with the intention of interesting and involving the students in the possibilities of a story, informed by theories of reading. These practices could be taken as illustrations of what Heap (1985: 265−6) has called taking the text 'off the page and into the culture', to turn 'boring maps' into meaningful texts. Our concern with these examples rests on the extent to which such- practices appear to entail a subordination of the student's knowledge to textual knowledge, and the extent to which game-like or quiz-like features characterize reading lessons. We are not unaware that the construction and maintenance of textual and teacher authority might be viewed by some as desirable outcomes of reading instruction or of schooling, but we do not share that view of what education in literacy is for.

CULTURE, LOGIC AND READING COMPREHENSION

In these early reading lessons, it often appears that teachers constitute students, for purposes of classroom discussion, essentially as sources of ideas and guesses. We have found that some lessons involve a great deal of this imaginative guessing practice, to the extent that students may come to assume that good guessers are treated by the teacher as good readers. Our transcripts provide evidence that students' 'thinking' in this context is assessed as good or not good against the implicit criteria underlying the teachers' questions, such that these guessing routines take the form of attempts to read the teacher's mind.

As Luke, de Castell and Luke (1983: 118) have pointed out, teachers describe texts in an 'individually selective manner'. Not only would each teacher be distinctive in how he or she constructs discourse, but even within a teacher's discourse there may be idiosyncratic or unpredictable variations. The student's task in participating in a lesson can thus be seen as the task of accomplishing coherence across the sequence of the teacher's utterances (cf. McHoul, 1982).

In example 7.17 below (from the same lesson as shown in examples 7.1 to 7.8 above), a year one teacher has completed an oral reading of the story and is questioning students about one of the pictures in the book.

Example 7.17

(Year one)

T   What else has he got on to keep him wet, uh dry.
Ss   hh wet
S   wet hh
T   Robert.
R   Boots?
T   Yes big, boots what-do-we-call those big boots?
S   Gumboots!
T   Two names that I know of, don't call out hands up, Nicolas did you have one? Yes Nicolas?
N   Gumboots.
T   Call them gumboots and there's another name too.
Ss   (   )
S   Galoshes.
T   Or galoshes that's three names 'cause I (could only) I didn't think of galoshes.
S   Rubber boots?

T I didn't think of— that's four 'cause I didn't think of (hh) rubber boots either the one I'm thinking of starts with whuh. (*4.0*)

S (   )

S Wet boots.

T Not wet boots.

S (   ) boots.

S Wellington [boots

T   [Good try though Tim, wellington boots yes wellington boots. And what's the other thing he's got on (*3.0*) for cold and wet.

S (   )

S (   ) coat.

T A big, big coat a big raincoat.

S (   )//

T   //Cold wet and how do you know it's night?

S Because it's//

T   //Apart from the fact it tells you in the story.

S Uh!

T Chris, I wonder if you can tell us. How do you know it's night from this picture?

S Uh! 'cause he's, ahh!

S Lamp.

T Yeah he's got big lamp, hasn't he. Can you see what he's got on underneath his

S   Pyjamas.

T   wet

weather clothes?

S hh

S Pyjamas.

T Do you think he sort of took a lot of time getting out of bed?

Ss [No.

Ss [Yes.

T Getting dressed rather?

Ss [Yes.

Ss [No.

T Did he take a lot of time getting dressed?

Ss [No.

Ss [Yes.
T   Have a look here what, what does this tell you?
S   p.j'.s
S   p–
T   He's still got his p.j.'s on hasn't he so, he [might
Ss   [(   )
T   have had to?
Ss (   )
S   Pyjamas.
S   (   )
T   He might have had to?
S   They're pyjamas.
S   Get out in a hurry.
T   In a hurry so perhaps it was some sort of an emergency.

This lengthy exchange concerning the farmer's apparel exemplifies a number of points. First, the teacher signalled explicitly that some of the intended answers are located not in the text but rather in the teacher's mind ('Two names that I know of ... the one I'm thinking of ... Apart from the fact that it tells you in the story ... he might have had to ...?'). This is an implicit lesson that school knowledge is located with the teacher. A second observation is that the farmer's apparel plays no part in the subsequent story line. The teacher appears (to us) to be elaborating on a detail of the illustration without linking this elaboration to the text as a story. What is conveyed is the absence of boundaries around the territory a teacher could choose to survey inside the context of teaching reading.

The teacher is displaying how to do a reading of the illustration, what to 'wonder' about, what counts as a resolution of the puzzles the teacher poses. Reading lessons in the early years of school characteristically contain considerable material which gives students access to how the teacher thinks. Such lessons confirm the importance of competence in answering teacher's questions about text as evidence of reading ability. The teacher's metatextual commentary here is a display not of knowledge of the text or of the story directly, but of acceptable observational and reasoning procedures. The reading and comprehension of texts may be viewed essentially as the reading and comprehension of the teacher. While the teacher does a reading of the text, students do a reading of the teacher. We see here that the technical aspects of reading become subordinated to the cultural resources necessary to answer a teacher's question (cf. Hammersley, 1977). This practice in following a teacher's line of commentary on a text is practice for answering questions in reading tests (cf. Heap, 1986).

The persistent involvement of students' background experience is, on face value, compatible with some cognitive theories of reading comprehension (see, e.g., Schallert, 1982). Such theories have stressed the need to locate material to be comprehended in the prior knowledge of the learner — a need which is encapsulated in the maxim: 'Comprehension is building bridges between the new and the known' (Pearson and Johnson, 1978: 24). From this viewpoint, comprehension is an internal psychological process by which an incoming message is structured and made concrete by the relevant organized knowledge of the reader. 'The meaning is not in the message. A message is a cryptic recipe that can guide a person in constructing a representation' (Anderson, 1977: 422). Thus, a useful activity associated with reading might be seen to be the teacher's calling into play those aspects of the background knowledge of the students that facilitate comprehension of the story.

It is possible to account for the questioning practices of the teacher, particularly in example 7.17, in terms of such an account of the comprehension process. However, some critical issues can be raised about the way in which this theory of reading was effected in the lesson. The teacher's 'backgrounding' questions seem rarely to draw the students further into the story, but rather can be seen as episodic digressions into details that the teacher sees as interest-ing, instructive or worth discussing. While such discussion may serve various instructional purposes, the point remains that the effect may well be to draw students away from the story.

A second consideration arises from the nature of teachers' evaluations of background knowledge answers. As we noted in reference to table 7.1 at the beginning of this chapter, in this particular lesson the teacher asked a total of 79 questions. Of these, 23 were stated explicitly to indicate that the location of the answer was in the teacher's mind. It should also be pointed out that of the questions drawing apparently on the students' background knowledge (e.g. 'What do we call these big boots?' in the excerpt above), many were reformulated to indicate that the teacher had particular answers in mind (e.g. 'Did he take a lot of time getting dressed?' in the excerpt above). Further, as indicated above, most of the teacher's echoes of acceptable student answers contained elaborations, enhancing the completeness or appropriateness of the students' responses. In yet other instances, students' answers were followed by evaluative comments signalling the specific frame of reference which should have been conveyed in a student's answer, as in the following example:

Example 7.18

('Cold Wet Night' lesson)

T   If you had a chance to be one of the things in our story which, or— someone in the story which would you like to be?
S   hh!
T   Carl?
C   The cricket. I mean the big weta.
T   [The big weta.
S   [Oh so would I.
T   Why would you like to be the big weta?
S   'Cause he comes last.
T   He comes last, but what's what happens to him that's so uh so good do you think?
S   'Cause he, he gets to stay in the bed.
T   He gets to stay in the bed.

This example is instructive in that the teacher is requesting personal opinions from the students which, it might be thought, are entirely within the discretion of the answerer (cf. Heap, 1985: 262—3). An acceptable answer to such a question would appear to reside neither in the text nor in the teacher's mind. The teacher none the less indicated that there is a proper rationale and frame of reference even for a personal preference. Prior to that specification, no guidance was given as to what grounds students should use to decide their preference.

Thus, another equally notable effect of forays into students' background knowledge and personal preferences can be seen when such questions are placed within the pattern of evaluative utterances used by teachers. Not only are students' abilities to demonstrate knowledge of words or memory for events in a story assessed by teachers, but teachers also pronounce upon the acceptability of students' contributions from their background knowledge and preferences. Teachers thereby claim and exercise the prerogative of the school to pronounce upon the acceptability of students' apparently personal feelings and aspects of their lives out-of-school, a prerogative recognized even by young students:

Example 7.19

(Taken from 'Cold Wet Night' lesson)

T   ... What do you think is the thing about the story that you like most?
S   ((*whispered eagerly*)) I know!

Exhortations to teachers to call upon and employ students' knowledge and feelings about various topics appear to personalize learning and render instruction more student-centred, a strategy that is also mirrored in 'reader-response' approaches to literary appreciation in the later years of schooling (Gilbert, 1987). However, the location of such techniques in a teacher-centred, evaluative organization of talk in the classroom may serve to expand the legislative boundaries of schooling into personal and social areas of the student's life, in ways that may carry no necessary entailment of the students' acquisition of skills such as reading, and no necessary connection with genuinely subjective responses to literature.

CONCLUSION

In this chapter, we have suggested that the latitude teachers display in questioning sequences is part of the demonstration to students of the breadth of the teacher's authority. The more episodic the diversions, the harder students must work to access the logic underlying the discussion, and how it relates to the words or the story. The more expansive the discussion, the more difficult is the task of making coherent the teacher's running metatextual commentary. The broader the range of background knowledge, imagining, inferring and guessing that students must produce in order to take part successfully in the public activity of reading lessons, the less reading lessons appear to be about the text at all.

Thus, while the apparent source of an answer lies in the student's background knowledge, in personal preferences, or in the illustrations in the book, the reformulative and evaluative utterances of the teacher can be seen to reveal that virtually all of the retrospectively correct or adequate answers are so found in relation to the teacher's ongoing construction of a reading of the story. In inspecting lessons of the kind we have illustrated here, we are drawn to the conclusion that it is the teacher's reading and the teacher's 'thinking' that are the targets of the students' guesses.

It is in this important sense that reading as an organized activity cannot be separated from the relation of teacher and student. The teacher invades and imbues the text with his or her own interpretation during the course of formal reading instruction. That interpretation is effected within a particular constitution of the student and the students' status in relation to both text and teacher.

It would appear more important in these kinds of lesson sequences for students to be in tune, culturally and intellectually, with the teacher, and to be able and willing to search for a 'cultural logic' underlying the teacher's individually selective attention to the detail of the text, than to be able to read the words. It could be seen to be irrelevant for these kinds of lessons that any student could read the words. It does not appear to be assumed that any student or all students can or cannot read the words. We may ask, What appears to be taught here? What is this a lesson in? We would conclude that these are essentially lessons in school culture, and more particularly, lessons in how school knowledge is generated and transmitted. We have seen that the materials of early reading instruction organize social relations — especially child—adult relations — in a particular way. They organize student—teacher relations in a complementary way. The conjunction of materials and methods that we have described forms the distinctive character of school-literate culture in its introductory forms.

We have shown in this chapter some possible ways in which teachers may orient students to written text. We recognize that teachers would use a more extensive range of interactional and conversational practices than our instances illustrate. But in observing practices such as those illustrated here, we have a basis for arguing that reading instruction in the early years of schooling plays a critical role in introducing young children to a number of central understandings about the acquisition of school-literacy: first, *whatever* the specific practices employed, students learn about the relative status of teacher and student with respect to textual knowledge; they learn about the breadth of the teacher's expertise, the forms and location of school knowledge, and the relative status of their own contributions to classroom talk. They learn these through immersion in the conversational routines that occur in classrooms. Secondly, students learn about adult constructions of their capacities and interests as children. Our materials indicate that the content of the books and the teacher's questions seem to dovetail. Teachers' questions effect the same continuities between child-readers and text-characters as do the stories. Finally, children learn about the possibilities and constraints that apply to textual interpretation.

On the basis of our materials, we are drawn to the notion of the 'set text': a particular interpretation of the story is settled through the teacher's reading and questioning; that reading and questioning is in turn predicated on the assumption that textual interpretation is a closed affair. We pose the question: are there other ways in which the relation of teacher, student and text could be constructed, given the institutional constraints and the conventional child—adult relations that characterize schooling?

8

Text as Topic: Some Conclusions and Implications for Children and Literacy

Having considered our analyses of the contents of beginning reading books and having indicated some of the ways in which texts are talked about in classrooms, it is useful to recall the Gedanken experiment we presented in chapter 1. This experiment involved imagining that a colonial power had developed a literacy programme for the indigenes it was administering. We argued that the documents used in this literacy programme could be treated as evidence of the linguistic, pedagogical and social theories informing the colonists' practices. Such a treatment, we proposed, affords some insights not only into the colonists' version of optimal literacy instruction but also into their views of social order and of the relationship between themselves and the indigenes within the terms of that social order. The materials could be examined for their match to the indigenous language, for the social content and categories used to order the social world and indirectly for the ways in which the colonial power assembles and displays its version of the indigenous culture to the indigines themselves.

Now imagine further that the documentation we provided of the contents of beginning reading materials and methods in formal instructional settings was in fact a documentation of the colonists' materials and methods in our Gedanken experiment. We may then attempt some answers to the set of questions that we posed in chapter 1. What might we say about how the colonists are trying to effect their literacy programme? In particular we can ask what might be the effects on the use of the indigenous language itself, on concepts such as 'knowing', 'thinking' and 'feeling', on the versions of themselves that the indigenes can find in the early reading materials, and on the general concept of literacy as a particular set of socially organized practices.

In using this analogy, we recognize that the 'indigines' in this case already participate in a social world mediated by print (Hall, 1986) and that they are, in other ways also, already members of the wider culture in which our 'colonists' work. Thus, it is to school-literacy that we have directed our attention here. The analogy is intended to set in high relief the cultural practices of adults in shaping the materials and methods of early literacy instruction in schools; it is not meant to endorse by implication a view of children as primitive or pre-competent.

HOW LANGUAGE IS REPRESENTED

First we address the version of language that is displayed in the BR books. We can note initially that English, in its written form, can express only a small subset of the stress and intonational features of spoken language. The novice reader acquires a communicative technology that represents only certain aspects of the native tongue, principally the morphological and lexical aspects. There is in English a separation of the linguistic from the extra-linguistic (prosodic and contextual) aspects of native oral communication when print is encountered.

Second, these books appear to be transitional between oral conventions and written conventions of communication, partly in that they contain a great deal of reported talk, partly in the relative frequency of first person reference and partly in the introduction of the speaker—writer distinction in narrative texts. We have shown, however, that the reported talk in fact represents a reshaping of natural oral interaction. Quite apart from the omission of many prosodic features and the neglect of repetition, overlapping speech and many other qualities common in ordinary talk, the forms and functions of dialogue in which the characters in the BR books engage contrast in a number of ways with the forms and functions that are evident in everyday talk.

We have also documented some conventions that operate in the portrayal of oral language on paper, such as the prevalence of question—answer sequences, the 'complete correct response' and the representation of routine oral language interaction in cross-generational and cross-gender talk among the characters. These features recall Walter Ong's point (1982: 1) that a developing research documentation of differences between primary oral and literate cultures' management of oral language use has led, among other things, to a reconsideration of the ways in which *oral* discourse is conducted among literates. This corpus of beginning reading material puts on display a version of everyday oral language use that has a literate bias — a bias that is especially suited to the organizational aspects of school life and to the epistemological basis of schooling.

We have also remarked on the strong preference for the story form, which has antecedents in pre-literate oral cultures, as a type of discourse recruited for literacy instruction. As we pointed out, however, the characteristic forms of stories that are presented with great frequency in these books lead to the inference that they in fact offer so little as sources of entertainment that their use and, by retrospective inference, their purpose in the first place was essentially pedagogical and expository. Gee has made a similar comment about the kind of 'oral narratives' that teachers want children to produce: preference is for the production of 'a form of speech-writing ... to a group of pretend strangers, for the purpose of displaying and/or learning academic literacy skills' (1985: 25).

Further, the words that occur most frequently in the BR texts are selected from a large set of many possible thousands of suitable monosyllabic and multisyllabic words. From a concern with the acquisition of decoding skill alone, many words that do not appear with any significant frequency or at all could be equally qualified candidates for use in these books. It is surely the case that an implicit cultural image of the child is guiding the selection of such key dimensions as *big* ($n=564$)/*little* ($n=652$) over, say, *right* ($n=9$)/*wrong* ($n=0$) or *rich* ($n=0$)/*poor* ($n=4$).

We see that in these texts the versions of language, rationality and order are built largely around the use of particular interpretive categories as the commonsense axes for describing and making sense of the world. This raises the obvious question of whether or not children would order their world in this way independently of their encounters with adult discourse about childhood.

HOW EXPERIENCE IS REPRESENTED

Just as the basic flow of everyday conversation is recast in this form of literate language, so, we argue, are basic categories of experience such as knowing, thinking and feeling. Again, these categories need to be regarded as social productions, and throughout this book we have stressed the significance of the BR texts in introducing school-endorsed versions of language use. This representation of basic cognitive and emotional experience can be seen in the examination of a number of features of the books. First, we have argued that the narrator's voice, while often playing an unobtrusive role in speaker identification and scene choreography in stories, organizes the major categories of interpretation and experience. In considering the comparison of everyday conversational interaction with the impersonal essay text form that dominates later school materials, we can regard the narration in these beginning reading books as introductory and transitional. Through the characters' speeches and the narrator's organizing work, sets of interpretive categories are consistently worked through the books — categories that pertain in particular to gender and generational relations. These categories, we have suggested, are derived from adult culture and are used to shape the apparent child consciousness presented in the books.

We have noted also the prevalence of perceptual and cognitive-process terms (*see, look*) and action descriptions (*go, come*) as the principal vehicles for conveying activity in the stories. Emotion and evaluation are comparatively rarely expressed in these books; we noted the infrequency of interpersonal expressions of emotion such as liking, loving, hating, and so on. It is as if this dimension of experience has been neglected in the interests of displaying organized activities and forms of attention. We may speculate that the books represent the starting point of a process that emphasizes factual, nominal contents as the major currency of schooling, a point that parallels Ong's description of the impact of print technology on Renaissance academies:

[the teacher had become] part of a corporation which was uncalculatingly but relentlessly reducing the personalist, dialoguing element in knowledge to a minimum in favour of an element which made knowledge something a corporation could traffic in, a-personal and abstract (almost as though it was something which existed outside a mind, as though one could have knowledge without anybody to do the knowing). (1958/1983: 152)

The origins of this process, we have argued, are evident in the BR books, even though the books portray 'actual dialogue'. Later school texts more clearly depersonalize the source of knowledge and the selection of descriptive and interpretive categories. As characters cease to speak for themselves, so the texts become apparently self-descriptive.

HOW THE SOCIAL ORDER IS REPRESENTED

Many of the social categories consistently worked into the materials relate to children and the adults and animals in their apparent immediate environment. That is to say that learning about knowing, thinking and feeling is simultaneously learning about endorsed versions of the social world as it comes to be put on paper. Our corpus of materials shows the persistent use of character-types selected apparently from the world of children, officially assembled for their own use in ways that are meant to apply to and order their own lives. In these beginning reading books we find that the readership is clearly constituted to be 'children'. That is, while there may be explicit race and gender dimensions in these books, and while certain indirect inferences may be drawn concerning the social class contexts of many of the characters and their activities, we would argue that it is the intergenerational relations that are built most persistently and explicitly into these reading materials. The school may prefer its clients to be middle class and white, but it demands that they be 'children'. Furthermore, school practices help students to assemble themselves into this category through repeated displays, both overt and covert, of models of childhood in material documents as well as by portraying preferred forms of interaction in the classroom and in the home.

With these observations in mind, we have asked whether or not, in the light of the analyses we have presented, these books can be said to be about children at all, or whether they are better seen (following Jenks and Speier) as devices through which adults display a preferred version of social order and the place of children in that order. The point is further reinforced by our observation that child-characters are consistently shown in contexts of child—adult relations, even though the adults may be absent from the fictional scene. Moreover, the books caricature the adult world as much as they do the child world — through omissions as much as through commissions — and both caricatures are sketched in outlines compatible with school-literate culture.

HOW LITERACY IS REPRESENTED

In the light of the analyses of beginning reading materials that we have presented in this book, what particular form of literacy seems to be effected through current schooling practices? The goals of literacy and the identification of those goals with abstract, objective and logical thought are part of a tradition which has characterized literacy as a somewhat utopian, culturally uplifting achievement. However appealing such abstract descriptions may be to some educators, it needs to be asserted that literacy must always be seen as a particular set of social practices (Street, 1984). Further, the form of literacy pervading modern schooling is only one of many possible forms. We have assumed that current school-based literacy practices are in large part visible in the materials that are used in the process of literacy acquisition.

The particular emphasis that schools place on students' management of literate modes of discourse (including hearing and talking as well as reading and writing) requires teachers and students to reshape oral language practices. In the early years of schooling, for instance, there is a preference for oral language uses that are book-like (cf. Michaels, 1981) and written texts that are not talk-like (cf. Michaels, 1987). We have shown how early reading materials assist in organizing these preferences.

Towards the end of formal schooling, there may be new preferences, for example to become in some respects less book-like, and to recover an apparently personal voice in a none the less literate pitch. These new emphases can be induced from a consideration of some external supervising examiners' remarks on the performance of final year high school students (as studied by Ozolins, 1981). We find many examples of examiners' complaints about the lack of 'personal involvement' of the students in the subjects of Literature, History, Social Studies and so on. These reports are written mainly to advise departments of education about the relative ease or difficulty of the examination questions used, but they reveal clearly the goal of a personalization of understanding that ostensibly underlies the markers' rhetoric. For example, consider the following (from Ozolins, 1981), the first of which is taken from a supervising examiner's report concerning an English Literature examination paper:

Many (by no means all) students write perfectly correctly, but their prose is still often rather stodgy, stiff, comparatively character-less; it has little liveliness or personal voice ... the best papers usually have an unobtrusive personal voice in the prose, carrying something of the student's own personality and live response ... (153)

And another from a History supervising examiner:

The great majority of ... candidates in British History demonstrated only too clearly that they had spent a year in a sterile, pointless and soul-destroying exercise, a negation of all history study even at the elementary level. It must be emphasised that unless a teacher or student explores issues for himself he is unlikely to develop any commitment to or any enthusiasm for the subject, or any insight into it. (150)

Ozolins argued that statements such as the above indicate that examiners are searching for distinctions in the students' work that reflect different levels of 'cultural capital' (Bourdieu, 1974; Bourdieu and Passeron, 1977) rather than merely for the technically competent production of factual information. It strikes us, moreover, that the examiners' remarks above are reminiscent of the reactions that a reader might have to the materials contained in the BR books — 'little liveliness or personal voice', little exploration of issues, 'comparatively character-less', little 'enthusiasm for the subject'. In the interests of parsimony, then, perhaps we need look no further than the books that students receive in schools, beginning with the very first reading materials, for one source of the examiners' complaints.

The point needs to be emphasized that students not only learn the techniques of reading and writing in early schooling but importantly they learn what specific sorts of relationships can be inferred or should be constructed between the written word and human experience from the types of text (and talk about text) they encounter in school. By participating in a variety of 'literate' discourses, across the school years, students may gain access to culturally acceptable forms of textual commentary. Where students' productions match valued forms of literate discourse, those productions are likely to be read or heard favourably, even though, as Ozolins has documented, the criteria for such assessments may shift from occasion to occasion. Both 'informational' and 'interpretive' discourses about textual material become hard currencies in schooling, although the problems remain for students of where and how to exchange such currencies, that is, the problems of precisely where and how to balance and diversify their investment portfolios.

LEARNING ABOUT TEXTUALITY

If literacy acquisition is to entail more than the technical competencies of reading and writing, then it needs to include learning about what literacy is and what it offers, how it is to be practised in school and elsewhere, and what the rationales for those sets of practices may be. This includes the study of textuality as a topic. As a starting point, the crafting process by which particular social purposes come to be translated into textual products needs to become a topic of learning in itself. Here 'crafting' refers to the entire textualizing activity from the layout of the written word, the format of the book including words and pictures, the style and content of lettering, the pictorial accompaniments, the selection of vocabulary, the portrayal of certain categories of characters and their attendant ways of behaving, the selection of particular written genres, and so on. The apparently simplistic nature of the content of many of the BR books is counter-balanced by the many interesting opportunities they offer for examining this textualizing process, in particular in light of the fact that they are probably the only sets of books that students will encounter in their whole school careers that attempt to portray their own everyday world to them.

With this in mind, we offer the following possibilities for practice that seem to be compatible with the notion of the study of the textualizing process as an aspect of early literacy learning.

The suggestions that follow should be regarded as only a subset of possible activities that could be incorporated into the kinds of instructional programme that are compatible with our analyses of beginning reading materials. It is this programmatic nature of early encounters with the written word that we wish to emphasize rather than the intrinsic merit of specific practices. Further, these suggestions are not necessarily new, in that they may be similar to practices informed by a variety of theories of reading pedagogy and they may be in use in many classrooms.

A final prefatory point to keep in mind concerns the widespread debate that occurs between advocates of contrasting early literacy programmes. Nowhere in this book have we suggested that the technicalities of learning to read and write (or hear or talk) in literate ways should be ignored or given a secondary place. These technical competencies are essential. Rather, we have adopted the view that teaching such skills can be facilitated by providing students with an explicit pragmatic and aesthetic framework for learning how to become literate. It should be clear from our remarks so far that current 'skills-based' approaches to early literacy instruction, as well as those current programmes that define themselves as 'meaning-based', only partly address the task of learning about literacy as we have developed it here.

We emphasize that the problems and possibilities afforded by books such as those we have analysed in the preceding chapters are problems and possibilities that are presented equally to the teacher and the student. We have given some attention to child-readers' access to and interpretation of such texts, but it is worth highlighting the point that the texts may also mediate, sometimes obviously and sometimes subtly, the sorts of practices teachers undertake.

A programme that focuses upon literacy as a topic of learning – including its social purposes and functions as well as the specific technical capacities that it requires – would take as its goal an understanding of the full ramifications of the notion that written texts are crafted products. The programme would take it for granted that textual material can be decomposed and recomposed for purposes of considering the writers' choices of formats, words, expressions, character categories and genres. One of its major purposes would be to explicate and to illustrate the particular conventions that have, due to certain historical processes, come to be associated with the way written materials are produced. These conventions relate not only to the graphic forms in which language is symbolized but also to the forms of expressing and knowing that are embodied in particular narrative and expository genres.

It seems to us that the functional basis of literacy is a topic that can be addressed at varying degrees of complexity continually throughout schooling. Young students could be encouraged to think about and discuss the reasons why people found a need or a want to read and write in the first place, and about why some sorts of people or groups of people might need or want to read and write more than others. Such activities could serve to ground the purposes of literacy and overcome some of the for-school-only assumptions that some students seem to hold with respect to their literacy learning. They could also lead students to think about and discuss the reasons why they themselves may currently or in the future need to read and write, and why, independently, they may wish to read and write, in and out of school. Such activities could focus not only on the pragmatic value of literacy skills but could also come to deal with their interpersonal possibilities, for instance, in allowing more careful selection of vocabulary and more deliberative structuring of discourse in general. Such activities could further assist students in addressing the question of the social valuation of literate discourse.

These approaches to literacy could be accompanied by projects in which the various attempts made by different cultures to develop writing systems are examined. Young students could experiment with different kinds of sound–symbol relationships and develop their own pictographic, ideographic, syllabic and alphabetical systems of communication. Such manipulations of sound–symbol relationships may assist in developing phonemic awareness (which some have argued is an important prerequisite of reading acquisition, see Ehri, 1979) and may also serve to place in perspective the particular form of the sound–symbol relationship that is currently in use in the parent script.

This programme could serve as a basis for the students' understanding of the plausibility (if not conventionality) of their invented spellings in their early attempts to write. We have observed, for instance, that some students seem reluctant to attempt to write a word they cannot spell, even though the teacher has indicated that invented spellings are acceptable in early drafts of written material. Our interpretation of this is that some students are aware that finally there is a right and a wrong way to spell, and they have not been convinced that the wrong way could be viewed as a principled attempt. Drawing attention to the many possible principled ways of visually mapping the sound system would be a concrete way of establishing the notion of conventionality, a notion surely more instructive than correctness (and historically more accurate). If some experimentation occurs around possible forms of the sound—symbol relationship, then the learning of writing and spelling could also entail explication of the relationship that is currently in force in the parent script, rather than the conventions being seen as arbitrary.

Such a notion could be taken further to suggest that students be encouraged to experiment with different ways of representing oral language events, for example, conversations, arguments, instructions and ceremonies, on paper. This mapping of oral language on to paper is the reverse and complement of finding different ways of reading print aloud, and the two exercises in conjunction may assist students in seeing some connections and differences between the resources and the constraints of the two mediums of communication. Through this practice students could locate some of the theoretical considerations about the oral—written relation outlined in chapter 1. This also could be used to ensure that the special qualities and values of oral language continue to be recognized in the classroom.

As others have suggested (e.g., Christie, 1985) students may also benefit from knowing about how to read and write the major text types or genres. Activities could be developed to explicate the communicational purposes of stories, fairy tales, or experiential or informational texts, and what might make effective or ineffective versions of texts of each type. In previous chapters we have noted many of the interesting possibilities that are offered by the BR books with respect to the mixing and blending not only of fantasy and reality contents but also of structural forms, such as the ventriloquized 'I' in the experiential texts and the pseudo-narrative expository forms of stories. While the contents of these different kinds of texts may seem at first glance to the teacher to be so simple as to offer little basis for interesting commentary or discussion, they are in fact uniquely rich when the process of their crafting becomes a topic. That is, their apparently impoverished nature as slices-of-life is more than counterbalanced by their intricacy and peculiarity as crafted texts.

Attempting to pursue further the central notion that textual materials are produced by particular people with particular purposes and knowledge for use in some set of social contexts, we suggest that even very young students could study different types of text for purposes of comparison with the books usually provided for school work. For example, children could bring and use as texts birthday cards, grocery lists, menus, instruction manuals, empty cereal boxes, advertisements, and so on. Some of these could be described as 'enabling' texts (that is, their comprehension enables the reader to perform some activity), as distinct from the 'reflective' texts typically encountered in school (see Heap, 1987 for further treatment of this distinction). Our point here is similar to other calls for expanding the range of reading materials used in schools to include kinds of texts commonly encountered outside school, to enhance functional literacy (e.g., Luke, 1988b). The importance and prevalence of such texts in everyday reading in the out-of-school world has been documented by Mikulecky (1982) and Heath (1983). There are many questions students could ask for each kind of text. What does a writer do or try to do when he or she writes? What aspects of the format and language are associated with the degree of clarity, appeal, or other qualities of the text? What interests does this writer display? How are these interests displayed? How does this writer comply with or experiment with words, sentences and genre conventions? Finally, what sort of person does this writer seem to be and what sort of reader is this text written for? Students could rework, parody, improve upon, or reply to these various texts as exercises in textual analysis.

Such activities would highlight for students some aspects of the comparison between the writer–reader relationship and the speaker–hearer relationship. Including many varieties of texts in an early reading programme may allow students to draw attention to details of texts which to adults are normally unremarkable, but which to children may signal new lines of curiosity about their everyday surroundings. That is, these texts may turn out to be instructive in unanticipated ways for both teacher and student.

THE READING—WRITING CONNECTION

Turning to the issue of students' written work in school, we note that conference or process writing curricula have become widespread. In such programmes, students share and discuss their ideas for stories, work through successive drafts of stories and 'publish' final drafts of stories. We would go further than most of these programmes on two counts. First, students can learn about the influence and efficacy of the written word most directly through the production of texts that someone else can use — that is, students could experiment with writing texts such as signposts, timetables, instructions to get to different parts of the school or the neighbourhood, messages to one another, advertisements for upcoming events, and so on. In this way the quality of their texts could be concretely confirmed. The writers themselves would be available to explain why certain formats, words and expressions were used. A steady consumption and production of 'everyday' stories, recounts or other reflective texts omit many of the consequential written forms that are used routinely in the wider culture. Second, we suggest that students' consecutive drafts of any texts — and the interactive work that produces them — could also be examined and compared to show how written materials might get to be the way they are. Such analysis involves more than the 'improvement' of successive drafts.

As a way of addressing directly the issue of textual authority, we suggest that, from their first encounters with written materials, young students be encouraged to rebuild and reshape stories and expositions, orally recounting or writing from their own perspective, or from other imagined perspectives (the Wolf in *Red Riding Hood*, the adults or the pets in the everyday stories, the novice's version of a set of instructions). Briefly we are endorsing here a programme that explores the implications of the notion that all written texts imply particular readerships and have particular purposes, and are thus reworkable. The review of young children's oral language competencies we presented in chapter 1 demonstrates that young students would not find the task of tailoring language to various contexts an alien notion. The point is to recruit these facilities with oral language to the problem of understanding the conventions of written language. It may well be that in the early years of schooling much of this reworking would focus on pictorial accompaniments, the use of colloquialisms, or the provision of alternative speeches from a variety of different characters. These narrative-based exercises, however, could form the basis for similar defeasibility studies of expository textual material.

The possibility of mismatches between what we would take to be the purposes of the text and the instructional strategies used by teachers in discussion was outlined in chapter 7. We suggest that if a text is taken to be a story in its function, then the subsequent need to answer informational and certain classes of inferential questions becomes inappropriate. Similarly, a teacher's evaluation of students' responses to apparently discretionary questions (such as preferences for certain characters, what might have happened next, what was the best part, and so on) seems to be inappropriate. This problem arises partly because most questions in the classroom are generated by the teacher, a tendency documented in a long tradition of classroom-observational research. With texts such as these, apparently about the everyday life of children, there seems ample opportunity for student-generated comments or questions. Out of school, children ask questions and make observations all the time.

It seems to us not a difficult matter for teachers to encourage students' questioning and discussion about everyday, contemporary stories. A route to this could be to draw on some of our observations in previous chapters to initiate some analytic work by students. For instance, students could draw attention to the possible peculiarity of many of the speeches and activities of apparently familiar and generic characters — girls, boys, fathers, mothers, and so on. We reiterate the point that the peculiarity of these characters, activities and scenes applies not only to groups of students viewed as ethnically or culturally different, but potentially to all students. It may be more difficult for the teacher to regard these child-characters as problematic versions of children than it is for the students. The observation that these story characters may be curious versions of children, adults, dogs and so on is not to debunk or dismiss these stories; rather, it explicitly allows the possibility that students can learn, from the earliest school years, to notice and describe an author-at-work in the text. This is a core realization in a programme addressed at the nature of literacy: students can be constituted as more than hearers of stories — they can, in addition, be constituted as analysts of texts.

This suggestion acquires more force when it is kept in mind that the contents of many of the early reading books that students encounter in school are centrally concerned with apparent versions of their own lives, or are written and selected for their special enjoyment and interest. Yet, in our examples, it is typically the teacher who decides what there is to talk about. A 'correct' interpretation is less important, with these types of reading materials, than is giving students prerogatives and strategies for generating topics and questions for themselves. These topics and questions will reveal more of their understanding than do their answers to the teacher's questions. Based on the analyses we presented in chapter 7, we recommend that interested teachers tape-record and transcribe some of their own instructional talk to examine the interpretive role they and their students play as questioners, commentators and evaluators.

The goal of some reading-related activities in classrooms might be to encourage students' interpretations and aesthetic responses to texts. Many teachers would claim to be encouraging students' own interpretations or reactions to stories, and not imposing their own, by organizing discourse through questions instead of announcements. However, we have shown that asking questions does not necessarily act to privilege students' ideas or conceal a teacher's interpretation, for questions themselves embody descriptions and interpretations of the text. Our view is that many young students could, from experience with question–answer sequences, easily arrive at the conclusion that the teacher's expertise extends beyond the mechanics of decoding and scribing into the area of knowing how the story should be heard and enjoyed. From our examinations of teachers' questions and reactions to students' comments, we concluded that teachers show themselves to be expert decoders, expert reactants to story content and expert assessors of a wide range of student interpretations. We see no need and no possibility for teachers to suppress their own interpretations and reactions to stories. But if multiple interpretations of texts are to be encouraged, then students need to conduct their own reasoned discussions as members of an interpretive community (cf. Hunsberger, forthcoming) a goal uniquely served by reading materials masquerading as reflections of the readers' world.

THE 'SET TEXT'

Part of our characterization of beginning school reading materials has entailed viewing them as precursors to the kinds of texts students will encounter in later years — precursors both to literary texts, to which students are to respond interpretively and aesthetically, and to informational/expository texts, from which students are to acquire factual knowledge. In schools, readings of both kinds of texts (and mixtures and hybrids) are routinely produced and assessed. School texts are 'set' in two senses: they are prescribed as material to be read, and preferred ways of reading them are established largely through textual, instructional and assessment practices. Indeed, this 'set-text' attitude seems to dominate much of educational practice from kindergarten through to graduate school; it is inferrable from the structure of the texts, the nature of classroom discourse, comments on students' written work, and even curriculum manuals and guidelines.

The process of textual interpretation often seems to be a process of accomplishing a single, 'correct' reading of a text (a point that applies also to classroom reconstructions of shared experiences). This issue is at the heart of many of our observations, as well as those of other writers such as Olson, concerning the authority and autonomy pretended to by school textual material. Our view is that a set-text attitude closes off many valuable approaches to textual interpretation, thereby seriously and unjustifiably constraining students' full access to literate practices and products.

There are at least two ways of attempting to erode the dominance and centrality of this attitude to school texts. The first is to increase the use of material from outside the school, especially textual materials that are not written primarily for students or even for children. A second approach is based on the continual contextualizing of the material presented in school books. An example of such activities would be pointing to strengths and limitations associated with the choices the writer has made in accessing certain sources and in using certain language forms in the presentation of information. This entails a redefinition of the textbook as a heuristic, as a device for shaping a discussion, a "machine for producing possible worlds" (Eco, 1979: 264). Again, we are led to the conclusion that beginning reading books are machines that are well designed for achieving such a redefinition.

WRITING FOR EARLY LITERACY

Our analyses and our interpretations of how the topic of literacy may form part of school learning have parallel implications for the producers of books for young students. The points that follow should be taken as a sample of devices — some of which can be found in existing books — that are compatible with a programme of literacy awareness of the sort we are suggesting, and that would facilitate the kinds of classroom activities we have outlined. These implications for writers are also built around a redefinition of the book, not as an object which attempts to submerge or obscure its own crafting, but rather as a text which draws explicit attention to its own history and character.

Our interest in how stories are written for use in early schooling recognizes that school books are written to be compatible with broad pedagogical theories and with educational and social policy concerns. We referred earlier to Luke's (1987b) historical account of the genesis of the modern basal reader in North America. A further reference point is offered in Rose's (1985) historical analysis of how a work of literature — Barrie's *Peter and Wendy* — was edited to be compatible with a notion of 'writing for the child' as this was understood in England in the early part of this century, and thus to be acceptable for use in elementary schools. Among the changes that were made to the original text were the removal of 'all syntax ... resonant of a classical literary style; all specific cultural and material references ...; all signs of play or parody of its own language ...; all those moments when the sexuality of the text becomes explicit ...; all episodes which disturb the logical narrative sequence of the story' (Rose, 1985: 101–2); and further,

Above all, the school version cuts out virtually all signs of the presence of an identifiable narrator, that is, a narrator who forces on the reader's attention the question of who is telling the story. The school version is told almost entirely by an anonymous third person narrator who never appears explicitly in the text to trouble its linguistic norms or its utterly sustained cohesion of address.

To varying extents, the texts that we have examined show similar absences. Rose claimed that these erasures were part of the process of making language and literature into objects of policy — 'policy by means of which the child's relationship to its culture can be defined' (1985: 92). This observation parallels our description of the implicit policy regarding the relations between children and culture in the kinds of texts currently produced for early schooling. Much of this present work has sought to describe how contemporary school reading materials constitute children, language and learning from text. Our analyses of these texts indicate a number of alternative treatments that could reverse these transformations in ways that could enliven the texts and the methods for teaching and learning with them.

For example, beginning school reading books could be produced that experiment with different sound—symbol relationships. Young students could be invited to read texts written in pictographs or ideographs, including materials that show how scripts might develop out of pictorial sketches, as in Chinese, or the Sumerian precursors to the English alphabet. The book itself thus explicitly draws attention to the relativistic nature of the particular sound — symbol conventions in use, and may serve as an analytic preparation for managing the parent script.

Similarly more books could be produced that experiment with a variety of ways of showing some sequence of events or some information on paper — through pictures, with talk bubbles, with different kinds and sizes of type and printing, and with differing degrees of writer visibility. Again, we argue that it is these variations that can form a foundation for learning about reading and writing as technologies. That is, children could learn about the choices made by writers in the presentation of experience on paper, and thus be led to consider explicitly the implication of particular choices and the neglect of others. This experimentation with the format of text presentation could be facilitated by books that constantly draw attention to the ways in which the discourse is structured by the conventions of written text. Multiple beginnings and endings could be provided; stories could be written from multiple perspectives; writers could make unexpected appearances in stories; the temporal sequencing of events could be varied; and a number of other devices found both in adult fiction and in films produced for adult and child audiences could be employed. Many of our suggestions are consistent with some recent theorizing about literacy instruction, capturing, for example, the idea that children could be led to read like writers and write like readers (Pearson and Tierney, 1984).

We also can imagine techniques whereby a book could personalize and locate its writer. These could include annotations concerning the writer's identity and intentions, running commentaries by the writer on why particular events were shown next or why particular characters did certain things, how the writer thought about what characters might do next in the production of the story, or how the writer might organize material to help informational learning. Such commentaries could entail experimentation with shifts in the fantasy—reality dimension, in which the writer may attempt to signal how the world of the story might intersect with what he or she imagines to be the real world of the reader and the real world of the writer. Commercially successful books for children have demonstrated that children can appreciate such sophisticated interplays between writer and reader.

The above points focus attention on the format and crafting of the books written for young students. The notion of crafting is also pertinent to the social contents of the texts — the ways in which the social world is constructed in the discourse by the writer. We have argued and demonstrated, principally in chapters 3 and 4, that one of the features of the BR books is the familiarity and blandness of their story contents. We are reminded of Bruner's remarks made many years ago concerning the issue of 'relevance' in educational practice:

A generation ago, the progressive movement urged that knowledge be related to the child's own experience and brought out of the realm of empty abstractions. A good idea was translated into banalities about the home, then the friendly postman and trashman, then the community, and so on. It is a poor way to compete with the child's own dramas and mysteries. (1966: 534)

It is not only that the contents are banal because of their familiarity; it is also that there seems to be rarely any attempt to query aspects of the apparently familiar and immediate social world of the reader. That is to say, the books offer both the child-reader and the teacher who wishes to use them in the classroom few direct avenues for questioning the presumptions built into the texts in sometimes subtle ways. As we noted in our analyses, while the social contents of the texts may appear familiar, they do not constitute 'idle discourse'.

We could consider as an example the problems we have located with respect to gender portraits. These are not resolved by equalizing print-time given to male and female characters or by substituting new activities for the same cast of characters. The relentless gendering of the social world of the books reinforces gender differences as critical parameters of social experience. Rather than patrolling the gender border in this diligent way, the books could aim to dissolve that border – in part by releasing characters from the constraints of gender-based definitions, and by showing that gender attributions and relations are themselves problems for both characters and readers. Many non-sexist books for children currently attempt to invite the reader to question gender differences and relations, not merely to accept and absorb them (see Davies, 1987, 1989).

We take seriously Bruner's point about attempting to deal with the actual 'dramas and mysteries' of childhood experience. However, we argue that adult-written books can typically represent only an adult's version of those dramas and mysteries and how to cope with them. None the less, an attempt to describe intense practical problems that adults know that children face day by day seems warranted. These experiences need not only concern the personal level (pain, frustration, joy, relief and so on), but may also deal with those struggles of childhood that are less visible to adults, such as difficulties relating to cross-age, cross-gender and cross-racial communication, and the maintenance of positive social relations within a socially complex and changeable world. The point remains, however, that, unless students' interpretations of such texts are privileged in the classroom, the texts become merely a device for an even more thorough adult colonization of children's experience.

It would seem to us incumbent on writers who wish to portray the culture of childhood in children's books to consult some of what we would regard as non-adultist accounts of children's and students' everyday lives – for example work by Corsaro (1979, 1981), Davies (1982, 1989), MacKay (1974a), Maynard (1985, 1986) and Speier (1976, 1982). Consulting such work would dramatically highlight the gap between the social world of the child in school-endorsed reading materials of the sort represented in the BR corpus and the social world of the child as these analysts have observed and documented it.

We endorse the suggestion that writers attempt to present events located in other cultures or other periods of history to illuminate what they take to be problems and joys facing children.

This is best done in words that are faithful to the construction of childhood that is appropriate to those other times and places, not through anachronistic or ethnocentric revisions of different social circumstances. Compatible with our remarks above, however, such attempts would need to be presented in open texts, which allow various solutions to problems to be considered by the reader rather than affording one interpretive account. When reading materials attempt to address what are taken to be serious problems facing children, our comments concerning the need for the book to draw attention to its own textualizing process become even more pertinent.

In addition, we see no reason why beginning school books need to portray versions of childhood as relentlessly as they do. The insistence that childhood is a separate and unique category of human existence is itself a historically relative notion: 'In medieval society the idea of childhood did not exist' (Ariés, 1982: 36); and over the centuries adult theorizations about childhood have varied remarkably (De Mause, 1982). In our culture, children can participate in many facets of adult culture, and adults shape and participate in child culture, no matter how distinctly these categories may be defined. The notion of childhood as a distinct form of life permeates much of educational discourse. We have argued that, while such a notion may be benevolent in its intent, its uses are not disinterested. This point parallels our comments above about gender: rather than drawing unproblematically on conventional categories, writers, educators and students can topicalize, question and reassemble them.

In presenting this range of ideas and alternatives, we recognize that texts of the kind we have described in this book may continue to be produced and used widely in classrooms. We have already stated that we regard their peculiarity as written texts as interesting and valuable resources in a programme that may be aimed to teach young children about the practices of literacy. As vehicles for teaching the technical competencies required to be literate, or for teaching about the conventions that apply in certain written genres, they contain peculiar and unique features. Thus, as resources for providing an opportunity for teachers and students to engage in what Heath calls 'literacy events' (1982, 1983), they offer a unique set of problems and possibilities. Heath's advice to researchers that literacy events must 'be interpreted in relation to the larger socio-cultural patterns which they may exemplify or reflect' (1982: 74) can also guide the teacher in the development of a stimulating instructional programme for the teacher and the students, in which the technicalities of literate competencies are embedded in a broader social communicative framework. Such a programme would also challenge the teacher to develop instructional approaches that permit the explicit viewing of textual construction in the context of school learning.

CONCLUSION

Reading and writing are communicative technologies that have come to characterize those cultures that need and wish to exchange ideas and information across time and space. As technologies, they can be seen as enabling historical consciousness and access to knowledge and ways of thinking outside one's own culture, whereby the utterances of different, distant and dead people are made accessible. In this sense, it is the writer whose words can persist and thus travel, and the reader who has potential access to a breadth of information, values and perspectives beyond the knowledge base and orthodoxy embodied in the oral wisdom of the tribe. Equally, reading and writing can be characterized as technologies that systematically privilege some voices and thus mute alternative descriptions of experience (a characterization more fully developed by Street, 1984).

The analyses and the interpretations we have offered in this book may be seen partly as our attempts to document how the potentially enabling functions of literacy can be limited or even reversed by current instructional materials and by the kind of activities that surround those materials in classrooms. That is, the uses to which schooling may put literacy can counter the very consciousness that many educators take to be the richest offering of the written word. On the other hand, we have found in the materials features that could assist in building that consciousness.

Our attention has been focused primarily on the nature of the texts that young children encounter in school, and we have found in those texts a pervasive 'naturalization' of a set of categories for describing the world, in which 'childhood' is most centrally placed. Our analyses of the contents of these early reading books lead us to conclude that, in large part, the process of early literacy instruction is the archetypal context in which school knowledge is forged into the relations between generations. Children's first contacts with school-literate knowledge, as encapsulated in materials and methods, are likely to be crucial for the adoption of attitudes toward the practices and purposes of literacy in and out of school. An awareness of the centrality of these materials in establishing the relations between generations in the school context has substantial implications not only for conducting early literacy instruction but also for understanding the ways in which knowing and knowledge are defined and conveyed in schools: 'What teachers teach is "not knowledge ... [but] preferred discourses", which are inscribed within institutions and everyday practices' (Whitty, 1985, citing Alvarado and Ferguson, 1983).

It is because the BR books apparently recruit the oral-language heritage and everyday experience of child-readers that they could form an equally central part of two contrasting educational projects. On the one hand, if these apparent representations of childhood, language and the social world are treated as natural descriptions, then the books would form part of a thorough-going project of socialization into school culture. This would entail, as we have shown, accepting the transformations of language, childhood and knowledge into the logic and categories of institutional discourse.

Alternatively, if the books are treated as documents of cultural policy, they could form part of a critical educational project in which such transformations are made visible and contestable. This latter project, in sharp contrast to the first, would equip the child-reader with principled and even privileged grounds for informed challenge, and is thereby a route to achieving what literacy, in its broadest and most enabling sense, can offer. Such an approach would also demarcate more clearly boundaries of the teacher's expertise while equipping the teacher with new orders of interest in the task of acquainting novice readers with written text. It is the features we have detailed in this book that make beginning school reading books ready and powerful accomplices in both of these contrasting educational projects.

In this book we have examined one corpus of textual materials to explore the relations between those materials, school practices and the wider cultural context in which the materials are produced and used. Other collections of materials and other records of classroom activities could be similarly studied as documents of literacy as social practice. It is in the belief that current and future theory, practice and research about literacy can be stimulated by careful analysis of the ways in which school-literacy is built that we have undertaken this work.

References

Alvarado, M. and Ferguson, B. (1983) The curriculum, media studies, and discursivity. *Screen*, 24, 20−32.

Anderson, R. C. (1977) The notion of schemata and the educational enterprise. In R. C. Anderson, R. J. Spiro and W. E. Montague (eds), *Schooling and the Acquisition of Knowledge*, Hillsdale, NJ: Erlbaum.

Aries, P. (1982) The discovery of childhood. In C. Jenks (ed.), *The Sociology of Childhood: Essential Readings*, London: Batsford.

Atkinson, J. M. and Heritage, J. (1984) *Structures of Social Action: Studies in Conversation Analysis*. Cambridge: Cambridge University Press.

Baker, C. D. and Freebody, P. (1986) Representations of questioning and answering in children's first school books. *Language in Society*, 15, 451−84.

Baker, C. D. and Freebody, P. (1987) 'Constituting the child' in beginning school reading books. *British Journal of Sociology of Education*, 8, 1, 55−76.

Baker, C. D. and Freebody, P. (1988) Possible worlds and possible people: interpretive challenges in beginning school reading books. *Australian Journal of Reading*, 11, 95−104.

Baker, C. D. and Freebody, P. (1989) Talk around text: constructions of textual and teacher authority in classroom discourse. In S. de Castell, A. Luke and C. Luke (eds), *Language, Authority and Criticism: Readings on the School Textbook*. London: Falmer Press.

Baker, C. D. and Perrott, C. (1988) The news session in infants and primary classrooms. *British Journal of Sociology of Education*, 9, 19−38.

Baker, G. P. and Hacker, P. M. S. (1984) *Language, Sense and Nonsense*. Oxford: Basil Blackwell.

Banfield, A. (1982) *Unspeakable Sentences: Narration and Representation in the Language of Fiction*. Boston, Mass.: Routledge and Kegan Paul.

Baron, J. (1979) Orthographic and word-specific mechanisms in children's reading of words. *Child Development*, 50, 60–72.

Bawden, N. (1976) A dead pig and my father. In G. Fox, G. Hammond, T. Jones, F. Smith and K. Sterck (eds), *Writers, Critics and Children*. London: Heinemann.

Bayley, N. (1956) Individual patterns of development. *Child Development*, 27, 45–74.

Beck, I. (1984) Developing comprehension: the impact of the directed reading lesson. In R. C. Anderson, J. Osborn and R. J. Tierney (eds), *Learning to Read in American Schools: Basal Readers and Content Texts*. Hillsdale, NJ.: Erlbaum.

Beck, I., McKeown, M. G., McCarlin, E. S. and Burkes, A. M. (1979) Instructional dimensions that may affect reading comprehension: examples from two commercial reading programs. Technical report no. 20, Learning Research and Development Center, University of Pittsburgh, Pittsburgh, Pennsylvania.

Beddis, R. (1982) *Places, Resources, and People* (Book 2). Oxford: Oxford University Press.

Bereiter, C. (1986) The reading comprehension lesson: a commentary on Heap's ethnomethodological analysis. *Curriculum Inquiry*, 16, 66–72.

Black, J. K. (1979) Assessing kindergarten children's communicative competence. In O. K. Garnica and M. L. King (eds), *Language, Children and Society: the Effect of Social Factors on Children Learning to Communicate*. Oxford: Pergamon Press.

Bourdieu, P. (1974) The school as a conservative force. In J. Eggleston (ed.), *Contemporary Research in the Sociology of Education*. London: Methuen.

Bourdieu, P. and Passeron, J-C. (1977) *Reproduction in Education, Society and Culture*. London: Sage.

Brewer, W. F. (1980) Literary theory, rhetoric, and stylistics: implications for psychology. In R. J. Spiro, B. C. Bruce and W. F. Brewer (eds), *Theoretical Issues in Reading Comprehension*. Hillsdale, NJ: Erlbaum.

Brewer, W. F. and Lichtenstein, E. H. (1982) Stories are to entertain: a structural-affect theory of stories. *Journal of Pragmatics*, 6, 473–86.

Brown, R. (1973) *A First Language: the Early Stages*. London: Allen and Unwin.

Bruner, J. S. (1959) Learning and thinking. *Harvard Educational Review*, 29, 184–92.

Bruner, J. S. (1966) The growth of mind. In J. F. Rosenblith and W.

Allinsmith (eds), *The Causes of Behavior: Readings in Child Development and Educational Psychology*, 2nd edn. Boston, Mass.: Allyn and Bacon, Inc.

Bryant, P. and Impey, L. (1986) The similarities between normal readers and developmental and acquired dyslexics. *Cognition*, 24, 121–37.

Byrne, B. (1986) Learning to read the first few items: evidence of a nonanalytic acquisition procedure in adults and children. Conference on Early Reading, Center for Cognitive Science, University of Texas, Austin.

Carroll, J. B., Davies, P. and Richman, B. (1971) *The American Heritage Word Frequency Book*. Boston, Mass.: Houghton Mifflin.

Cazden, C. B. (1981) Social context of learning to read. In J. T. Guthrie (ed.), *Comprehension and Teaching: Research Reviews*. Newark, Del.: International Reading Association.

Chafe, W. L. (1985) Linguistic differences produced by differences between speaking and writing. In D. R. Olson, N. Torrance and A. Hildyard (eds), *Literacy, Language and Learning*. Cambridge: Cambridge University Press.

Christie, F. (1985) Curriculum genres: towards a description of the construction of knowledge in schools. Working Conference on Interaction of Spoken and Written Language in Educational Settings. Armidale College of Advanced Education, Armidale, New South Wales.

Cicourel, A. V. (1972) Cross modal communication: the representational context of sociolinguistic information processing. In R. Shuy (ed.), *Monograph Series on Language and Linguistics*, 23rd annual round table. Washington: Georgetown University Press.

Cicourel, A. V. (1974) The acquisition of social structure: toward a developmental sociology of language and meaning. In J. D. Douglas (ed.), *Understanding Everyday Life*, Chicago: Aldine.

Corsaro, W. (1979) "We're friends, right?": children's use of access rituals in a nursery school. *Language in Society*, 8, 315–36.

Corsaro, W. (1981) Entering the child's world – research strategies for field entry and data collection in a preschool setting. In J. L. Green and C. Wallatt (eds), *Ethnography and Language in Educational Settings*, Norwood, NJ: Ablex.

Davies, B. (1982) *Life in the Classroom and Playground: the Accounts of Primary School Children*. London: Routledge and Kegan Paul.

Davies, B. (1983) The role pupils play in the social construction of classroom order. *British Journal of Sociology of Education*, 4, 55–69.

Davies, B. (1987) The accomplishment of genderedness in pre-school children. In A. Pollard (ed.), *Children and their Primary Schools*, London: Falmer Press.

Davies, B. (1989) *Frogs and Snails and Feminist Tales: Pre-School Children and Gender*. Sydney: Allen and Unwin.

De Mause, L. (1982) The evolution of childhood. In C. Jenks (ed.), *The Sociology of Childhood: Essential Readings*, London: Batsford.

Eco, U. (1979) *The Role of the Reader*. Bloomington: Indiana University Press.

Edwards, A. D. (1980) Patterns of power and authority in classroom talk. In P. Woods (ed.), *Teacher Strategies: Explorations in the Sociology of the School*, London: Croom Helm.

Edwards, A. D. (1981) Analysing classroom talk. In P. French and M. MacLure (eds), *Adult—Child Conversation*, London: Croom Helm.

Ehri, L. (1979) Linguistic insight: threshold of reading acquisition. In T. G. Waller and G. E. MacKinnon (eds), *Reading Research: Advances in Theory and Practice*, vol. 1, New York: Academic Press.

Ferreiro, E. and Teberosky, A. (1982) *Literacy Before Schooling*. London: Heinemann.

Fishman, P. (1978) Interaction: the work women do. *Social Problems*, 25, 397—406.

Freebody, P. (1983) Narrative discourse: stimulating involvement and comprehension. In N. Stewart-Dore and P. van Homrigh (eds), *Reading: Techniques, Materials, and Organization*, Brisbane: Australian Reading Association.

Freebody, P. (1984) Context, language, and strategies in learning from text. In P. Kidston and D. Patullo (eds), *Reading and Writing: Implications for Teaching*, Brisbane: Australian Reading Association.

Freebody, P. and Baker, C. D. (1985) Children's first school books: introductions to the culture of literacy. *Harvard Educational Review*, 55, 381—98.

Freebody, P. and Baker, C. D. (1987) The construction and operation of gender in children's first school books. In A. Pauwels (ed.), *Women and Language in Australian and New Zealand Society*, Sydney: Australian Professional Publications.

Freebody, P., Baker, C. D. and Gay, J. (1987) The use of expressive words in children's first school books. *Language and Communication*, 7, 25—38.

Freund, J. (1969) *The Sociology of Max Weber*. New York: Vintage Books.

Garfinkel, H. (1967) *Studies in Ethnomethodology*. New Jersey: Prentice-Hall.

Garnica, O. K. (1979) The boys have the muscles and the girls have the sexy legs: adult—child speech and the use of generic person labels. In O. K. Garnica and M. L. King (eds), *Language, Children and Society: the Effect of Social Factors on Children Learning to Communicate*, Oxford: Pergamon Press.

Gee, J. P. (1985) The narrativization of experience in the oral style. *Journal of Education*, 167, 9—35.

Gilbert, P. (1987) Post reader-response: the deconstructive critique. In B. Corcoran and E. Evans (eds), *Readers, Texts, Teachers*, Upper Montclair, NJ: Boynton/Cook.

Goldman, S. R. (1985) Inferential reasoning in and about narrative texts. In A. C. Graesser and J. B. Black (eds), *The Psychology of Questions*, Hillsdale, NJ: Erlbaum.

Green, J. L., Harker, J. O. and Golden, J. (1987) Lesson construction: differing views. In G. Noblit and W. Pink (eds), *Schooling in Social Context: Qualitative Studies*, Norwood, NJ: Ablex.

Grice, H. P. (1975) Logic and conversation. In P. Cole and J. L. Morgan (eds), *Syntax and Semantics*, vol. 3, *Speech Acts*, New York: Seminar Press.

Hall, N. (1986) *The Emergence of Literacy*. London: Edward Arnold.

Hall, W. S. and Guthrie, L. F. (1980) On the dialect question and reading. In R. J. Spiro, B. C. Bruce and W. F. Brewer (eds), *Theoretical Issues in Reading Comprehension*, Hillsdale, NJ: Erlbaum.

Hall, W. S. and Nagy, W. E. (1984) *Spoken Words: Effects of Situation and Social Group on Word Usage and Frequency*. Hillsdale, NJ: Erlbaum.

Halliday, M. A. K. (1980) *Spoken and Written Language*. Geelong, Victoria: Deakin University Press.

Hammersley, M. (1977) School learning: the cultural resources required by pupils to answer a teacher's question. In P. Woods and M. Hammersley (eds), *School Experience: Explorations in the Sociology of Education*, London: Croom Helm.

Hart, N. (1974) *Theoretical Background, Procedures Used, and a Partial Analysis of Five-and-a-half Year Old Children's Language* (Research report no. 1). Brisbane: Mt Gravatt Teachers' College.

Havelock, E. A. (1976) *Origins of Western Literacy*. Monograph Series Number 14, Ontario Institute for Studies in Education, Toronto.

Heap, J. L. (1982) The social organization of reading assessment: reasons for eclecticism. In G. C. F. Payne and E. C. Cuff (eds), *Doing Teaching: the Practical Management of Classrooms*. London: Batsford.

Heap, J. L. (1985) Discourse in the production of classroom knowledge: reading lessons. *Curriculum Inquiry*, 15, 245—79.

Heap, J. L. (1986) Cultural logic and schema theory: a reply to Bereiter. *Curriculum Inquiry*, 16, 73—86.

Heap, J. L. (1987) Reading as cultural activities: enabling and reflective texts. Unpublished paper, Ontario Institute for Studies in Education, Toronto.

Heap, J. L. (forthcoming) Applied ethnomethodology: looking for the local rationality of reading activities. *Human Studies*.

Heath, S. B. (1982) What no bedtime story means: narrative skills at home and school. *Language in Society*, 11, 49–76.

Heath, S. B. (1983) *Ways with Words*. Cambridge: Cambridge University Press.

Hildyard, A. and Olson, D. R. (1978) Literacy and the specialization of language. Unpublished manuscript, Ontario Institute for Studies in Education, Toronto.

Hoffman, M. (1981) Children's reading and social values. In N. Mercer (ed.), *Language in School and Community*, London: Edward Arnold.

Hunsberger, M. (forthcoming) Students and textbooks: which is to be master? *Phenomenology* + Pedagogy.

Jackson, S. (1982) *Childhood and Sexuality*. Oxford: Basil Blackwell.

Jenks, C. (1982) Introduction: constituting the child. In C. Jenks (ed.), *The Sociology of Childhood: Essential Readings*, London: Batsford.

Kantor, R. N. (1978) Anomaly, inconsiderateness, and linguistic competence. In D. Lance and D. Gulstad (eds), *Papers from the 1977 Mid-American Linguistics Conference*, Columbia: University of Missouri.

Klare, G. R. (1975) Assessing readability. *Reading Research Quarterly*, 10, 62–102.

Luke, A. (1987a) Making Dick and Jane: historical genesis of the modern basal reader. *Teachers College Record*, 89, 91–116.

Luke, A. (1987b) Open and closed texts: a theoretical model for the critical analysis of curricular narratives. Unpublished manuscript, James Cook University, Townsville, Queensland.

Luke, A. (1988a) *Literacy, Textbooks and Ideology*. London: Falmer Press.

Luke, A. (1988b) Functional literacy in the classroom. *Australian Journal of Reading*, 11, 4–10.

Luke, A., de Castell, S. and Luke, C. (1983) Beyond criticism: the authority of the school text. *Curriculum Inquiry*, 13, 111–27.

McClelland, J. L. and Rumelhart, D. E. (1981) An interactive activation model of context effects in letter perception. part 1: An account of basic findings. *Psychological Review*, 88, 375–407.

McDermott, R. P. (1976) Kids make sense: an ethnographic account of the interactional management of success and failure in one first grade classroom. Unpublished doctoral dissertation, Stanford University, California.

McHoul, A. W. (1978) The organization of turns at formal talk in the classroom. *Language in Society*, 7, 183–213.

McHoul, A. W. (1982) *Telling How Texts Talk: Essays on Reading and Ethnomethodology*. London: Routledge and Kegan Paul.

MacKay, R. (1974a) Conceptions of children and models of socialization. In R. Turner (ed.), *Ethnomethodology*, Harmondsworth: Penguin.

MacKay, R. (1974b) Standardized tests: objective/objectified measures of 'competence'. In A. V. Cicourel, K. H. Jennings, S. H. M. Jennings K. C. W. Leiter, R. MacKay, H. Mehan, and D. R. Roth, *Language Use and School Performance*, New York: Academic Press.

McKeown, G. P. (1986) Assessment of the match between oral discourse and literate language: a comparison of the talk of Aboriginal and non-Aboriginal children and the texts they read in school. Unpublished thesis, University of New England, New South Wales.

McKeown, G. P. and Freebody, P. (1988) The language of aboriginal and non-aboriginal children and the texts they encounter in schools. *Australian Journal of Reading*, 11, 115–26.

MacLure, M. and French, P. (1980) Routes to right answers: on pupils' strategies for answering teachers' questions. In P. Woods (ed.), *Pupil Strategies: Explorations in the Sociology of the School*, London: Croom Helm.

MacLure, M. and French, P. (1981) A comparison of talk at home and at school. In G. Wells, *Learning through Interaction*, Cambridge: Cambridge University Press.

Maynard, D. W. (1985) On the functions of social conflict among children. *American Sociological Review*, 50, 207–23.

Maynard, D. W. (1986) Offering and soliciting collaboration in multi-party disputes among children (and other humans). *Human Studies*, 9, 261–285.

Mehan, H. (1974) Accomplishing classroom lessons. In A. V. Cicourel, K. H. Jennings, S. H. M. Jennings, K. C. W. Leiter, R. MacKay, H. Mehan and D. R. Roth, *Language Use and School Performance*, New York: Academic Press.

Mehan, H. (1979) *Learning Lessons: Social Organization in the Classroom*. Cambridge, Mass.: Harvard University Press.

Mercer, J. (1975) *The Other Half: Women in Australian Society*. Harmondsworth: Penguin.

Michaels, S. (1981) "Sharing time": children's narrative styles and differential access to literacy. *Language in Society*, 10, 423–42.

Michaels, S. (1985) Hearing the connections in children's oral and written discourse. *Journal of Education*, 167, 36–56.

Michaels, S. (1987) Text and context: a new approach to the study of classroom writing. *Discourse Processes*, 10, 321–46.

Mikulecky, L. (1982) Job literacy: the relationship between school preparation and workplace actuality. *Reading Research Quarterly*, 17, 400–19.

Mishler, E. G. (1976) Conversational competence among first graders. Conference on Language, Children and Society, Ohio State University, Columbus.

Mulkay, M. (1985) *The Word and the World: Explorations in the Form of Sociological Analysis.* London: Allen and Unwin.

Murdoch, P. (1974) *Duyfken and the First Discoveries of Australia.* Sydney: Antipodean Press.

Ninio, A. and Bruner, J. S. (1978) The achievement and antecedents of labelling. *Journal of Child Language*, 5, 1–14.

Olson, D. R. (1977a) From utterance to text: the bias of language in speech and writing. *Harvard Educational Review*, 47, 257–81.

Olson, D. R. (1977b) The languages of instruction: the literate bias of schooling. In R. C. Anderson, R. J. Spiro and W. E. Montague (eds), *Schooling and the Acquisition of Knowledge.* Hillsdale, NJ: Erlbaum.

Olson, D. R. (1980) On the language and authority of textbooks. *Journal of Communication*, 30, 186–96.

Olson, D. R. (1982) What is said and what is meant in speech and writing. *Visible Language*, 16, 151–61.

Olson, D. R. (1983) Sources of authority in the language of the school: a response to "Beyond Criticism". *Curriculum Inquiry*, 3, 129–30.

Olson, D. R. (1985) "See! Jumping!": some oral language antecedents of literacy. In H. Goelman, A. Oberg, and F. Smith (eds), *Awakening to Literacy*, London: Heinemann.

Olson, D. R. and Astington, J. W. (1986) Talking about text: how literacy contributes to thought. Boston University Conference on Language Development, Boston, Mass.

Ong, W. (1958/1983) *Ramus, Method and the Decay of Dialogue.* Cambridge, Mass.: Harvard University Press.

Ong, W. (1982) *Orality and Literacy.* London: Methuen.

Oxford English Dictionary (1971) Compact Edition. London: Oxford University Press.

Ozolins, U. (1981) Victorian HSC examiners' reports: a study of cultural capital. In H. Bannister and L. Johnson (eds), *Melbourne Working Papers 1981*, Parkville, Victoria: Sociology Research Group in Cultural and Educational Studies.

Pauwels, A. (1984) Research into gender differences in language: a feminist approach. In R. Burns and B. Sheehan (eds), *Women and Education.* Proceedings of the Twelfth Annual Conference of the Australian and New Zealand Comparative and International Education Society, La Trobe University, Victoria, Australia.

Payne, G. and Hustler, D. (1980) Teaching the class: the practical management of a cohort. *British Journal of Sociology of Education*, 1, 49–66.

Payne, G. and Ridge, E. (1985) "Let them talk": an alternative approach to language development in the infant school. In G. C. F. Payne and E. C. Cuff (eds), *Crisis in the Curriculum*, London: Croom Helm.

Pearson, P. D. and Johnson, D. D. (1978) *Teaching Reading Comprehension*. New York: Holt, Rinehart and Winston.

Pearson, P. D. and Tierney, R. J. (1984) On becoming a thoughtful reader: learning to read like a writer. In A. C. Purves and O. Niles (eds), *Becoming Readers in a Complex Society*. 83rd Yearbook of the National Society for the Study of Education. Chicago: NSSE.

Pellegrini, A. D., Brody, G. H and Stoneman, Z. (1987) Children's conversational competence with their parents. *Discourse Processes*, 10, 93–106.

Perera, K. (1984) *Children's Writing and Reading: Analysing Classroom Language*. Oxford: Basil Blackwell.

Phillips, T. (1983) Now you see it, now you don't. *English in Education*, 17, 32–41.

Romaine, S. (1984) *The Language of Children and Adolescents: the Acquisition of Communicative Competence*. Oxford: Basil Blackwell.

Rose, J. (1985) State and language: *Peter Pan* as written for the child. In C. Steedman, C. Urwin and V. Walkerdine (eds), *Language, Gender and Childhood*, London: Routledge and Kegan Paul.

Rosen, H. (1972) The language of textbooks. In A. Cashdan and E. Grugeon (eds), *Language in Education*, London: Routledge and Kegan Paul.

Rubin, A. A. (1980) A theoretical taxonomy of the differences between oral and written language. In R. J. Spiro, B. C. Bruce and W. F. Brewer (eds), *Theoretical Issues in Reading Comprehension*. Hillsdale, NJ: Erlbaum.

Rumelhart, D. E. (1977) Toward an interactive model of reading. In S. Dornic (ed.), *Attention and Performance* IV. Hillsdale, NJ: Erlbaum.

Sacks, H. (1974) On the analysability of stories by children. In R. Turner (ed.), *Ethnomethodology*. Harmondsworth: Penguin.

Schallert, D. L. (1982) The significance of knowledge: a synthesis of research related to schema theory. In W. Otto and S. White (eds), *Reading Expository Material*, New York: Academic Press.

Schegloff, E. A. (1968) Sequencing in conversational openings. *American Anthropologist*, 70, 1075–95.

Schegloff, E. A. (1984) On questions and ambiguities in conversation. In J. M. Atkinson and J. Heritage (eds), *Structures of Social Action: Studies in Conversation Analysis*, Cambridge: Cambridge University Press.

Speier, M. (1976) The child as conversationalist: some culture contact features of conversational interactions between adults and children. In M. Hammersley and P. Woods (eds), *The Process of Schooling*, London: Routledge and Kegan Paul.

Speier, M. (1982) The everyday world of the child. In C. Jenks (ed.), *The Sociology of Childhood: Essential Readings*. London: Batsford.

Stewig, J. W. and Higgs, M. (1973) Girls grow up to be mommies: a study of sexism in children's literature. *School Library Journal*, 98, 236−41.

Street, B. V. (1984) *Literacy in Theory and Practice*. Cambridge: Cambridge University Press.

Tannen, D. (1982) The oral/literate continuum in discourse. In D. Tannen (ed.), *Spoken and Written Language: Exploring Orality and Literacy*, Norwood, NJ: Ablex.

Tannen, D. (1985) Relative focus on involvement in oral and written discourse. In D. R. Olson, N. Torrance and A. Hildyard (eds), *Literacy, Language and Learning*. Cambridge: Cambridge University Press.

Twer, S. (1972) Tactics for determining persons' resources for depicting, contriving and describing behavioural episodes. In D. Sudnow (ed.), *Studies in Social Interaction*, New York: The Free Press.

Walker, S. (1981) Teacher−pupil question−answer sequences: some problems of analysis. In L. Barton and S. Walker (eds), *Schools, Teachers and Teaching*, Sussex: Falmer.

Walton, C. (1986) Aboriginal children learning to write: Kriol and Walpiri speakers in an English-speaking classroom. Unpublished thesis, University of New England, New South Wales.

Wells, G. (1979) Variation in child language. In P. Fletcher and M. Garman (eds), *Language Acquisition*, Cambridge: Cambridge University Press.

Wells, G. (1981) *Learning through Interaction: the Study of Language Development*. Cambridge: Cambridge University Press.

Wells, G. (1985a) *Language Development in the Pre-school Years*. Cambridge: Cambridge University Press.

Wells, G. (1985b) Preschool literacy-related activities and success in school. In D. R. Olson, N. Torrance and A. Hildyard (eds), *Literacy, Language and Learning*, Cambridge: Cambridge University Press.

Wells, G. and Montgomery, M. (1981) Adult−child interaction at home and at school. In P. French and M. MacLure (eds), *Adult−Child Conversation*, London: Croom Helm.

Whitty, G. (1985) *Sociology and School Knowledge*. London: Methuen.

Widdowson, J. (1976) The language of the child culture: pattern and tradition in language acquisition and socialization. In S. Rogers (ed.), *They Don't Speak Our Language: Essays on the Language World of Children and Adolescents*, London: Edward Arnold.

Willes, M. J. (1983) *Children into Pupils*. London: Routledge and Kegan Paul.

Willows, D. M., Barwick, D. and Hayvren, M. (1981) The content of school readers. In G. E. MacKinnon and T. G. Walker (eds), *Reading Research: Advances in Theory and Practice*, vol. 2, New York: Academic Press.

Women on Words and Images. (1972) *Dick and Jane as Victims: Sex Stereotyping in Children's Readers*. Princeton, NJ: National Organisation for Women.

Wootton, A. J. (1981a) Children's use of address terms. In P. French and M. MacLure (eds), *Adult—Child Conversation*, London: Croom Helm.

Wootton, A. J. (1981b) The management of grantings and rejections by parents in request sequences. *Semiotica*, 37, 59—89.

Wootton, A. J. (1981c) Two request forms of four year olds. *Journal of Pragmatics*, 5, 511—23.

Materials Reference List

Jacaranda Press (1967, 1970, 1980) Endeavour reading programme. Milton, Qld: Jacaranda.

Jacaranda Press (1970) Stage 1 library. Milton, Qld: Jacaranda.

Jacaranda Press (1982) Expressways: Levels 1, 2, 3. Milton, Qld: Jacaranda.

Mount Gravatt Reading Series (1977) Level 1. Brisbane, Qld: Addison–Wesley.

Murray, W. (1964, 1965) The Ladybird Key Words reading scheme. Loughborough: Wills and Hepworth Ltd.

New South Wales Department of Education (1954) Primary readers. Sydney: Department of Education Press.

Randell, B. (1966) Methuen caption books. London: Methuen.

Rasmussen, D. and Goldberg, L. (1973) Basic reading series. North Ryde, NSW: Science Research Associates.

Reading Rigby (1983) Get Ready books, sets A, B, C. Brisbane: Qld: Rigby Education.

Schools Council (1970) Breakthrough to Literacy: Schools Council Programme. London: Longman.

Schools Publication Branch, Department of Education, New Zealand (1966) Ready to Read. London: Methuen.

Young Australia Language Development Scheme (1966, 1967) Basic readers. Melbourne, Vic.: Thomas Nelson.

Young Australia Series (1980) Basic reader 1. Melbourne, Vic.: Thomas Nelson.

Appendix 1

Vocabulary Contents of the Beginning Reading Corpus

Some readers may find it informative and useful to have access to a summary of the vocabulary contents of the entire Beginning Reading corpus. While table 2.3 provides a listing of the 50 most frequent words in the corpus, this appendix reports all of the distinct words in the corpus, listed in alphabetical order to make it easy to locate particular items. Included here is the raw frequency (F) and frequency per thousand words of running text (F/1,000) for each distinct word in the corpus.* Since this book reports only a sample of the vocabulary analyses that could be performed on the BR corpus, readers may wish to consult this appendix to examine further some of our claims or to pursue other aspects of the nature of early reading vocabulary.

---

* Computational linguists have employed a range of indices of word frequency at varying degrees of technicality and with differing theoretical/mathematical assumptions. Carroll, Davies and Richman (1971), for instance, argued that the distribution of distinct word types in their corpus conformed closely to a log-normal model. They developed a rescaled logarithmic index (SFI) to indicate the frequency of an item with respect to a theoretical lognormal population curve. This index can readily be computed from the values contained in this appendix, should the reader wish to make direct comparisons, by using the formula SFI = 10 (log [raw frequency/83,838] + 10). Such comparisons are not inappropriate given that the BR corpus distribution also closely approximates a lognormal model.

WORD	F	F/1,000	WORD	F	F/1,000	WORD	F	F/1,000
A	2,360	28.15	AS	175	2.09	BEATEN	1	0.01
ABOARD	3	0.04	ASK	11	0.13	BEATER	6	0.07
ABOUT	112	1.34	ASKED	144	1.72	BEATING	1	0.01
ABOVE	2	0.02	ASKS	33	0.39	BEAUTIFUL	10	0.12
ABRACADABRA	1	0.01	ASLEEP	7	0.08	BEAUTY	1	0.01
ABSURD	1	0.01	ASTRIDE	1	0.01	BEAVER	1	0.01
ACROSS	12	0.14	AT	615	7.34	BECAUSE	12	0.14
ACT	6	0.07	ATE	8	0.10	BECKONED	1	0.01
AEROPLANE	2	0.02	ATTIC	2	0.02	BECOME	1	0.01
AEROPLANES	1	0.01	AUNTIE	12	0.14	BED	133	1.59
AFRAID	7	0.08	AUNTY	3	0.04	BED'S	1	0.01
AFTER	137	1.63	AUSTRALIAN	1	0.01	BEDS	5	0.06
AFTERNOON	35	0.42	AWAKE	3	0.04	BEDTIME	14	0.17
AGAIN	112	1.34	AWAY	214	2.55	BEE	23	0.27
AGAINST	1	0.01	AWFUL	2	0.02	BEEHIVES	1	0.01
AGO	2	0.02	AXE	1	0.01	BEEN	28	0.33
AGREED	1	0.01	B	9	0.11	BEES	13	0.16
AIR	2	0.02	BABY	89	1.06	BEETLE	2	0.02
AIRPORT	3	0.04	BACK	94	1.12	BEFORE	31	0.37
AL	14	0.17	BACKWARDS	1	0.01	BEG	2	0.02
ALAN	7	0.08	BACON	1	0.01	BEGAN	52	0.62
ALAN'S	3	0.04	BAD	75	0.89	BEGINS	1	0.01
ALIVE	5	0.06	BAG	84	1.00	BEHIND	1	0.01
ALL	299	3.57	BAGS	5	0.06	BEING	2	0.02
ALLIGATORS	1	0.01	BAKE	4	0.05	BELIEVE	1	0.01
ALMOND	1	0.01	BAKED	2	0.02	BELL	4	0.05
ALONE	2	0.02	BAKER	6	0.07	BELLOWED	1	0.01
ALONG	58	0.69	BAKER'S	2	0.02	BELLS	3	0.04
ALWAYS	5	0.06	BAKING	1	0.01	BEN	17	0.20

Word	Count	Freq	Word	Count	Freq	Word	Count	Freq
AM	244	2.91	BALL	113	1.35	BEN'S	2	0.02
AMBULANCE	1	0.01	BALLOON	12	0.14	BEND	1	0.01
AN	80	0.95	BALLOONS	1	0.01	BENT	1	0.01
AND	2,362	28.17	BAM	10	0.12	BERRIES	1	0.01
ANDREW	77	0.92	BANANA	3	0.04	BESIDE	10	0.12
ANDREW'S	12	0.14	BANANAS	8	0.10	BESS	10	0.12
ANDY	16	0.19	BAND	9	0.11	BEST	43	0.51
ANGEL	1	0.01	BANG	22	0.26	BET	1	0.01
ANGELS	2	0.02	BANK	4	0.05	BETTER	22	0.26
ANGRY	1	0.01	BARE	5	0.06	BETTY	12	0.14
ANIMAL	4	0.05	BARK	2	0.02	BETTY'S	1	0.01
ANIMALS	31	0.37	BARKED	18	0.21	BETWEEN	1	0.01
ANN	12	0.14	BARKING	1	0.01	BICYCLE	2	0.02
ANNA	10	0.12	BARKS	4	0.05	BICYCLES	1	0.01
ANOTHER	8	0.10	BARLEY	1	0.01	BIG	564	6.73
ANSWERED	21	0.25	BASKET	15	0.18	BIGGER	25	0.30
ANTONIO	2	0.02	BASKETS	3	0.04	BIGGEST	1	0.01
ANY	12	0.14	BAT	20	0.24	BIKE	8	0.10
ANYONE	10	0.12	BATH	3	0.04	BIKES	1	0.01
ANYTHING	9	0.11	BATHROOM	2	0.02	BILL	52	0.62
ANYWHERE	3	0.04	BATTERING	1	0.01	BILLY	20	0.24
APPLE	23	0.27	BATTLE	1	0.01	BIM	6	0.07
APPLE-PIE	1	0.01	BE	199	2.37	BIMBO	6	0.07
APPLES	62	0.74	BEACH	7	0.08	BIN	17	0.20
ARE	585	6.98	BEAK	1	0.01	BIRD	65	0.78
AREN'T	1	0.01	BEANS	2	0.02	BIRDS	38	0.45
ARM	2	0.02	BEAR	150	1.79	BIRDS'	1	0.01
ARMS	5	0.06	BEAR'S	1	0.01	BIRTHDAY	32	0.38
AROUND	18	0.21	BEARS	20	0.24	BISCUITS	8	0.10
ART	1	0.01	BEARS'	1	0.01	BIT	28	0.33
ARTICHOKE	1	0.01	BEAT	8	0.10	BITE	4	0.05

WORD	F	F/1,000	WORD	F	F/1,000	WORD	F	F/1,000
BITS	2	0.02	BRIGHTENED	1	0.01	CAMEL	1	0.01
BLACK	47	0.56	BRING	15	0.18	CAMP	1	0.01
BLACKIE	14	0.17	BRINGING	1	0.01	CAN	933	11.13
BLACKY	20	0.24	BROKE	3	0.04	CAN'T	32	0.38
BLADE	1	0.01	BROOM	1	0.01	CANDLES	2	0.02
BLANKET	1	0.01	BROTHER	19	0.23	CANDLESTICK	1	0.01
BLANKET'S	1	0.01	BROW	1	0.01	CANNOT	138	1.65
BLEW	8	0.10	BROWN	110	1.31	CANS	11	0.13
BLOCK	2	0.02	BROWN'S	8	0.10	CAP	27	0.32
BLOCKS	1	0.01	BRUCE	15	0.18	CAPE	1	0.01
BLOOD	1	0.01	BRUCE'S	2	0.02	CAPER	2	0.02
BLOW	38	0.45	BRUSH	3	0.04	CAPS	5	0.06
BLOWING	2	0.02	BUBBLE	5	0.06	CAR	174	2.08
BLOWN	1	0.01	BUBBLES	3	0.04	CARAVAN	15	0.18
BLOWS	2	0.02	BUCKET	10	0.12	CARD	7	0.08
BLUE	46	0.55	BUCKLE	1	0.01	CARDBOARD	1	0.01
BLUEBIRD	5	0.06	BUD	1	0.01	CARDS	2	0.02
BOAT	156	1.86	BUDGIE	2	0.02	CARE	1	0.01
BOATS	63	0.75	BUFFALO	1	0.01	CAROLS	1	0.01
BOB	58	0.69	BUG	42	0.50	CARRIAGES	1	0.01
BOB'S	3	0.04	BUGS	2	0.02	CARRIED	1	0.01
BOBBING	1	0.01	BUILD	9	0.11	CARROT	3	0.04
BOG	1	0.01	BUILDING	2	0.02	CARROTS	14	0.17
BONE	7	0.08	BULLDOZERS	1	0.01	CARRY	12	0.14
BONES	2	0.02	BUMBLE	1	0.01	CARS	13	0.16
BOO	2	0.02	BUMP	31	0.37	CART	16	0.19
BOOK	26	0.31	BUMPED	5	0.06	CARTONS	1	0.01
BOOKS	8	0.10	BUMPITY	30	0.36	CASE	1	0.01
BOOM	3	0.04	BUMPS	2	0.02	CASTLE	10	0.12

Word	Count	Freq	Word	Count	Freq	Word	Count	Freq
BOTTLE	2	0.02	BUMPY	3	0.04	CAT	224	2.67
BOTTLES	1	0.01	BUNNY	47	0.56	CAT'S	1	0.01
BOUGH	1	0.01	BURNING	1	0.01	CATCH	62	0.74
BOUNCE	1	0.01	BURNT	2	0.02	CATERPILLAR	2	0.02
BOUNCING	1	0.01	BURROWING	1	0.01	CATS	10	0.12
BOW	1	0.01	BURY	1	0.01	CAUGHT	1	0.01
BOWED	2	0.02	BUS	169	2.02	CAVE	3	0.04
BOWL	31	0.37	BUSES	3	0.04	CAVES	1	0.01
BOX	109	1.30	BUSH	20	0.24	CHAINS	1	0.01
BOXER	35	0.42	BUSTLE	1	0.01	CHAIR	28	0.33
BOXES	12	0.14	BUSY	3	0.04	CHAIRS	10	0.12
BOY	141	1.68	BUT	192	2.29	CHANGE	1	0.01
BOY'S	4	0.05	BUTCHER	1	0.01	CHANGING	1	0.01
BOYS	101	1.20	BUTTER	1	0.01	CHARLES	1	0.01
BRANCH	2	0.02	BUTTERFLY	3	0.04	CHARLEY	3	0.04
BRANCHES	3	0.04	BUY	8	0.10	CHASES	1	0.01
BRAND	1	0.01	BUZZ	27	0.32	CHEER	1	0.01
BRAVE	5	0.06	BUZZING	2	0.02	CHEESE	6	0.07
BRAY	1	0.01	BY	121	1.44	CHEESES	1	0.01
BREAD	13	0.16	C	4	0.05	CHERRIES	1	0.01
BREAK	1	0.01	CAB	10	0.12	CHEST	1	0.01
BREAKFAST	7	0.08	CAGE	2	0.02	CHESTER	1	0.01
BREAKFAST'S	1	0.01	CAGES	1	0.01	CHICKEN	1	0.01
BREAKS	1	0.01	CAKE	42	0.50	CHICKENS	1	0.01
BREEZE	1	0.01	CAKES	36	0.43	CHICKS	3	0.04
BRIAN	7	0.08	CALF	25	0.30	CHIEF	1	0.01
BRICK	1	0.01	CALF'S	1	0.01	CHILDREN	293	3.49
BRICKS	4	0.05	CALL	13	0.16	CHILDREN'S	1	0.01
BRIDE	1	0.01	CALLED	101	1.20	CHIMNEY	6	0.07
BRIDGE	13	0.16	CALLING	2	0.02	CHIMNEY-BOX	3	0.04
BRIGHT	7	0.08	CAME	128	1.53	CHIMPANZEE	1	0.01

WORD	F	F/1,000	WORD	F	F/1,000	WORD	F	F/1,000
CHIN	12	0.14	COSTUMES	1	0.01	DAN	82	0.98
CHINNY	5	0.06	COSY	1	0.01	DANCE	17	0.20
CHIPS	2	0.02	COT	5	0.06	DANCED	5	0.06
CHOCOLATE	7	0.08	COULD	61	0.73	DANCING	6	0.07
CHOPS	4	0.05	COULDN'T	2	0.02	DANGER	24	0.29
CHRISTMAS	20	0.24	COUNT	2	0.02	DARK	3	0.04
CHUG	6	0.07	COUNTER	1	0.01	DAUGHTER	4	0.05
CHUNK	1	0.01	COUNTRY	6	0.07	DAVID	60	0.72
CIRCUS	53	0.63	COURSE	6	0.07	DAVID'S	1	0.01
CLAMOURING	1	0.01	COURTYARD	1	0.01	DAVIS	7	0.08
CLANG	6	0.07	COUSIN	7	0.08	DAY	127	1.51
CLAP	1	0.01	COUSINS	1	0.01	DAYS	6	0.07
CLAPPED	6	0.07	COVERED	1	0.01	DEAD	2	0.02
CLASS	11	0.13	COW	58	0.69	DEAL	1	0.01
CLATTERING	1	0.01	COW'S	1	0.01	DEAN	2	0.02
CLAWING	1	0.01	COWBOY	2	0.02	DEAN'S	1	0.01
CLAWS	1	0.01	COWBOYS	1	0.01	DEAR	31	0.37
CLEAN	16	0.19	COWS	42	0.50	DEARLY	1	0.01
CLEANED	5	0.06	CRAB	2	0.02	DEEDS	1	0.01
CLEANER	4	0.05	CRACKING	1	0.01	DEEP	1	0.01
CLEAR	1	0.01	CRACKLES	5	0.06	DELICATESSEN	1	0.01
CLEVER	26	0.31	CRADLE	3	0.04	DELL	3	0.04
CLIFFS	2	0.02	CRANE	1	0.01	DEN	15	0.18
CLIMB	5	0.06	CRASH	25	0.30	DICKORY	3	0.04
CLIMBED	2	0.02	CRASHED	4	0.05	DICKY	1	0.01
CLIMBING	1	0.01	CRASHES	1	0.01	DID	185	2.21
CLIMBS	2	0.02	CRAWL	4	0.05	DIDDLE	8	0.10
CLOCK	3	0.04	CRAWLED	1	0.01	DIDN'T	12	0.14
CLOSE	3	0.04	CREAM	9	0.11	DIE	7	0.08

Word	Count	Freq	Word	Count	Freq	Word	Count	Freq
CLOSER	?	0.01	CREATURES	3	0.04	DIG	25	0.30
CLOTHES	3	0.04	CREEK	1	0.01	DIGGER	57	0.68
CLOUD	3	0.04	CREEP	15	0.18	DILLAR	1	0.01
CLOUDS	3	0.04	CRIED	34	0.41	DINNER	3	0.04
CLOUT	1	0.01	CRIES	1	0.01	DINOSAUR	2	0.02
CLOVER	2	0.02	CROCODILE	1	0.01	DIP	9	0.11
CLOWN	36	0.43	CROSS	1	0.01	DISAPPOINTED	1	0.01
CLOWN'S	5	0.06	CROSSING	2	0.02	DISH	11	0.13
CLOWNS	4	0.05	CROW	1	0.01	DISTANCE	1	0.01
COAT	27	0.32	CROWN	2	0.02	DITCHES	2	0.02
COATS	1	0.01	CRUSHES	1	0.01	DIVE	1	0.01
COBWEB	6	0.07	CRY	11	0.13	DO	308	3.67
COCOA	1	0.01	CRYING	8	0.10	DOCK	3	0.04
COCONUT	1	0.01	CRYSTALS	1	0.01	DOCTOR	6	0.07
COD	2	0.02	CUB	17	0.20	DOCTORS	3	0.04
COLD	8	0.10	CUB'S	1	0.01	DOES	19	0.23
COLIN	1	0.01	CUDDLED	1	0.01	DOESN'T	2	0.02
COLLAR	1	0.01	CUP	17	0.20	DOG	224	2.67
COLOUR	6	0.07	CUPBOARD	3	0.04	DOGS	10	0.12
COLOURS	4	0.05	CUPS	1	0.01	DOING	17	0.20
COME	593	7.07	CURE	1	0.01	DOLL	45	0.54
COMES	87	1.04	CURTAIN	1	0.01	DOLL'S	12	0.14
COMING	19	0.23	CUT	15	0.18	DOLLAR	1	0.01
COOK	1	0.01	D	4	0.05	DOLLS	10	0.12
COOKIES	3	0.04	DAD	156	1.86	DOLLY	1	0.01
COOKING	1	0.01	DAD'S	9	0.11	DON	31	0.37
COOL	1	0.01	DADDY	128	1.53	DON'T	52	0.62
COPY-CAT	3	0.04	DADDY'S	3	0.04	DONE	3	0.04
CORN	1	0.01	DADS	1	0.01	DONKEY	7	0.08
CORNER	3	0.04	DAIRY	3	0.04	DONKEYS	1	0.01
CORNFLAKES	1	0.01	DAM	1	0.01	DOOR	68	0.81

WORD	F	F/1,000	WORD	F	F/1,000	WORD	F	F/1,000
DOOR'S	2	0.02	EIGHT	4	0.05	FEATHERS	4	0.05
DOORS	6	0.07	ELBOW	3	0.04	FED	7	0.08
DOT	3	0.04	ELEPHANT	46	0.55	FEED	11	0.13
DOT'S	1	0.01	ELEPHANT'S	1	0.01	FEEL	8	0.10
DOUGHNUTS	1	0.01	ELEPHANTS	5	0.06	FEET	17	0.20
DOVES	1	0.01	ELEVATORS	1	0.01	FELICITY	1	0.01
DOWN	311	3.71	ELF	38	0.45	FELIPE	1	0.01
DOWNSTAIRS	3	0.04	ELF'S	1	0.01	FELL	14	0.17
DRAGON	24	0.29	ELIZABETH	57	0.68	FELLOW	1	0.01
DRAGONFLY	1	0.01	ELIZABETH'S	1	0.01	FELT	1	0.01
DRAGONS	5	0.06	ELSE	1	0.01	FENCE	2	0.02
DRAIN	2	0.02	EMPTY	3	0.04	FERDY	1	0.01
DRAW	22	0.26	EMU	1	0.01	FESTIVAL	1	0.01
DRAWER	1	0.01	END	3	0.04	FETCH	2	0.02
DRAWING	2	0.02	ENGINE	10	0.12	FEW	1	0.01
DRAWS	12	0.14	ENGLISHMAN	1	0.01	FIDDLE	3	0.04
DREAM	1	0.01	ENOUGH	1	0.01	FIDDLES	1	0.01
DREAMS	1	0.01	ENTERTAIN	5	0.06	FIELD	1	0.01
DRESS	11	0.13	ENTRANCE	3	0.04	FIERCE	2	0.02
DRESSED	5	0.06	ESCALATOR	3	0.04	FIG	2	0.02
DRESSES	2	0.02	EVEN	1	0.01	FIGHT	2	0.02
DRESSING	2	0.02	EVER	11	0.13	FILL	4	0.05
DRESSING-UP	1	0.01	EVERY	33	0.39	FILLED	2	0.02
DREW	11	0.13	EVERYONE	30	0.36	FIND	73	0.87
DRINK	14	0.17	EVERYTHING	3	0.04	FINDS	7	0.08
DRINKING	1	0.01	EVERYWHERE	10	0.12	FINE	6	0.07
DRINKS	3	0.04	EVIL	1	0.01	FINGER	5	0.06
DRIVE	2	0.02	EXIT	5	0.06	FINGERS	3	0.04
DRIVER	40	0.48	EXPLODE	1	0.01	FIONA	1	0.01

Word	N	Freq.	Word	N	Freq.	Word	N	Freq.
DRIVING	2	0.02	EYE	2	0.02	FIRE	37	0.44
DROP	7	0.08	EYES	13	0.16	FIRE-PLACE	1	0.01
DROPPED	7	0.08	F	3	0.04	FIREMAN'S	1	0.01
DROVE	9	0.11	FACE	10	0.12	FIREMEN	1	0.01
DRUM	1	0.01	FACES	2	0.02	FIRST	34	0.41
DRUMS	1	0.01	FACTORS	1	0.01	FISH	156	1.86
DRY	4	0.05	FACTORY	10	0.12	FISHED	3	0.04
DUCK	15	0.18	FAIRIES	3	0.04	FISHERMAN	1	0.01
DUCKLING	4	0.05	FAIRY	3	0.04	FISHING	8	0.10
DUCKLINGS	2	0.02	FALL	2	0.02	FIT	17	0.20
DUCKS	2	0.02	FAN	46	0.55	FITTING	1	0.01
DUG	7	0.08	FANCY	1	0.01	FIVE	43	0.51
DUMPLINGS	1	0.01	FANCY-DRESS	1	0.01	FIX	16	0.19
DURING	1	0.01	FAR	23	0.27	FIXED	1	0.01
DUST	1	0.01	FARE	1	0.01	FIXING	2	0.02
DWARFS	1	0.01	FARM	100	1.19	FIZZ	3	0.04
E	31	0.37	FARM-HOUSE	1	0.01	FLAG	1	0.01
EACH	11	0.13	FARMER	9	0.11	FLAGS	1	0.01
EAGER	1	0.01	FARMER'S	5	0.06	FLAMES	1	0.01
EAR	3	0.04	FARMERS	1	0.01	FLAMING	2	0.02
EARLY	3	0.04	FARMYARD	3	0.04	FLAP	1	0.01
EARS	15	0.18	FAST	21	0.25	FLASH	2	0.02
EAST	1	0.01	FASTER	13	0.16	FLASHES	1	0.01
EAT	114	1.36	FAT	98	1.17	FLAT	7	0.08
EATING	11	0.13	FATHER	255	3.04	FLAVOURS	2	0.02
EATS	4	0.05	FATHER'S	4	0.05	FLEA	6	0.07
EDAM	1	0.01	FATHERS	8	0.10	FLEW	3	0.04
EDGE	1	0.01	FAY	1	0.01	FLIES	3	0.04
EEL	1	0.01	FEAR	1	0.01	FLOOR	5	0.06
EGG	12	0.14	FEARFUL	1	0.01	FLOORS	1	0.01
EGGS	35	0.42	FEATHER	1	0.01	FLORA	1	0.01

WORD	F	F/1,000	WORD	F	F/1,000	WORD	F	F/1,000
FLOSS	1	0.01	GAMES	10	0.12	GRANDFATHER	33	0.39
FLOWER	12	0.14	GARDEN	58	0.69	GRANFATHER'S	4	0.05
FLOWERS	62	0.74	GARDENS	5	0.06	GRANDMA	11	0.13
FLOWS	1	0.01	GARY	4	0.05	GRANDMOTHER	133	1.59
FLUFF	1	0.01	GATE	19	0.23	GRANDMOTHER'S	31	0.37
FLUFFY	1	0.01	GATE'S	2	0.02	GRANDPA	9	0.11
FLUTES	1	0.01	GATES	3	0.04	GRAPES	1	0.01
FLY	49	0.58	GATHERED	1	0.01	GRASS	14	0.17
FLYING	2	0.02	GATHERING	1	0.01	GRAZING	1	0.01
FOAL	6	0.07	GAVE	27	0.32	GREAT	11	0.13
FOALS	2	0.02	GAY	5	0.06	GREECE	1	0.01
FOG	14	0.17	GEE	4	0.05	GREEK	1	0.01
FOLLOW	1	0.01	GEESE	1	0.01	GREEN	101	1.20
FOOD	12	0.14	GENTLE	1	0.01	GREEN'S	2	0.02
FOOT	5	0.06	GENTLY	1	0.01	GREENWOOD	3	0.04
FOOTBALL	7	0.08	GEORGIE	2	0.02	GREET	1	0.01
FOR	627	7.48	GET	393	4.69	GREW	7	0.08
FOREST	3	0.04	GETS	37	0.44	GREY	31	0.37
FORK	1	0.01	GETTING	3	0.04	GRIND	2	0.02
FOUND	7	0.08	GHOST	1	0.01	GROCER	6	0.07
FOUR	24	0.29	GHOSTIE	2	0.02	GROUND	3	0.04
FOX	60	0.72	GIANT	6	0.07	GROW	5	0.06
FOX'S	3	0.04	GIANTS	14	0.17	GROWLED	1	0.01
FOXES	1	0.01	GIGGLE	2	0.02	GROWS	3	0.04
FRANCE	2	0.02	GINGER	17	0.20	GRRR	43	0.51
FRANCIS	1	0.01	GINGERBREAD	2	0.02	GRUFF	16	0.19
FRANCISCO	1	0.01	GIRAFFE	11	0.13	GRUMP	1	0.01
FRANK	8	0.10	GIRL	88	1.05	GRUMPY	7	0.08
FRED	1	0.01	GIRL'S	2	0.02	GRUNTS	1	0.01

Word	Count	Freq	Word	Count	Freq	Word	Count	Freq
FREDA	1	0.01	GIRLS	78	0.93	GUESS	9	0.11
FREE	2	0.02	GIVE	60	0.72	GUM	4	0.05
FRESH	1	0.01	GIVES	27	0.32	GUN	10	0.12
FRIDAY	5	0.06	GLAD	19	0.23	GUNS	1	0.01
FRIDGE	1	0.01	GLOW	1	0.01	GUS	16	0.19
FRIEND	67	0.80	GLUE	1	0.01	GUTTER	1	0.01
FRIEND'S	2	0.02	GO	641	7.65	GYM	6	0.07
FRIENDS	61	0.73	GOAT	31	0.37	H	3	0.04
FRIGHT	3	0.04	GOATS	20	0.24	HA	10	0.12
FRIGHTENED	8	0.10	GOBBLE	3	0.04	HAD	304	3.63
FRISKING	1	0.01	GOD	3	0.04	HAIR	12	0.14
FRISKY	1	0.01	GOD-MOTHERS	1	0.01	HAIRY	2	0.02
FRITZ	1	0.01	GOES	21	0.25	HALF	2	0.02
FROG	61	0.73	GOING	272	3.24	HALL	2	0.02
FROG'S	1	0.01	GOLD	6	0.07	HALLS	1	0.01
FROGS	3	0.04	GOLDEN	16	0.19	HALLWAY	2	0.02
FROM	83	0.99	GOLDFISH	1	0.01	HAM	49	0.58
FRONT	11	0.13	GOLDILOCKS	17	0.20	HAMMER	1	0.01
FROTHY	1	0.01	GONE	6	0.07	HAMMERING	1	0.01
FROZEN	1	0.01	GOOD	222	2.65	HAND	17	0.20
FRUIT	2	0.02	GOOD-BYE	21	0.25	HANDBAG	2	0.02
FRY	1	0.01	GOODBYE	5	0.06	HANDS	5	0.06
FULL	10	0.12	GOODNESS	1	0.01	HAPPED	1	0.01
FUN	168	2.00	GOODNIGHT	3	0.04	HAPPEN	2	0.02
FUNNELS	1	0.01	GOODS	1	0.01	HAPPENED	9	0.11
FUNNY	149	1.78	GOOSE	2	0.02	HAPPENS	1	0.01
FUR	10	0.12	GOT	188	2.24	HAPPILY	2	0.02
FURRY	1	0.01	GOUDA	1	0.01	HAPPINESS	1	0.01
FURTHER	1	0.01	GOWN	1	0.01	HAPPY	71	0.85
G	4	0.05	GRAIN	1	0.01	HAPPY'S	2	0.02
GAME	22	0.26	GRANDAD	7	0.08	HARD	6	0.07

WORD	F	F/1,000	WORD	F	F/1,000	WORD	F	F/1,000
HARRY	7	0.08	HIS	273	3.26	I'VE	43	0.51
HAS	181	2.16	HISS	2	0.02	ICE	9	0.11
HAT	137	1.63	HIT	45	0.54	ICE-CREAM	2	0.02
HATS	15	0.18	HITS	1	0.01	ICECREAM	2	0.02
HAUNTED	5	0.06	HIVES	2	0.02	ICING	1	0.01
HAVE	483	5.76	HOED	1	0.01	IDEA	7	0.08
HAVEN'T	1	0.01	HOG	4	0.05	IDEAS	1	0.01
HAVING	4	0.05	HOGLEG	8	0.10	IF	62	0.74
HAY	4	0.05	HOIST	1	0.01	ILL	1	0.01
HE	1,037	12.37	HOITY	1	0.01	IN	1,199	14.30
HE'S	15	0.18	HOLD	6	0.07	INCH	3	0.04
HEAD	12	0.14	HOLDING	5	0.06	INDIAN	3	0.04
HEADED	1	0.01	HOLE	3	0.04	INDIANS	1	0.01
HEADMASTER	11	0.13	HOLES	3	0.04	INFANT	1	0.01
HEADS	2	0.02	HOLIDAY	10	0.12	INJECTION	1	0.01
HEALTHY	1	0.01	HOLIDAYS	11	0.13	INK	4	0.05
HEAR	36	0.43	HOME	185	2.21	INSECT	3	0.04
HEARD	16	0.19	HOOD	23	0.27	INSIDE	16	0.19
HEARTS	1	0.01	HOOK	1	0.01	INSTEAD	1	0.01
HEAT	1	0.01	HOOKED	2	0.02	INTO	256	3.05
HEAVY	1	0.01	HOORAY	20	0.24	IRON	2	0.02
HEDGEHOG	2	0.02	HOP	45	0.54	IS	1,496	17.84
HEE-HAW	2	0.02	HOPE	10	0.12	ISLAND	7	0.08
HEEL	1	0.01	HOPPED	4	0.05	ISLANDS	1	0.01
HEELS	1	0.01	HOPPING	1	0.01	ISN'T	1	0.01
HEIGH-HO	1	0.01	HOPSCOTCH	1	0.01	IT	982	11.71
HELEN	23	0.27	HORACE	11	0.13	IT'S	115	1.37
HELLO	58	0.69	HORNER	1	0.01	ITS	17	0.20
HELMET	1	0.01	HORSE	84	1.00	J	4	0.05

HELMETS	1	0.01	HORSE'S	3	0.04	JABS	3	0.04
HELP	270	3.22	HORSES	43	0.51	JACK	346	4.13
HELPED	22	0.26	HOSE	14	0.17	JACK'S	6	0.07
HELPERS	1	0.01	HOSED	4	0.05	JACK-IN-THE-BOX	12	0.14
HELPING	5	0.06	HOSPITAL	6	0.07	JAM	33	0.39
HELPS	37	0.44	HOT	57	0.68	JAN	26	0.31
HEN	70	0.83	HOUSE	249	2.97	JANE	482	5.75
HEN-HOUSE	2	0.02	HOUSE-BOAT	9	0.11	JANE'S	24	0.29
HENS	19	0.23	HOUSES	11	0.13	JAPAN	1	0.01
HER	248	2.96	HOW	46	0.55	JAR	5	0.06
HERE	686	8.18	HOWLED	6	0.07	JAWS	3	0.04
HERE'S	2	0.02	HUFF	4	0.05	JEAN	2	0.02
HERS	1	0.01	HUFFED	4	0.05	JELLIES	1	0.01
HERSELF	2	0.02	HUG	4	0.05	JELLY	14	0.17
HEY	4	0.05	HUGE	2	0.02	JENNY	21	0.25
HICKORY	3	0.04	HUGGED	1	0.01	JENNY'S	1	0.01
HID	15	0.18	HULLO	4	0.05	JESSIE	4	0.05
HIDE	5	0.06	HUM	2	0.02	JET	12	0.14
HIDE-AND-SEEK	3	0.04	HUNGRY	7	0.08	JETHRO	1	0.01
HIDING	5	0.06	HURRAH	11	0.13	JETTED	1	0.01
HIGH	3	0.04	HURRIED	1	0.01	JEWELS	2	0.02
HIGHER	2	0.02	HURRY	17	0.20	JIG	14	0.17
HILL	78	0.93	HURRYING	1	0.01	JIGGLED	6	0.07
HILL'S	2	0.02	HURT	5	0.06	JILL	254	3.03
HILL-TOP	1	0.01	HUSBAND	1	0.01	JILL'S	6	0.07
HILLS	2	0.02	HUSTLE	1	0.01	JIM	116	1.38
HILLSIDE	2	0.02	HUT	9	0.11	JIM'S	6	0.07
HIM	260	3.10	I	1,885	22.48	JIMPKIN	5	0.06
HIMSELF	6	0.07	I'D	2	0.02	JOAN	10	0.12
HIP	2	0.02	I'LL	95	1.13	JOB	7	0.08
HIPS	1	0.01	I'M	161	1.92	JOE	4	0.05

WORD	F	F/1,000	WORD	F	F/1,000	WORD	F	F/1,000
JOEY	1	0.01	KOALAS	1	0.01	LISA'S	3	0.04
JOHN	19	0.23	L	5	0.06	LISTEN	1	0.01
JOHN'S	1	0.01	LA	1	0.01	LIT	1	0.01
JONES	10	0.12	LABELS	1	0.01	LITTLE	652	7.78
JOURNEY	2	0.02	LADEN	1	0.01	LIVE	53	0.63
JUDGE	5	0.06	LADY	3	0.04	LIVED	17	0.20
JUG	5	0.06	LAKE	7	0.08	LIVES	29	0.35
JUICE	5	0.06	LAMB	1	0.01	LIVING	1	0.01
JUICY	1	0.01	LAMBS	19	0.23	LIZARD	1	0.01
JUMBO	1	0.01	LAND	1	0.01	LIZARDS	1	0.01
JUMP	154	1.84	LANDED	1	0.01	LOAD	1	0.01
JUMPED	39	0.47	LAP	16	0.19	LOG	30	0.36
JUMPER	1	0.01	LARGE	2	0.02	LOGS	1	0.01
JUMPING	3	0.04	LAST	5	0.06	LONG	31	0.37
JUMPKIN	5	0.06	LATE	1	0.01	LONGED	1	0.01
JUMPS	20	0.24	LAUGH	20	0.24	LOOK	569	6.79
JUNGLE	7	0.08	LAUGHED	102	1.22	LOOK-OUT	2	0.02
JUST	61	0.73	LAUGHING	3	0.04	LOOKDOWN	1	0.01
K	4	0.05	LAUGHS	2	0.02	LOOKED	170	2.03
KANGAROO	26	0.31	LAUGHTER	1	0.01	LOOKING	19	0.23
KANGAROOS	2	0.02	LAUNCHING	1	0.01	LOOKS	71	0.85
KATE	3	0.04	LAWN	5	0.06	LOOSE	3	0.04
KATHY	11	0.13	LAY	5	0.06	LOOSER	2	0.02
KATHY'S	1	0.01	LEAF	2	0.02	LORRY	2	0.02
KEEN	2	0.02	LEAPED	1	0.01	LOST	19	0.23
KEEP	24	0.29	LEARN	3	0.04	LOT	10	0.12
KEEPS	3	0.04	LEAVE	1	0.01	LOTS	23	0.27
KEN	44	0.52	LEAVES	6	0.07	LOUDER	3	0.04
KENNEL	1	0.01	LED	4	0.05	LOUDLY	1	0.01

Word	Count	Freq	Word	Count	Freq	Word	Count	Freq
KEPT	9	0.11	LEFT	11	0.13	LOVE	13	0.16
KETTLE	12	0.14	LEG	25	0.30	LOVED	2	0.02
KEY	3	0.04	LEGS	9	0.11	LOVELY	3	0.04
KICK	1	0.01	LET	142	1.69	LOVES	7	0.08
KICKED	1	0.01	LET'S	53	0.63	LOW	2	0.02
KICKING	2	0.02	LETS	10	0.12	LUG	2	0.02
KILL	5	0.06	LETTER	24	0.29	LUNCH	25	0.30
KIM	13	0.16	LETTERS	2	0.02	M	5	0.06
KIMOND	1	0.01	LETTUCE	3	0.04	MACDONALD	1	0.01
KIND	6	0.07	LIBRARY	4	0.05	MACHINE	8	0.10
KING	20	0.24	LICK	3	0.04	MACHINES	1	0.01
KIP	8	0.10	LICKED	1	0.01	MAD	15	0.18
KISSED	2	0.02	LID	18	0.21	MADE	49	0.58
KISSES	1	0.01	LIDS	1	0.01	MAGIC	89	1.06
KIT	46	0.55	LIE	2	0.02	MAGICIAN	25	0.30
KIT'S	2	0.02	LIFE	2	0.02	MAGICIAN'S	1	0.01
KITCHEN	4	0.05	LIFEBOATS	1	0.01	MAKE	240	2.86
KITE	6	0.07	LIFT	1	0.01	MAKE-BELIEVE	16	0.19
KITTEN	59	0.70	LIFTED	1	0.01	MAKES	20	0.24
KITTEN'S	2	0.02	LIGHT	5	0.06	MAKING	15	0.18
KITTENS	33	0.39	LIGHTNING	1	0.01	MAN	187	2.23
KNEE	9	0.11	LIGHTS	1	0.01	MAN'S	3	0.04
KNEES	1	0.01	LIKE	406	4.84	MANDY	9	0.11
KNELT	1	0.01	LIKED	60	0.72	MANDY'S	3	0.04
KNIFE	4	0.05	LIKES	127	1.51	MANY	10	0.12
KNOCK	3	0.04	LINDA	3	0.04	MAP	2	0.02
KNOCKED	1	0.01	LINE	10	0.12	MARCHING	1	0.01
KNOCKING	1	0.01	LINES	6	0.07	MARGARET	4	0.05
KNOW	99	1.18	LION	8	0.10	MARK	34	0.41
KNOWS	7	0.08	LIONS	2	0.02	MARK'S	1	0.01
KOALA	13	0.16	LISA	9	0.11	MARMALADE	1	0.01

WORD	F	F/1,000	WORD	F	F/1,000	WORD	F	F/1,000
MARRIED	2	0.02	MONSTER	13	0.16	NEWSPAPER	1	0.01
MARRY	2	0.02	MOO	19	0.23	NEWSPAPERS	1	0.01
MARY	61	0.73	MOON	34	0.41	NEXT	50	0.60
MARY'S	4	0.05	MOP	18	0.21	NIBBLE	3	0.04
MAST	1	0.01	MOPS	4	0.05	NICE	1	0.01
MASTS	1	0.01	MORE	49	0.58	NIGHT	8	0.10
MAT	34	0.41	MORN	1	0.01	NIGHT-TIME	1	0.01
MATTER	4	0.05	MORNING	43	0.51	NIMBLE	1	0.01
MAX	21	0.25	MOST	1	0.01	NINE	5	0.06
MAX'S	1	0.01	MOSTLY	1	0.01	NIP	12	0.14
MAY	123	1.47	MOTHER	289	3.45	NO	295	3.52
MAYBE	11	0.13	MOTHER'S	2	0.02	NOBODY	2	0.02
MCGREGOR	5	0.06	MOTHERS	15	0.18	NOD	1	0.01
ME	354	4.22	MOUNTAIN	2	0.02	NOISE	1	0.01
MEADOW	1	0.01	MOUSE	69	0.82	NOON	1	0.01
MEAN	1	0.01	MOUTH	1	0.01	NOR	2	0.02
MEANS	1	0.01	MOVING	1	0.01	NOSE	20	0.24
MEANTIME	1	0.01	MR	235	2.80	NOT	439	5.24
MEASURE	2	0.02	MRS	23	0.27	NOTHING	4	0.05
MEAT	2	0.02	MUCH	23	0.27	NOTHING'S	1	0.01
MEDICINE	1	0.01	MUD	20	0.24	NOW	237	2.83
MEEOW	34	0.41	MUM	93	1.11	NUMBER	1	0.01
MEET	18	0.21	MUM'S	3	0.04	NUMBERS	3	0.04
MEETING	1	0.01	MUMBLE	1	0.01	NURSE	3	0.04
MEETS	3	0.04	MUMMY	92	1.10	NURSERY	1	0.01
MELTING	1	0.01	MUMS	1	0.01	NURSES	4	0.05
MEN	41	0.49	MUNCHING	1	0.01	NUT	20	0.24
MERRY	3	0.04	MUST	80	0.95	NUTS	10	0.12
MERRY-GO-ROUND	1	0.01	MUSTN'T	1	0.01	O	3	0.04

Word	Count	%	Word	Count	%	Word	Count	%
MERRY-OH	1	0.01	MUTTER	2	0.02	O'CLOCK	11	0.13
MESS	6	0.07	MUTTON	1	0.01	ODD	1	0.01
MET	21	0.25	MY	481	5.74	OF	413	4.93
MEW	18	0.21	MYSELF	24	0.29	OFF	98	1.17
MEWING	1	0.01	N	4	0.05	OH	182	2.17
MICE	1	0.01	NAIL	1	0.01	OK	1	0.01
MICHAEL	12	0.14	NAME	4	0.05	OLD	113	1.35
MID-TASTY	1	0.01	NAMED	2	0.02	OLIVES	1	0.01
MIGHTY	1	0.01	NAMES	1	0.01	ON	666	7.94
MILK	112	1.34	NAN	59	0.70	ONCE	44	0.52
MILKING	6	0.07	NANNY	1	0.01	ONE	196	2.34
MILKMAN	3	0.04	NAP	31	0.37	ONE'S	8	0.10
MILKS	1	0.01	NARROW	1	0.01	ONES	15	0.18
MILL	1	0.01	NAT	7	0.08	ONLY	3	0.04
MILLER	1	0.01	NAUGHTY	10	0.12	ONTO	2	0.02
MIRROR	2	0.02	NEAR	24	0.29	OPEN	18	0.21
MISS	159	1.90	NEARBY	1	0.01	OPENED	13	0.16
MISSING	2	0.02	NEARER	1	0.01	OPENS	1	0.01
MISTAKEN	1	0.01	NEAT	1	0.01	OR	58	0.69
MITTENS	7	0.08	NECK	1	0.01	ORANGE	6	0.07
MIX	1	0.01	NECKLACE	1	0.01	ORANGES	2	0.02
MIXTURE	1	0.01	NECTAR	1	0.01	ORCHARDS	1	0.01
MOLLY	31	0.37	NEED	23	0.27	OSTRICH	4	0.05
MOLLY'S	2	0.02	NEEDS	2	0.02	OTHER	54	0.64
MOM	9	0.11	NELL	11	0.13	OTHERS	4	0.05
MOMOTARO	29	0.35	NELL'S	1	0.01	OTTER	3	0.04
MOMOTARO'S	4	0.05	NEST	6	0.07	OUR	84	1.00
MONDAY	1	0.01	NESTS	2	0.02	OUT	341	4.07
MONEY	14	0.17	NET	19	0.23	OUTER	1	0.01
MONKEY	46	0.55	NEVER	34	0.41	OUTSIDE	5	0.06
MONKEYS	5	0.06	NEW	85	1.01	OVEN	1	0.01

WORD	F	F/1,000	WORD	F	F/1,000	WORD	F	F/1,000
OVER	55	0.66	PEGS	3	0.04	PLAYMATE	1	0.01
OW	1	0.01	PEN	28	0.33	PLAYS	13	0.16
OWL	3	0.04	PENCIL	5	0.06	PLAYTIME	3	0.04
OWN	23	0.27	PENNY	10	0.12	PLEASANT	2	0.02
OX	21	0.25	PENNYFEATHER	43	0.51	PLEASE	82	0.98
P	3	0.04	PEOPLE	7	0.08	PLEASED	2	0.02
PACK	3	0.04	PERCHED	1	0.01	PLOP	2	0.02
PACKED	1	0.01	PERFECT	1	0.01	PLUM	2	0.02
PAD	5	0.06	PERHAPS	17	0.20	PLUMP	1	0.01
PADDOCK	23	0.27	PET	67	0.80	POINTED	1	0.01
PADDOCKS	1	0.01	PETALS	1	0.01	POINTS	1	0.01
PAGE	2	0.02	PETE	9	0.11	POLAR	2	0.02
PAIL	2	0.02	PETE'S	2	0.02	POLICE	22	0.26
PAINT	19	0.23	PETER	617	7.36	POLICEMAN	5	0.06
PAINTED	6	0.07	PETER'S	13	0.16	POLLY	7	0.08
PAINTING	13	0.16	PETS	26	0.31	POND	9	0.11
PAINTS	2	0.02	PETTICOAT	6	0.07	PONIES	2	0.02
PAL	43	0.51	PHEASANT	10	0.12	PONY	35	0.42
PAL'S	2	0.02	PHONED	1	0.01	PONY'S	1	0.01
PALACE	15	0.18	PIANO	1	0.01	POOH	5	0.06
PALS	2	0.02	PICK	1	0.01	POOL	18	0.21
PAM	80	0.95	PICKED	3	0.04	POOL'S	1	0.01
PAM'S	10	0.12	PICKING	1	0.01	POOLS	5	0.06
PAMELA	31	0.37	PICKLE	1	0.01	POOR	4	0.05
PAMELA'S	3	0.04	PICNIC	6	0.07	POP	16	0.19
PAN	25	0.30	PICTURE	22	0.26	PORGIE	2	0.02
PANCAKE	4	0.05	PICTURES	7	0.08	PORTHOLES	1	0.01
PANDA	2	0.02	PIE	7	0.08	POSSUM	14	0.17
PANS	2	0.02	PIG	180	2.15	POSTER	1	0.01

Word	Count	Freq	Word	Count	Freq	Word	Count	Freq
PAPER	6	0.07	PIG'S	2	0.02	POSTMAN	2	0.02
PAPERS	1	0.01	PIGEONS	2	0.02	POT	52	0.62
PARENTS	11	0.13	PIGLET	4	0.05	POTS	3	0.04
PARK	4	0.05	PIGPEN	14	0.17	POUND	2	0.02
PARROT	2	0.02	PIGS	66	0.79	POUR	4	0.05
PARTY	40	0.48	PIGS'	1	0.01	POURING	1	0.01
PASS	1	0.01	PILE	1	0.01	PRANCING	1	0.01
PAST	3	0.04	PILLOW	4	0.05	PRESENT	3	0.04
PASTING	1	0.01	PIN	7	0.08	PRESENTS	5	0.06
PAT	125	1.49	PINE	1	0.01	PRETEND	2	0.02
PAT'S	2	0.02	PINK	12	0.14	PRETTY	13	0.16
PAT-A-CAKE	2	0.02	PINKY	8	0.10	PRICK	1	0.01
PATCH	16	0.19	PINNED	5	0.06	PRINCE	8	0.10
PATH	9	0.11	PINS	2	0.02	PRINCESS	48	0.57
PATHS	1	0.01	PIRATE	7	0.08	PRINCESSES	1	0.01
PATRICK	6	0.07	PIT	55	0.66	PRODUCTS	3	0.04
PATS	6	0.07	PLACE	34	0.41	PROMISE	12	0.14
PATTED	2	0.02	PLAIN	1	0.01	PROMISED	3	0.04
PAUL	8	0.10	PLAN	7	0.08	PROMISES	2	0.02
PAWS	2	0.02	PLANE	2	0.02	PUDDING	1	0.01
PAY	1	0.01	PANNED	1	0.01	PUDDLES	3	0.04
PEACE	1	0.01	PLANS	1	0.01	PUFF	21	0.25
PEACH	10	0.12	PLANTED	1	0.01	PUFFED	4	0.05
PEANUTS	1	0.01	PLANTING	1	0.01	PULL	34	0.41
PEARS	2	0.02	PLANTS	2	0.02	PULLED	6	0.07
PEAS	3	0.04	PLATE	2	0.02	PULLS	13	0.16
PECKING	2	0.02	PLATES	1	0.01	PUMP	5	0.06
PEG	22	0.26	PLAY	358	4.27	PUMPED	2	0.02
PEG'S	2	0.02	PLAYED	16	0.19	PUMPKIN	12	0.14
PEGLEG	15	0.18	PLAYGROUND	4	0.05	PUMPS	1	0.01
PEGLEG'S	1	0.01	PLAYING	23	0.27	PUP	21	0.25

WORD	F	F/1,000	WORD	F	F/1,000	WORD	F	F/1,000
PUPPET	28	0.33	REMEMBERED	4	0.05	RUSTLE	1	0.01
PUPPETS	17	0.20	RETURNED	1	0.01	S	6	0.07
PUPPY	33	0.39	RHYMES	1	0.01	SACK	5	0.06
PURPLE	2	0.02	RIBBON	4	0.05	SAD	97	1.16
PURR	6	0.07	RIBBONS	1	0.01	SADDLE	3	0.04
PURRING	2	0.02	RICE	10	0.12	SADLY	2	0.02
PUSH	11	0.13	RICHARD	14	0.17	SAFE	1	0.01
PUSHED	6	0.07	RID	4	0.05	SAFELY	2	0.02
PUSHING	1	0.01	RIDE	83	0.99	SAID	1,719	20.50
PUSSY	3	0.04	RIDES	8	0.10	SAIL	6	0.07
PUSSYCAT	1	0.01	RIDING	24	0.29	SAILING	3	0.04
PUT	163	1.94	RIGHT	9	0.11	SAILOR	8	0.10
PUTS	40	0.48	RIM	1	0.01	SAILORS'	1	0.01
PUTTING	7	0.08	RIN-TIN-TIN	32	0.38	SAILS	1	0.01
PUZZLES	1	0.01	RINALDO	64	0.76	SALAMI	1	0.01
PUZZLING	1	0.01	RINALDO'S	1	0.01	SALLY	9	0.11
QU	3	0.04	RING	12	0.14	SAM	89	1.06
QUARTER	2	0.02	RINGING	2	0.02	SAM'S	10	0.12
QUEEN	3	0.04	RINGMASTER	6	0.07	SAME	1	0.01
QUICK	4	0.05	RIP	19	0.23	SAMSON	17	0.20
QUICKLY	10	0.12	RIPE	2	0.02	SAN	5	0.06
QUIET	1	0.01	RIPPLED	1	0.01	SAND	9	0.11
QUIETLY	1	0.01	RIPPLES	1	0.01	SANDMAN'S	1	0.01
QUILL	2	0.02	RISE	1	0.01	SANDPIT	5	0.06
R	4	0.05	RIVER	28	0.33	SANDWICH	3	0.04
RABBIT	81	0.97	RIVERS	1	0.01	SANDWICHES	7	0.08
RABBITS	43	0.51	RM	4	0.05	SANDY	64	0.76
RACE	22	0.26	ROAD	17	0.20	SANG	3	0.04
RACES	4	0.05	ROAM	1	0.01	SAP	7	0.08

Word	Count	%	Word	Count	%	Word	Count	%
RADIO	1	0.01	ROAR	4	0.05	SAT	128	1.53
RAG	11	0.13	ROB	3	0.04	SATURDAY	14	0.17
RAG'S	1	0.01	ROBBED	1	0.01	SAUCER	6	0.07
RAGBAG	5	0.06	ROBIN	72	0.86	SAUSAGES	3	0.04
RAGS	17	0.20	ROBIN'S	4	0.05	SAW	118	1.41
RAIL	2	0.02	ROCK	9	0.11	SAY	115	1.37
RAILWAY-LINE	1	0.01	ROCKET	2	0.02	SAYS	655	7.81
RAIN	20	0.24	ROCKS	2	0.02	SCALED	1	0.01
RAINBOW	2	0.02	ROD	3	0.04	SCAMP	1	0.01
RAINCOAT	3	0.04	RODE	13	0.16	SCARECROW	10	0.12
RAINDROPS	3	0.04	RODS	1	0.01	SCARECROW'S	1	0.01
RAINED	3	0.04	ROLL	2	0.02	SCARED	3	0.04
RAINING	5	0.06	ROLLED	2	0.02	SCARES	1	0.01
RAINY	2	0.02	ROLLS	1	0.01	SCARF	1	0.01
RAISE	1	0.01	ROMPED	1	0.01	SCARY	4	0.05
RAM	2	0.02	RON	10	0.12	SCAT	2	0.02
RAMS	1	0.01	ROOF	4	0.05	SCHOLAR	1	0.01
RAN	375	4.47	ROOM	26	0.31	SCHOOL	168	2.00
RAT	25	0.30	ROOMS	2	0.02	SCHOOL'S	1	0.01
RATTLE	1	0.01	ROUND	52	0.62	SCHOOLS	2	0.02
RATTLING	1	0.01	ROW	8	0.10	SCRATCH	38	0.45
RAY	1	0.01	ROY	2	0.02	SCRATCHED	4	0.05
REACH	1	0.01	RUB	1	0.01	SCRATCHING	1	0.01
REACHING	1	0.01	RUBS	1	0.01	SCREECH	2	0.02
READ	66	0.79	RUG	8	0.10	SCRUB	1	0.01
READING	3	0.04	RULER	1	0.01	SCRUNCH	1	0.01
READS	7	0.08	RULES	1	0.01	SCURRYING	1	0.01
READY	75	0.89	RUN	176	2.10	SEA	73	0.87
RED	259	3.09	RUNNING	9	0.11	SEAGULL	1	0.01
REDBREAST	2	0.02	RUNNY	2	0.02	SEASONS	1	0.01
REMEMBER	11	0.13	RUNS	24	0.29	SEAT	2	0.02

WORD	F	F/1,000	WORD	F	F/1,000	WORD	F	F/1,000
SECOND	9	0.11	SHOUTED	56	0.67	SMILED	1	0.01
SECRET	4	0.05	SHOUTS	1	0.01	SMOKE	1	0.01
SECRETS	1	0.01	SHOW	64	0.76	SNAIL	5	0.06
SEE	573	6.83	SHOW-AND-TELL	5	0.06	SNAILS	1	0.01
SEE-SAW	14	0.17	SHOWED	22	0.26	SNAKE	15	0.18
SEED	4	0.05	SHOWING	1	0.01	SNAKES	2	0.02
SEED'S	1	0.01	SHOWS	1	0.01	SNAPPED	1	0.01
SEEK	1	0.01	SHRINK	1	0.01	SNIFF	4	0.05
SEEM	1	0.01	SHUT	3	0.04	SNIFFLE	2	0.02
SEEMS	1	0.01	SHY	1	0.01	SNOW	9	0.11
SEEN	15	0.18	SICK	13	0.16	SNOWMAN	3	0.04
SEES	19	0.23	SID	18	0.21	SO	85	1.01
SEIZED	1	0.01	SID'S	3	0.04	SOCK	1	0.01
SELL	1	0.01	SIDE	4	0.05	SOFT	3	0.04
SELLING	1	0.01	SIGHT	1	0.01	SOFTLY	2	0.02
SENT	3	0.04	SIGNAL	1	0.01	SOLDIER	1	0.01
SET	10	0.12	SILK	1	0.01	SOME	354	4.22
SETTING	1	0.01	SILLY	10	0.12	SOMEBODY	1	0.01
SEVEN	9	0.11	SILVER	2	0.02	SOMEDAY	1	0.01
SEVEN-THIRTY	1	0.01	SILVER-SCALED	1	0.01	SOMEONE	9	0.11
SHAGGY	1	0.01	SILVER-SHINY	1	0.01	SOMETHING	166	1.98
SHALL	79	0.94	SIM	25	0.30	SOMETIMES	15	0.18
SHAPE	2	0.02	SIM-SAM	3	0.04	SONG	2	0.02
SHAPES	5	0.06	SING	9	0.11	SOON	87	1.04
SHARE	1	0.01	SINGING	2	0.02	SORRY	1	0.01
SHARP	3	0.04	SINGS	1	0.01	SOUND	25	0.30
SHAVING	1	0.01	SINK	1	0.01	SOUNDS	6	0.07
SHE	493	5.88	SIP	3	0.04	SOUP	1	0.01
SHE'LL	7	0.08	SISTER	27	0.32	SPACE	1	0.01

Word	Count	Freq	Word	Count	Freq	Word	Count	Freq
SHE'S	4	0.05	SIT	68	0.81	SPACE-SUITS	1	0.01
SHED	44	0.52	SITS	17	0.20	SPACESHIP	3	0.04
SHEDS	3	0.04	SITTING	3	0.04	SPANISH	3	0.04
SHEEP	11	0.13	SIX	22	0.26	SPARE	3	0.04
SHEET	6	0.07	SIZE	2	0.02	SPARROWS	2	0.02
SHELF	1	0.01	SKIP	6	0.07	SPECIAL	2	0.02
SHELL	3	0.04	SKIPPING-ROPE	1	0.01	SPEED	3	0.04
SHELLING	1	0.01	SKIPS	1	0.01	SPELL	3	0.04
SHELLS	4	0.05	SKUNK	1	0.01	SPELLS	4	0.05
SHELVES	1	0.01	SKY	16	0.19	SPIDER	19	0.23
SHH	2	0.02	SLEEP	42	0.50	SPIDER-WISH	1	0.01
SHINE	2	0.02	SLEEPING	1	0.01	SPIKED	2	0.02
SHINING	1	0.01	SLEEPS	1	0.01	SPILT	2	0.02
SHIP	13	0.16	SLEEPY	1	0.01	SPIN	1	0.01
SHIPS	12	0.14	SLEEPYHEAD	1	0.01	SPLASH	48	0.57
SHIRLEY	2	0.02	SLICE	1	0.01	SPLASHED	9	0.11
SHIRLEY'S	1	0.01	SLICES	2	0.02	SPLASHING	1	0.01
SHIRT	1	0.01	SLIDE	2	0.02	SPLENDID	1	0.01
SHIRTS	1	0.01	SLIDES	1	0.01	SPLOSH	3	0.04
SHOE	10	0.12	SLIPPERS	3	0.04	SPLUTTER	3	0.04
SHOES	7	0.08	SLIPPERY	2	0.02	SPOILS	1	0.01
SHOO	7	0.08	SLOW	5	0.06	SPOKE	7	0.08
SHOOK	6	0.07	SLOWER	3	0.04	SPOOK	2	0.02
SHOP	88	1.05	SLOWLY	2	0.02	SPOON	5	0.06
SHOPPING	7	0.08	SLOWS	1	0.01	SPORT	2	0.02
SHOPS	27	0.32	SLUMPY	1	0.01	SPOT	4	0.05
SHORT	5	0.06	SLURP	1	0.01	SPOTS	47	0.56
SHORTENING	2	0.02	SMALL	28	0.33	SPRANG	1	0.01
SHOULD	24	0.29	SMASH	1	0.01	SPREADS	2	0.02
SHOULDN'T	1	0.01	SMELL	1	0.01	SPRING	2	0.02
SHOUT	6	0.07	SMELLS	2	0.02	SPRINKLED	1	0.01

WORD	F	F/1,000	WORD	F	F/1,000	WORD	F	F/1,000
SPRINKLER	1	0.01	STREETS	1	0.01	TALL	13	0.16
SPRY	1	0.01	STRETCHED	1	0.01	TAN	56	0.67
SPUN	1	0.01	STRING	8	0.10	TANK	1	0.01
SQUARK	2	0.02	STRUCK	1	0.01	TAP	53	0.63
SQUASHED	1	0.01	STUCK	3	0.04	TASTY	1	0.01
SQUAWK	1	0.01	STY	1	0.01	TAT	2	0.02
SQUEAL	1	0.01	SUCH	7	0.08	TAXI	13	0.16
SQUEALS	1	0.01	SUDDENLY	3	0.04	TEA	101	1.20
SQUEEZES	1	0.01	SUDS	1	0.01	TEACHER	49	0.58
SQUELCH	1	0.01	SUE	53	0.63	TEACHER'S	1	0.01
SQUIRMS	1	0.01	SUE'S	3	0.04	TEACHES	1	0.01
SQUIRREL	20	0.24	SUGAR	5	0.06	TEACHING	1	0.01
SQUIRRELS	6	0.07	SUIT	3	0.04	TEAPOT	1	0.01
STABLE	5	0.06	SUKEY	6	0.07	TEAS	2	0.02
STAIRS	2	0.02	SUMMER	3	0.04	TEASING	1	0.01
STALKING	1	0.01	SUN	72	0.86	TED	17	0.20
STAMP	1	0.01	SUNDAY	2	0.02	TED'S	5	0.06
STAND	4	0.05	SUNNY	2	0.02	TEDDY	2	0.02
STANDING	8	0.10	SUNSET	3	0.04	TEETH	4	0.05
STAR	29	0.35	SUNSHINE	5	0.06	TELEPHONE	1	0.01
STAR'S	3	0.04	SUNTAN	2	0.02	TELEPHONES	1	0.01
START	27	0.32	SUPER-MARKET	1	0.01	TELEVISION	7	0.08
STARTING	1	0.01	SUPERMARKET	9	0.11	TELL	48	0.57
STARTS	33	0.39	SUPPOSE	1	0.01	TELLING	1	0.01
STATION	36	0.43	SURE	15	0.18	TELLS	26	0.31
STAY	21	0.25	SURGERY	1	0.01	TEN	45	0.54
STAYED	1	0.01	SURPRISE	97	1.16	TENT	4	0.05
STAYS	1	0.01	SURPRISED	3	0.04	TENTS	1	0.01
STEERING	1	0.01	SURPRISES	12	0.14	TERRY	5	0.06

Word	Count	%	Word	Count	%	Word	Count	%
STEP	1	0.01	SUSAN	110	1.31	THAN	3	0.04
STEPPED	1	0.01	SUSAN'S	4	0.05	THANK	102	1.22
STEPS	5	0.06	SWALLOW	2	0.02	THANKED	4	0.05
STEVE	3	0.04	SWALLOWED	37	0.44	THANKS	4	0.05
STICK	3	0.04	SWEET	8	0.10	THAT	237	2.83
STICKS	5	0.06	SWEETS	23	0.27	THAT'S	57	0.68
STILL	8	0.10	SWIM	14	0.17	THE	5,874	70.06
STILTS	1	0.01	SWIMMING	18	0.21	THEIR	102	1.22
STIR	4	0.05	SWIMS	1	0.01	THEIRS	1	0.01
STOLE	1	0.01	SWING	8	0.10	THEM	225	2.68
STOLEN	3	0.04	SWISH	1	0.01	THEN	224	2.67
STONE	1	0.01	SWISS	1	0.01	THERE	252	3.01
STONES	1	0.01	SWOOPING	1	0.01	THERE'S	9	0.11
STOOD	6	0.07	I	3	0.04	THESE	3	0.04
STOP	92	1.10	TABLE	34	0.41	THEY	762	9.09
STOPPED	39	0.47	TACK	1	0.01	THEY'LL	1	0.01
STOPS	5	0.06	TAD	20	0.24	THEY'RE	6	0.07
STORE	2	0.02	TADPOLE	1	0.01	THEY'VE	1	0.01
STORED	1	0.01	TAG	51	0.61	THIMBLE	1	0.01
STORIES	36	0.43	TAIL	31	0.37	THIN	3	0.04
STORM	5	0.06	TAILS	2	0.02	THING	8	0.10
STORMS	1	0.01	TAINA	4	0.05	THING'S	1	0.01
STORY	45	0.54	TAKE	118	1.41	THINGS	76	0.91
STORY-BOOK	2	0.02	TAKEN	5	0.06	THINK	28	0.33
STORY-LAND	3	0.04	TAKES	10	0.12	THINKING	2	0.02
STOWAWAY	4	0.05	TAKING	6	0.07	THIRD	5	0.06
STRAIGHT	1	0.01	TALE	1	0.01	THIS	351	4.19
STRANGE	2	0.02	TALK	46	0.55	THISTLE	1	0.01
STRAW	4	0.05	TALKED	3	0.04	THONG	1	0.01
STREAM	2	0.02	TALKING	4	0.05	THORN	1	0.01
STREET	46	0.55	TALKS	21	0.25	THOSE	9	0.11

WORD	F	F/1,000	WORD	F	F/1,000	WORD	F	F/1,000
THREAT	1	0.01	TOWARDS	2	0.02	UNDRESS	1	0.01
THREE	80	0.95	TOWER	1	0.01	UNHAPPY	2	0.02
THREW	1	0.01	TOWN	10	0.12	UNIFORM	1	0.01
THROAT	1	0.01	TOY	72	0.86	UNLOADING	1	0.01
THRONE	1	0.01	TOY-BOX	17	0.20	UNLOCKED	1	0.01
THROUGH	15	0.18	TOYS	43	0.51	UNTIL	5	0.06
THRUST	1	0.01	TRACK	18	0.21	UP	448	5.34
THUMB	2	0.02	TRACTOR	8	0.10	UPON	20	0.24
THUMP	7	0.08	TRAFFIC	1	0.01	UPSET	2	0.02
THUNDER	2	0.02	TRAILER	2	0.02	UPSIDE	1	0.01
TICKET	1	0.01	TRAIN	55	0.66	UPSTAIRS	2	0.02
TICKETS	1	0.01	TRAINS	7	0.08	UPWARDS	1	0.01
TICKLE	8	0.10	TRAMPOLINE	2	0.02	US	187	2.23
TICKLED	6	0.07	TRAP	7	0.08	USE	7	0.08
TIE	1	0.01	TRAPPING	1	0.01	USED	1	0.01
TIED	2	0.02	TRAVEL	2	0.02	V	4	0.05
TIG	19	0.23	TREACLE	1	0.01	VAN	33	0.39
TIGER	33	0.39	TREASURE	3	0.04	VANISH	1	0.01
TIGERS	1	0.01	TREASURES	5	0.06	VANS	2	0.02
TIGHT	2	0.02	TREE	118	1.41	VASE	2	0.02
TIGHTY	1	0.01	TREE-HOUSE	2	0.02	VAT	1	0.01
TILL	1	0.01	TREES	58	0.69	VELVETY	1	0.01
TIM	43	0.51	TRICK	9	0.11	VERY	95	1.13
TIM'S	1	0.01	TRICKS	16	0.19	VILLAGE	4	0.05
TIME	118	1.41	TRICYCLE	4	0.05	VILLAGERS	1	0.01
TIMES	6	0.07	TRIED	9	0.11	VINE	6	0.07
TIMOTHY	55	0.66	TRIP	7	0.08	VIOLIN	2	0.02
TIMOTHY'S	1	0.01	TRIPPED	1	0.01	VISCOUNT	3	0.04
TIN	31	0.37	TROLL	12	0.14	VISIT	1	0.01

TIN-PAN	2	0.02	TROUSERS	2	0.02	VOICE	13	0.16
TINS	2	0.02	TRUCK	24	0.29	W	5	0.06
TINY	2	0.02	TRUCKS	4	0.05	WAG	91	1.09
TIP	4	0.05	TRUE	3	0.04	WAG'S	2	0.02
TIP-TOE	7	0.08	TRUNK	2	0.02	WAGGON-LOAD	2	0.02
TIRED	1	0.01	TRY	1	0.01	WAGON	1	0.01
TO	2,327	27.76	TUB	1	0.01	WAIT	14	0.17
TOAST	1	0.01	TUCK	1	0.01	WAITED	2	0.02
TOASTER	2	0.02	TUCKED	1	0.01	WAITING	3	0.04
TOASTS	2	0.02	TUCKING	1	0.01	WAKE	8	0.10
TODAY	56	0.67	TUG	41	0.49	WALK	60	0.72
TOES	3	0.04	TUGS	1	0.01	WALKED	13	0.16
TOGETHER	14	0.17	TUMBLED	1	0.01	WALKING	10	0.12
TOITY	1	0.01	TUMBLING	2	0.02	WALKS	3	0.04
TOLD	13	0.16	TURKEY	2	0.02	WALL	10	0.12
TOM	100	1.19	TURN	5	0.06	WALLABY	2	0.02
TOM'S	13	0.16	TURNED	2	0.02	WALLS	5	0.06
TOMATO	1	0.01	TURNIPS	8	0.10	WANT	260	3.10
TOMMY	6	0.07	TURNS	2	0.02	WANTED	28	0.33
TOMORROW	11	0.13	TURTLE	3	0.04	WANTS	92	1.10
TONGUE	1	0.01	TWINS	1	0.01	WARM	9	0.11
TONY	3	0.04	TWO	117	1.40	WAS	327	3.90
TOO	267	3.18	TWOPENNY	1	0.01	WASH	1	0.01
TOOK	39	0.47	TYRE	7	0.08	WASHED	1	0.01
TOOT	22	0.26	U	2	0.02	WASHING	3	0.04
TOOTH	6	0.07	UGLY	12	0.14	WASN'T	3	0.04
TOOTH'S	1	0.01	UMBRELLA	4	0.05	WATCH	17	0.20
TOP	66	0.79	UMPIRE	3	0.04	WATCHED	1	0.01
TOSS	1	0.01	UNCLE	1	0.01	WATCHING	1	0.01
TOSSING	1	0.01	UNDER	33	0.39	WATER	217	2.59
TOUCH	1	0.01	UNDERNEATH	1	0.01	WATER'S	1	0.01

WORD	F	F/1,000	WORD	F	F/1,000	WORD	F	F/1,000
WATERED	1	0.01	WHO	97	1.16	WORE	1	0.01
WATERMELON	1	0.01	WHO'S	4	0.05	WORK	101	1.20
WAVE	7	0.08	WHOLE	2	0.02	WORKED	10	0.12
WAVED	8	0.10	WHY	34	0.41	WORKING	4	0.05
WAVES	9	0.11	WIBBLES	1	0.01	WORKS	4	0.05
WAY	26	0.31	WICKED	2	0.02	WORM	1	0.01
WE	741	8.84	WIDE	14	0.17	WORMS	1	0.01
WE'LL	9	0.11	WIG	7	0.08	WOULD	39	0.47
WE'RE	1	0.01	WILL	456	5.44	WOW	2	0.02
WE'VE	6	0.07	WILLIAM	9	0.11	WRIGGLED	6	0.07
WEALTHY	1	0.01	WILSON	11	0.13	WRITE	22	0.26
WEAR	4	0.05	WILSON'S	1	0.01	WRITES	2	0.02
WEARING	3	0.04	WIN	15	0.18	WRITING	1	0.01
WEASEL	1	0.01	WIND	41	0.49	X	2	0.02
WEATHER	2	0.02	WINDOW	29	0.35	Y	1	0.01
WEB	5	0.06	WINDOWS	10	0.12	YACHT	2	0.02
WEDDING	1	0.01	WINDY	1	0.01	YAM	5	0.06
WEEK	1	0.01	WINS	3	0.04	YAMS	1	0.01
WEIGH	1	0.01	WIRE	2	0.02	YAP	8	0.10
WELCOME	1	0.01	WIRI	42	0.50	YAPPY	1	0.01
WELL	72	0.86	WIRI'S	3	0.04	YARD	3	0.04
WENDY	19	0.23	WISE	1	0.01	YEAR	2	0.02
WENT	341	4.07	WISH	58	0.69	YELL	1	0.01
WERE	66	0.79	WISHED	10	0.12	YELLOW	67	0.80
WEST	1	0.01	WISHES	3	0.04	YES	360	4.29
WET	60	0.72	WISHING	29	0.35	YESTERDAY	2	0.02
WHALE	1	0.01	WITCH	6	0.07	YET	6	0.07
WHAT	282	3.36	WITCHES	3	0.04	YIP	3	0.04
WHAT'S	11	0.13	WITH	588	7.01	YIPPEE	1	0.01

WHATEVER	1	0.01	WIZARD	7	0.08	YORK	2	0.02
WHEAT	4	0.05	WIZARDS	2	0.02	YOU	1,268	15.12
WHEE	6	0.07	WOBBLE	1	0.01	YOU'LL	4	0.05
WHEELBARROW	1	0.01	WOBBLES	2	0.02	YOU'RE	2	0.02
WHEELS	1	0.01	WOKE	1	0.01	YOU'VE	1	0.01
WHEN	142	1.69	WOLF	57	0.68	YOUNG	7	0.08
WHENEVER	1	0.01	WOMAN	18	0.21	YOUR	141	1.68
WHERE	162	1.93	WON'T	7	0.08	YOURSELVES	1	0.01
WHERE'S	8	0.10	WONDER	11	0.13	YOWL	2	0.02
WHEREVER	3	0.04	WONDERFUL	2	0.02	YUM	3	0.04
WHICH	16	0.19	WONKY	1	0.01	Z	2	0.02
WHIRL	1	0.01	WOOD	5	0.06	ZEBRA	2	0.02
WHISKERS	85	0.01	WOODMAN	5	0.06	ZIGZAG	1	0.01
WHISPER	1	0.01	WOODS	45	0.54	ZIP	6	0.07
WHISPERED	2	0.02	WOOF	28	0.33	ZOO	29	0.35
WHISPERING	1	0.01	WORD	27	0.32	ZOOM	1	0.01
WHITE	44	0.52	WORDS	18	0.21			

Appendix 2

Conversation Transcription Conventions

/	latched turns (no intervening pause)
//	heard as interruption
[	said simultaneously; overlaps at this point (see also Note below)
co:old	extended vowel or consonant
(4.0)	approximate length of pause in seconds
(( ))	transcriber's description
( )	untranscribable
(mouse)	uncertain transcription
h, hh	aspirant sound
so-he-is	words said very quickly
ALONG	words read from text
?	interrogative or upward intonation
.	downward intonation
, or –	minor pause
– –	longer pause
...	beginning or continuation of talk omitted
must	emphasis
T	teacher
S(s)	student(s)
J	initial of name of student speaking where this can be inferred

Note: In the Sally and Ann transcript (example 1.1), the symbol // indicates talk overlapped at this point by next utterance.

Index